Learning Windows™ Programming with Virtual Reality

LIMITED WARRANTY AND DISCLAIMER OF LIABILITY

Learning Windows™ Programming with Virtual Reality

Christopher D. Watkins, President
Algorithm, Inc.
Roswell, GA

Russell J. Berube, Jr.
Brookside Systems, Inc.
Bartlett, IL

AP PROFESSIONAL

Boston   San Diego   New York
London   Sydney   Tokyo   Toronto

AP PROFESSIONAL
1300 Boylston Street, Chestnut Hill, MA 02167

An Imprint of ACADEMIC PRESS, INC.
A Division of HARCOURT BRACE & COMPANY

United Kingdom Edition published by
ACADEMIC PRESS LIMITED
24–28 Oval Road, London NW1 7DX

Library of Congress Cataloging-in-Publication Data
Watkins, Christopher
    Learning Windows Programming with Virtual Reality / Christopher D. Watkins, Russell J. Berube, Jr.
        p.   cm.
    Includes bibliographical references and index.
    ISBN 0-12-737842-1 — ISBN 0-12-737843-X (disk)
    1. Windows (Computer programs)   2. Virtual reality.   I. Title.
QA76.76.W56W38   1995
006—dc20
                                                                            95-12025
                                                                                CIP

Printed in the United States of America
95 96 97 98   IP   9 8 7 6 5 4 3 2 1

Contents

List of Illustrations

Acknowledgments

The outline for this book was generated by Christopher D. Watkins, Russell J. Berube Jr., and Stephen R. Marenka. The VR engine technical text was written by Christopher D. Watkins and Christopher Laurel. The Microsoft Windows technical text was written by Russell J. Berube Jr. The writing of the general virtual reality text was done primarily by Stephen Marenka with contributions to the human perception section by Vincent Mallette of the Georgia Institute of Technology. The graphics engine for Windows application was written primarily by Christopher Laurel. The Windows human interface was written by Russell J. Berube Jr. Last-minute formatting anomalies contributed by Stephen R. Marenka. Vincent Mallette acted as technical/copy editor for the book.

All of the software in this book was written in C using Borland C++ version 3.1. The Borland C++ software was furnished by Borland International, 1800 Green Hills Road, Scotts Valley, CA 95066.

Thanks to WATCOM of 415 Phillip Street, Ontario, Canada, N2L 3X2 for supplying the WATCOM compiler version 10.0.

Thanks go to director Michael Sinclair of the Georgia Institute of Technology Multimedia Technology Laboratory for his help in obtaining information on simulation.

Thanks go to director James D. Foley and Larry Hodges of the Georgia Institute of Technology College of Computing Graphics, Visualization & Usability (GVU) Center for their information on virtual reality systems and simulation research.

Thanks to Toni Emerson, Cybrarian Extraordinaire of the HIT Lab, for providing information about the HIT Lab's virtual environments research programs and for her excellent work making VR resources available through the Web and sci.virtual-worlds.

Thanks go to Ken Welton and Michael Glaser of Lavista Systems, Inc., Tucker, Georgia for supplying equipment necessary for the completion of this book.

Algorithm, Inc., of 3776 Lavista Road, Suite 100A, Atlanta, Georgia 30084, produces tools for ray tracing, volume rendering, 3-D modeling and VR, animation, image processing and interactive image warping and morphing. Contact us at the above address or call/fax (404) 998-7934 for more information regarding our products. We can also be seen on the internet at http://www.algorithm.com/ or cwatkins@algorithm.com.

And special thanks again go to our parents, wives, soon-to-be wives and friends for their patience with us during this project. It's nice to know that we actually have friends after it. Well, I guess it's nice to know that we have friends at all—tee hee hee.

And once again, a most grand thanks to the Coca-Cola Company and to the Jolt Cola Company for providing cola and to Snapple for providing tea to keep us awake long enough to complete this project. We have also learned about Cheetos. . . .

Biographies

Christopher D. Watkins is founder and president of *Algorithm, Inc.*, an Atlanta-based scientific research and engineering company that produces software for medical imaging and visualization, photorealistic rendering, virtual reality, and animation. His latest focus is bringing large companies and individuals on-line to the internet—look for *The Internet Edge* (AP Professional, 1995). He is an electrical engineer, an experienced programmer, and coauthor of *Photorealism and Ray Tracing in C* (M&T Books, 1992) and *Virtual Reality ExCursions* (AP Professional, 1994). He received his degrees from The Georgia Institute of Technology and is a member of the IEEE Computer Graphics Society and of the ACM/SIGGRAPH. Hobbies include guitar, and more guitar. Come check out his Algorithm, Inc. home page at http://www.algorithm.com/

Russell J. Berube Jr. is the founder and original president of Neoteric Systems, Inc., a design and manufacturing company specializing in leading-edge microprocessor-based systems for industrial and military use. After leaving NSI, Mr. Berube founded Brookside Systems, Inc., a Chicago-based consulting company specializing in microcontroller systems and Windows consulting. He attended Brown University and the University of Rhode Island. He is a member of the ACM. His hobbies include fishing, bridge, and poker tournaments.

Stephen R. Marenka is a founder and the Chief Engineer of Akneram Industries. He specializes in human--computer interfaces, intelligent control systems, and data reduction techniques for multiplatform and internetworked computers. He is a member of the IEEE Computer and Control Systems societies and the ACM's SigChi. His degrees are from the Georgia Institute of Technology. He is the coauthor of several books including *Virtual Reality ExCursions* (AP Professional, 1994) and *The Internet Edge* (AP Professional, 1995).

Christopher Laurel works as a software developer for On Ramp, Inc., where he is fortunate enough to have his favorite hobby—3-D computer graphics—as a job focus. He graduated from St. Olaf College with degrees in mathematics and physics in spite of a consuming interest in computers. Chris enjoys skiing, playing the drums, and several other things which he would mention if he didn't detest writing about himself in the third person. He would like to acknowledge a debt to the Free Software Foundation and the developers of Linux, whose software made possible the initial versions of wt.

PART I

WINDOWS PROGRAMMING

CHAPTER 1

INTRODUCTION TO WINDOWS PROGRAMMING

Introduction

Before we begin, some items to be aware of.

- You should have or be able to obtain the Windows SDK documentation from Microsoft. These are the definitive documents in regard to the Windows API function descriptions, messages, structure definitions, etc. Without these, you're pretty much lost.

- This book is not the be-all and end-all of learning Windows. There are some subjects not covered at all. However, what we do talk about is gone into in detail.

It's about programming and virtual reality; the prize is a C-language virtual reality application for Windows. What makes it different? In addition to teaching you **what** to write to create a Windows application, we're more concerned you learn **how and why** you do certain things. Of course, you'll learn how to create a 3-D virtual environment and manipulate it. Very exciting stuff.

This is going to be informal. I want to pass along thoughts I've had and things I've learned while programming for the last 30 years. Nothing earth-shattering; rather, quietly beneficial precepts which have seen me through more software development than I care to remember, which the best programmers implement intuitively. You should be familiar with the C language; this isn't intended to be a primer. Also, we're not going to attempt to teach you all about Windows or virtual reality; that would require a good deal more than one book. What we will do is take a few selected topics and give you a thorough understanding of them. Hopefully, once you get the hang of it, you'll be able to puzzle out some other mysteries by yourself.

When I started programming, we really had machines which contained 4K core (that's right, core!) and communicated via an ASR-33 teletype over a 20mA current loop. I wrote editors, assemblers, linkers, compilers, operating systems, you name it. Everything fit in 2—3K and we brought in 1—2K overlays from the disk. Simply amazing. Now, compilers routinely require hundreds of kilobytes, and even moderate applications can run into megabytes. On the other hand, they also perform some impressive tasks: on-line help systems are expected, as is all sorts of magic-at-the-touch-of-a-button. So who got the short end of the mouse? Writing simpler (relative to today's programs) applications on cumbersome equipment back then, or the huge, complex, and sophisticated applications of today? To tell you the truth, I think we had it easier (though we did have to walk barefoot through three miles of snow every morning just to get to the mainframe...) and that's why this book was created, to help you on that journey.

My Dad always says: "*Although a loaf of bread is taller than a jar of peanut butter, the wise man also prefers jelly.*" Now, I have no idea what that means, but whenever I'm stuck, I whip it out. Conversation pretty much stops when I do, so it must be fairly profound. In any event, I'm stuck: I like Microsoft (and Windows), at the moment. But there have been times, particularly at 3 A.M., after staring at a CRT for hours, not being able to determine what's wrong, when I would have happily bombed the company into oblivion. Once I've finally figured out what's wrong and gotten things working, however, everything's wonderful again. Usually I find the problem is mine; I didn't follow my own precepts, and that's gotten me into trouble.

Windows is complicated, and getting more so by the minute. It has its problems. Like all systems, it has design flaws and some bugs, and some features are so complex to use that the total amount of documentation required to fully understand their proper implementation is staggering. This brings me to my first few profound thoughts:

Any system that requires more than a few sentences to explain is too complex. Something's wrong.

I'm not talking about explaining the physical implementation of something; that can obviously take up quite some space. I'm speaking of concepts here. I've seen this time and again—programs which weren't properly structured to begin with; patches and fixes being stuck on like bandages, the whole thing beginning to look like a beautiful girl with warts. Well, a program is an explanation to a computer. If you can't explain it simply to a machine, what makes you think you understand it?

If it doesn't flow smoothly, it's wrong.

Throw it away, *now*, before it costs too much to maintain. You'll know when you've got it right—it fits, it's simple, it's elegant. Best of all, it works.

Simple is elegant.

If you don't believe me, look at the universe. Fairly complicated as things go, but when you pull it apart, it's layer upon layer of simple, beautifully designed systems. I suspect that pattern repeats all the way to the bottom (if there is one). Which (if you haven't figured it out yet) is the way I recommend programs be written.

Program creation comes in three phases: design, implementation, and documentation (I consider debugging part of implementation). You need all three for a successful product. Designing from the hip will get you shot in the foot.

Take your time.

If I had only one piece of advice to give, this probably wouldn't be it (I think all my advice profound), but it's not bad. Time taken now, ensuring the design is correct, will be recovered so many times during implementation and documentation that you may actually finish a project when you said you would!

So, What Are We Going to Do?

When we decided to write this book, we needed to define an application which provided a platform for the teaching of our two master concepts: virtual reality and Windows implementation. After kicking it around for a few days on the phone, discounting a number of ideas, we came up with a ride through a pinball machine, in the pinball, and when we hit on the idea of *Plunging into Virtual Reality* (plunging, pinball, get it?) we knew that was it.

The Basic Concept, Application-wise

So, what's our application going to do? Once we know that, we can decide what it's going to look like. Expressed as simply as possible, we want to create an application that:

Provides the user with a view onto a 3-D modeled environment through which he can navigate.

All of the concepts expressed above are put to use now. Let's take apart our statement of intention and see what develops.

Provides the user with a view. From this we understand we're going to need a graphics display system of some sort.

3-D modeled environment. From this we understand we're going to need a 3-D modeling system.

through which he can navigate. From this we understand we're going to need a user interface and a set of navigation controls.

We can arrive at the simple flowchart in Figure 1.1 from an understanding of these statements.

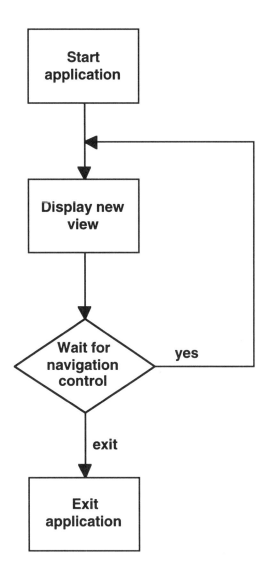

Figure 1.1—Simplified application flowchart

The question now is how to get from the simple flowchart to a working application which is obviously much more complex. The solution reveals itself in the approach to the problem—do it the way nature does complex things: recursively.

The solution to a complex problem lies in the ability to perceive it as a recursive group of less complex problems

Let's examine each part of the flowchart and begin to break it down.

Start Application

As you would expect, application startup is system-specific, though some things never change: initialization of global data and external subsystems, i.e., DLLs.

Display New View

The mechanics of displaying the new view requires us to define how, what method we'll use to move the view from the CPU memory to the display. Since we're generating a 3-D environment consisting of polygons, two choices present themselves: bitmaps and high-level polygon drawing. We'll explore both possibilities.

Wait for Navigation Control

We now need to decide what controls we'll support. We can't decide on the specifics of the control implementation yet, but we should have a good idea of what controls we need to implement. These are listed in Table 1.1.

We also need to wait. A process which must be handled with care in Windows. We'll talk about this a little further on also.

Table 1.1—Navigation controls

Description
Viewer look azimuth (left/right)
Viewer look elevation (up/down)
Automatic or manual pinball motion
Manual pinball azimuth
Manual pinball velocity
Manual update
Stop motion

Exit Application

If anything, Windows is overly sensitive to the condition it's left in when an application exits. You are responsible for clearing up any messes you've made and freeing any resources you've used.

You should be able so see, if ever so faintly, a glimmer in the distance of what it is we're going to produce. By repeating this process of breaking down each requirement, again and again, into simpler requirements, you'll find your complex task becomes manageable.

But first, we need to have an understanding of Windows.

CHAPTER **2**

WINDOWS

Windows

Windows consists of three basic programs:

- The kernel (KRNL286.EXE or KRNL386.EXE) controls and allocates all computer resources to manage memory, load applications, and schedule program execution and other tasks.

- USER.EXE creates and maintains windows on the screen, carrying out all requests to create, move, size, or remove a window. USER.EXE also handles requests regarding the icons and other components of the user interface. USER.EXE directs input to the appropriate application from the keyboard, mouse, and other input sources.

11

- GDI.EXE controls the Graphics Device Interface, which executes graphics operations that create images on the system display and other devices.

A Simple Description

Windows is a system which allows multiple applications to share the same physical computer and display device by assigning each application its own virtual display area, called a window. A window is a rectangular area to which an application can write output or from which it can receive input. Windows can overlap, and an application can own and control more than one window at a time. Windows communicates with each of the applications through the use of a mailbox called a message queue. Applications in turn communicate with

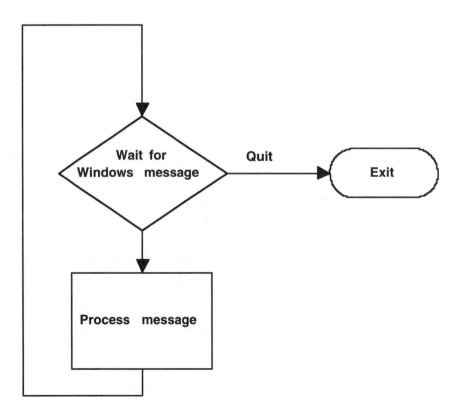

Figure 2.1—Windows application components

Windows through their responses to messages and through a series of functions provided by Windows called **API**s (Application Program Interfaces). These functions are fully described in the Microsoft SDK *Programmer's Reference, Volume 2: Functions*.

The basic structure of a Windows application is shown in Figure 2.1. That's really all there is to a Windows application. Once initialization has been completed, the application simply sits in the message loop, idling (other applications are active then) until a message is received. When a message finally is received, it's passed to the message processor, which either takes an action specific to the application, or ignores the message by passing it back to Windows.

Prior to version 4.0 (Chicago), Windows can be described as a *non-preemptive, round-robin, message-based, event-driven, multitasking scheduler and library of graphics functions*. To some extent it "sits" on top of DOS and to some extent it replaces DOS. For our purposes, we're going to assume Windows simply replaces DOS. Before we go any further, let's examine our description of Windows.

Non-preemptive

Once an application gains control, Windows won't take that control away; indeed, it can't. That means, any application can literally bring Windows to a screeching halt if it doesn't play nice with the other applications.

Each Windows application is responsible for giving up control on a periodic basis. Failure to do so causes all other applications to stop responding.

The periodic release of control is assured by the code used in the recommended Windows application paradigm. However, you must always keep in mind it's your responsibility to ensure that code is executed and frequently! For example, the (seemingly innocent) code fragment:

```
do {test <condition>} while(<condition> is true);
```

will bring Windows to a screeching halt if <condition> never goes false. So what takes control away from us? Nothing. Each application voluntarily gives up control, allowing other applications to run. Each application performs a very polite dance with all others while Windows fiddles.

Have you ever seen a juggler who kept a number of plates spinning atop long, thin poles? Remember him dashing among the poles, giving each a spin every so often? Think of him as Windows and the plates as the applications, we can even take the analogy so far as to think of the poles as the message queue. If each plate doesn't receive some attention from the juggler on a periodic basis, it'll come crashing down.

Round-Robin, Message-Based

The pole on which each plate sits is the means by which the juggler (Windows) transfers energy (information) to the plate (application). This "pole" is called the *message queue*. Windows contains a single queue (list) in which it places the messages it creates for all the applications. Version 4, "Chicago," contains a message queue per application. Every Windows application contains the code shown in Figure 2.2. It's well known to all Windows programmers, being the heart and soul of each application's link to Windows. The code fragment searches the queue for any message addressed to it. If found, the message is removed from the queue and given to the application to be processed. If there currently are no messages for an application, it gives control to the next in line. At some point, each application has examined the queue and processed all available messages. When that happens, the dance just starts all over again from the front. That circular motion is known as *round-robin* processing.

Figure 2.2—Get message loop

```
while (GetMessage(&Message, NULL, 0, 0))
{
  TranslateMessage(&Message);
  DispatchMessage(&Message);
}
return(Message.wParam);
```

GetMessage() does just what it sounds like: searches the message queue for any messages for the calling application. If none are found, Windows internally calls the next application, which presumably will execute virtually the same code itself. If a message is retrieved, it's processed by **TranslateMessage()** (for the moment, consider that a no-op) and handed to **DispatchMessage()**, which causes the message to be given to the function identified by the **lpfnWndClass** member of the **WNDCLASS** structure passed to the **RegisterClass()** function during startup.

Note that **GetMessage()** is within a **while()** loop, **GetMessage()** returns TRUE as long as the retrieved message is *not* **WM_QUIT**. Until that message is retrieved, **GetMessage()** will stay in the **while()** loop, retrieving and dispatching messages.

Event-Driven, Multitasking

What are these messages that Windows slings around? What's so important? They're each a predefined milestone, an *event* occurring within an application. Each time an *event* occurs, Windows generates and passes a message to the application associated with the event. For example, if a user changes the size of a window, a **WM_SIZE** message is generated. Moving a window causes a **WM_MOVE** message to be sent to the application. Being able to distinguish which application caused the event allows each message to be sent only to the appropriate application. Thus, Windows can support more than one application at a time (multitasking).

Library of Graphics Functions

Probably the single most significant accomplishment of Microsoft has been the creation and adoption of a set of common standards which have been defined by Microsoft and the various hardware manufacturers for Windows. Windows is popular enough, has enough visibility, enough "clout," that hardware manufacturers ensure their products conform with and "speak" to Windows.

You, the programmer, no longer need to contend with the vagaries of individual hardware systems. Windows protects you and wraps each device in a logical blanket called a **device context,** or **DC** for short. When you want to draw a line on the display or on a printer, you tell Windows where to start the line and where to end the line. That's it. Windows figures out how to talk to the actual hardware.

Getting Started

This next paragraph is repeated a few times in a few ways. It's important that you understand this concept.

The basic difference between Windows and most other operating systems can be understood by looking at something as simple as keyboard input. In most systems, an application issues a function called something on the order of **SuspendMeUntilThereIsAKeystroke()** which causes the application to wait until a key is pressed. Other applications execute while this one is suspended. Everything is straightforward. Windows is different. You don't suspend waiting for a keystroke. Your application is *constantly running;* Windows comes along and says **here is a keystroke, what do you want to do with it?** Understand that, and you've got Windows knocked.

Just as every C language application requires a function called **main()**, every Windows application requires a function called **WinMain()**. This is the function first called (as far as the programmer is concerned) by Windows. The WinMain() function must contain the code to create the application window and the *Get message loop* as described in Figure 2.2.

In addition to **WinMain()**, a Windows application must contain a CALLBACK function to process the messages sent to it. This function can be given any name, though typically it's called **WndProc()**. That's it. No other functions are required for a Windows application.

There are two types of functions so far as Windows is concerned:

- WINAPI

- CALLBACK

They are both defined as **_far _pascal**, but the important distinction is that a WINAPI function is a Windows function you call, while a CALLBACK function is your function that Windows calls.

In the **WinMain()** function two things must be done:

- register a window class

- create a window

Why register a window class? Why not simply create a window and be done with it? All the parameters for a window could be passed in a call to a window-creation function. Generic classes are needed so common windows, specifically buttons, scroll bars, checkboxes, etc., can be handled. If that's the case, you'll need to register a class to attach to the window you create. Just as importantly, you need to define the function that is going to process the messages Windows sends to your application. Once that's done, creating an instance of the specified class window allows Windows to attach a message processing function (your **WndProc()** function) to an application.

One other thing that may not be obvious: Your window need not be visible, nor must it be an overlapped window. As long as you create a valid class, reference a valid message processor function, and create a valid window, you're in business.

If those two goals are successfully accomplished and the application makes it into the *Get message loop,* then it need only concern itself with message handling from there on out.

Message handling is what the **WndProc()** function is there for. Actually, there's only one message that absolutely must be processed, and that's the **WM_DESTROY** message. You must execute the **PostQuitMessage()** function when sent **WM_DESTROY**. Do that, and your application is at least following the basic rules established by Windows.

User Interface

Windows accepts physical user input from a keyboard, a mouse or a pen; pen input is beyond the scope of this book.

Keyboard Input

Your application receives keyboard input from the messages:

WM_CHAR
WM_KEYDOWN

WM_KEYUP
WM_SYSKEYDOWN
WM_SYSKEYUP

The WM_CHAR message is a combination of a WM_KEYDOWN followed by a WM_KEYUP message. The WM_SYSKEYDOWN and UP are identical to the WM_KEYDOWN and UP, except the SYSKEY messages indicate the ALT key is being pressed. Each time a key is pressed, Windows sends a WM_KEYDOWN message. When the key is released, Windows sends a WM_KEYUP message followed by a WM_CHAR message.

Windows treats the keyboard in the same manner as any other program: keys have codes; type a key and the code is sent to the program. The problem is, what code and which program? The most widely accepted character code in use today is ASCII. Its 128 different character codes suffice for all of the letters, numbers, punctuation, and carriage control. But the best part is an ASCII character fits very nicely in 8 bits, one byte. The keyboard, however, contains more characters than just the normal letters and numbers. There are cursor control arrows, function keys, and a host of editing controls. What about these?

Windows solves the problem through the use of *virtual key codes*. These are 8-bit codes which incorporate the additional keys found on graphics keyboards. Appendix B of the Microsoft SDK *Programmer's Reference, Volume 3: Messages, Structures and Macros* contains the virtual key codes.

Now the question becomes, which application gets the character when one is typed? That depends on which window has the focus. Which window, not application. An application can contain multiple windows, and only one of them will receive the character; that window is the one with the **focus**. The input focus is closely related to the **active window**. The active window is either an application's main window or a child window of that application. Windows highlights the title bar of the active application's window. If the active window is a child of an application, then typically it has a focus rectangle drawn around it.

Menus

In addition to simple keystrokes, input to Windows can take the form of menu selections. Within Windows you can create menus. When a menu selection is made, Windows generates a WM_COMMAND message. Also, Windows supports a feature called *keyboard accelerators* where keystrokes are associated with a menu item. Windows translates a keystroke into a WM_COMMAND message if it is found in a simple lookup table.

Mouse Input

Mouse input is somewhat different. We want to know when a mouse button is clicked, and we also want to know where the mouse is whenever it is moved. Windows provides a number of messages regarding the mouse:

> **WM_LBUTTONDOWN**
> **WM_LBUTTONUP**
> **WM_MBUTTONDOWN**
> **WM_MBUTTONUP**
> **WM_RBUTTONDOWN**
> **WM_RBUTTONUP**
> **WM_MOUSEMOVE**

These messages are sent to an application whenever a mouse button (**L/M/R**) is clicked or released or when the mouse is being moved. These messages are only sent to the window across which the mouse is moving. But suppose we want to track the mouse? If we note when a mouse button is clicked down and then follow the mouse-move messages, what happens if the user releases the mouse over another window, not us? Windows provides for that with the **SetCapture()** and **ReleaseCapture()** functions. Regardless of where the mouse is, once an application requests mouse capture, all mouse messages are sent to that application.

Windows also passes the mouse position with every mouse message. This brings up another question: position relative to what? Well, for mouse messages, the position is relative to the *client area* of the window. Which means, *unless you've changed the mapping mode,* the upper left corner of the window, excluding the title and frame, is coordinate (0, 0) and the lower right corner is (x-1, y-1) where x **is the width of the client area in pixels and** y **is the height of the client area in pixels**. Figure 2.3 shows the difference between *screen coordinates* and *client coordinates*.

Figure 2.3—Window coordinates

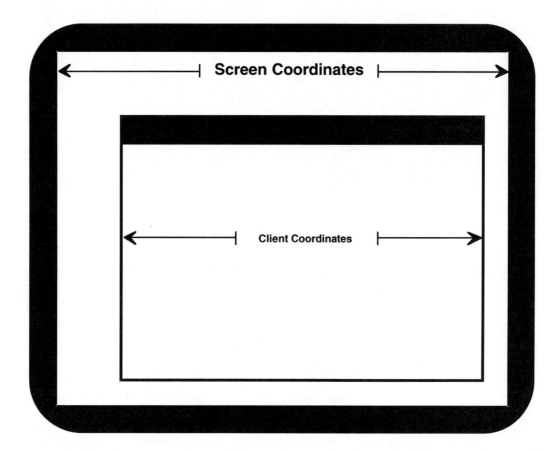

Windows provides two functions for getting information about your window location and size: **GetWindowRect()** and **GetClientRect()**. **GetWindowRect()** returns a rectangle structure which contains the screen coordinates of the perimeter of the window. A returned rectangle of 50, 75, 300, 400 describes a window with an upper left corner at pixels (50, 75) and a lower right corner at pixels (300, 400) *relative to the upper left corner of the display*. **GetClientRect()**, on the other hand, would return a rectangle of 0, 0, 250, 325, where 250 and 325 would be the width and height of the client area of the window. **GetClientRect()** *always* returns an upper left corner of 0, 0. Actually, it probably wouldn't return 250, 325, but something smaller. Remember this is the actual client area size so the returned rectangle will be minus any borders, captions, scroll bars, etc.

Child Window Control

You can also control the application through the use of child windows. These include the standard Windows child window classes: buttons, checkboxes, listboxes, scrollbars, etc. Or you can roll your own. You create a child window control in the same manner as any other window. Register a class if it's not standard and create a window, putting it where you want. The key part is the **CreateWindow()** parameters. From the *Microsoft SDK Programmer's Reference, Volume 2: Functions*:

```
HWND     CreateWindow(lpszClassName, lpszWindowName, dwStyle, x, y, nWidth, nHeight,
hwndParent, hmenu, hinst, lpvParam)
```

The particular parameter we're interested in is the *hmenu*. When creating a child window (*hwndParent* not NULL), *hmenu* is not a handle to a menu; rather, it is a unique id value used to identify the child window. When? When Windows, surprise, sends the application a WM_COMMAND message indicating something is going on with the child window.

Graphics

Graphics functions are the concern of GDI.EXE. This includes line and shape drawing, area fill, text output and bitmap processing. Windows supports these functions through the use of **GDI objects** such as **pens**, **brushes**, **fonts**, and **bitmaps**. We'll use all of these objects in the application.

Device Context

Before continuing, you need to meet an old friend, the **device context**. One of the major goals for Windows was (and is) physical device independence, from the application point of view. An application should ideally be able to draw a line on any device, printer, display, plotter, etc., without caring about the physical commands required to perform the task. Windows does that, but there's more. If I'm drawing a line from the upper left corner to the upper right corner, I need to know some of the physical characteristics of the device I'm working with, which seems to defeat device independence.

Both issues are addressed through a device context. To perform any operation with a device, the device must first be connected to a device context, sort of a logical blackboard you get to scribble on. Once connected, and there are a number of methods, you can access the device's physical characteristics using **GetDeviceCaps()**. Each physical device supported by Windows has an associated **device driver**, software written (probably by the device's manufacturer) according to the rules established by Windows.

Pens

Windows draws lines with imaginary pens. You can create your own, specifying thickness, style, and color.

Brushes

Windows "paints" with imaginary brushes. These are used to fill in enclosed figures and paint the background of a window. They can be mixed with bitmaps for some interesting effects. Brushes are themselves small bitmaps.

Fonts

Windows displays text using fonts, which are collections of printing characters of a specific physical shape. If you have a typewriter, it has a single font; the characters it can produce are fixed in metal. Changing the typing element changes the font. You can create your own fonts or use those provided by other vendors.

Bitmaps

Windows is most efficient in displaying images when they are bitmaps, rather than a **metafile**, which is a series of individually drawn elements.

The virtual world you see in PIVR is a bitmap, updated every time the world view changes. So in order to understand what's happening in PIVR, you're going to need to understand bitmaps. Prepare yourself; this is a rather lengthy explanation.

Bitmaps

Take a close-up look at the display screen of your computer. Use a magnifying glass if you have one. You'll see the display area is composed of thousands of clustered dots, a red, a green, and a blue (RGB) bunched together as shown in Figure 2.4. These are the **primary colors**. Each cluster of three dots is called a *pixel*. Each dot is a minute quantity of a phosphor, which gives off light of the appropriate color when stimulated. That stimulation comes from three electron guns at the back of the display, one for each of the primary colors.

Figure 2.4—Physical pixel layout

But the best part is the way the human eye works. Put two or more colored dots close together and the eye "sees" a different color. Stand about 10 feet away from this book and look at Figure 2.4. You should see a yellow strip between the red and green bars and a cyan strip between the green and blue. This phenomenon is called **dithering**. Each of the electron guns is in turn controlled by a signal from the video card in your computer. For purposes of simplicity, we're going to assume that the control signal from the video card is a linear voltage from 0 to some maximum, with a value of 0 producing no color at the pixel being stimulated while a maximum value produces maximum saturation of the selected color. By varying the control voltage from 0 to maximum, all intensities of a hue can be achieved. With all three guns working simultaneously, any color can be achieved.

True Color Images

Envision a structure which contains a value for each of the three primary colors. Each value will in turn control the video card, which controls the electron gun which irradiates the phosphor. To simplify matters, each value in the structure will be a byte, so it can contain a value from 0 to a maximum of 255. This gives us 256 different intensities for each of the primary colors or (256 x 256 x 256) 16,777,216 total colors. Figure 2.5 shows an example of this structure, called an **RGB triple**.

Figure 2.5—RGB triple

RED	GREEN	BLUE

A system capable of displaying 16M simultaneous colors is called **true color** capable. Unfortunately, because of hardware constraints and other considerations, it's far less expensive to support display of far fewer colors. In fact, the most popular display methodology allows for the display of 256 simultaneous colors. We're going to look at bitmaps which support both display systems.

Picture a picture, then picture that picture on your display. Picture the pixels that the picture covers as a rectangular grid. Each row of pixels is called a **scan line**. Picture that for every pixel in the picture, there is a color structure that we just spoke about which governs the color of the pixel. The color structure determines the intensities of red, green, and blue that make up the pixel. An array of color structures is required to describe the pixels in one scan line and an array of scan line, color structure arrays is required to describe the entire picture. That array of arrays is a bitmap.

Consider a true color bitmap. Each pixel in the image is described by an RGB triple. If we have a 10x20 pixel image the space required to describe the image colors is 10x20x3 or 600 total bytes. Let's leave aside the question of support structures such as file headers for the moment. Clearly, these 600 bytes completely describe the colors of the image, regardless of whose video card or display we wish to use. If a pixel is described by an RGB triple which has a value of 255,0,0, then regardless of hardware, this describes a pixel of maximum red intensity and no green or blue intensity. The actual colors may vary from display to display or from display to color printer, but the relative effects should be identical. Indeed, what we have created is a **device-independent bitmap (DIB)**. Figure 2.6 shows the correspondence between an RGB triple and the associated pixel in an image.

Figure 2.6—True color image

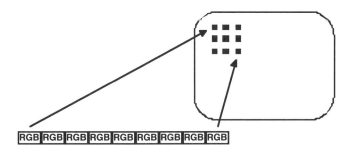

256-Color Images

Let's consider the alternative to a true color image we mentioned, a 256 simultaneous color image. How is this accomplished, and why would we want to do it at all? The how is by use of a device called a **palette**, the wooden gizmo used by artists to hold the paints currently mixed and being used. Any color on the palette can be replaced with another, but there's only room for so many colors at one time. Picture a video card which contains a hardware palette which contains 256 entries, each an RGB triple. If we have the ability to read and write the entries in the palette, we can create a picture by loading the palette entries with the colors used in our image. How the actual hardware functions isn't important to this discussion. *But now, each pixel in the image is described by an index into the palette instead of an actual RGB triple*. We no longer require an RGB triple for each pixel. Since we know (by definition) there are no more than 256 colors, we can replace an RGB triple with a single byte that is an index into the palette which contains the actual RGB triples. Figure 2.7 shows this concept. The vertical stack of RGB triples is the palette, while the array of RGB triples present in a true color image has been replaced by the values (in this example) 3, 2, 0, 1, ... which are palette indices. The first byte, which still corresponds to the first pixel in the picture, contains the value 3, which tells the hardware to display the RGB triple value in palette entry 3 whenever the first pixel is displayed. The last byte, corresponding to the last pixel in the picture, contains the value 2, which tells the hardware to display the RGB triple value palette entry 2 whenever the last pixel is displayed.

Figure 2.7—256-color image

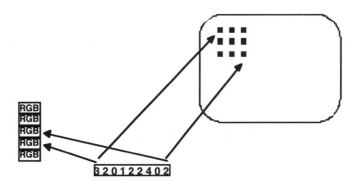

The 256-color image format is somewhat more complex than the true color: it must contain both the image pixels (as palette indices) and the actual colors with which the palette is to be loaded when the image is displayed. Note, however, that since the image format contains absolute RGB values, the 256-color image is also a device-independent bitmap format. Since the hardware required to support a 256-color palette image is less expensive than true color hardware and the image is one-third the size (plus the overhead for the palette), 256-color images are the norm when dealing with Windows.

If you've followed the discussion so far, then you realize the palette technique can be used for images with any maximum number of colors. The limit in the lower end being monochrome, you don't need a palette when you're only concerned with turning a pixel on or off; since there's no color involved, a single bit suffices to describe a pixel. At the other end is a true color image. You wouldn't require a palette of RGB triples and an additional set of palette indices when you already had the individual pixels described in terms of their absolute color. You're wasting space in that case.

So, if we have a true color image, a pixel appears on the display screen when we send a complete three-byte RGB triple to the video card. For a 256-color image, a pixel appears when we send a one-byte value to the video card, which uses that as an index into the hardware palette. That returns an RGB triple from the palette which is the final pixel color.

System Palette

Suppose we predefined the colors that were available. That does us no good for a true color image, but with a 256 (or less) color image we can now eliminate the palette requirement from the image. Since it's using predefined colors, there's no requirement for it to contain a palette. Well, that's only 256 x 3 (768) bytes. Who cares? If you're asking that question, you haven't been around computers long enough. You can buy 1 MB for $130.00 or thereabouts nowadays. I remember when 4KB of core cost $9,000.00! At one time, everything was done in the holy name of saving memory. Every byte saved meant one more feature might be squeezed in....

In any event, we have another image format, which is similar to a palette image format with the single difference that the actual palette has been removed, reducing the size of the image. But we pay a price (of course): The image has become a **device-dependent bitmap (DDB)**. Or perhaps a better phrase would be palette-dependent. The end result is the same, however: I can't give you an image unless I know the palette you're using is identical to mine.

As usual, reality is somewhere in the middle, between a predefined palette and a completely definable palette. Windows reserves 20 of the 256 colors and leaves the rest for each application. By reserving 20 colors, Windows guarantees the colors it uses to draw its components, window frames, buttons, highlights, etc., will always be available and will be consistent. That basic, 20-color-only palette is called the **system palette** in Windowspeak.

Stored Bitmap Formats

Bitmaps are stored either as files (normally .BMP) or as resources in a .EXE file. The only difference between the two formats is that the .BMP file format contains an additional structure, a **BITMAPFILEHEADER**, which precedes the remaining information.

Figure 2.8—Bitmap file structure

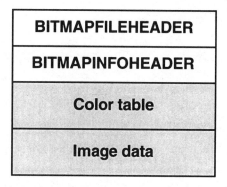

Figure 2.8 shows the structure of a bitmap file. The PIVR application is structured to use bitmaps stored as resources within the .EXE file. The application contains code to load and process bitmaps both as resources and files. While we're here, we'll restrict ourselves to a discussion of the various bitmap components.

BITMAPFILEHEADER

The first is the **BITMAPFILEHEADER**. This structure is located at the beginning of a bitmap file. Table 2.1 describes the structure.

BITMAPINFO

Remember, a bitmap stored as a resource in an executable file doesn't have a BITMAPFILEHEADER structure. It begins where a bitmap file continues, with a **BITMAPINFOHEADER** structure. There is another structure, a **BITMAPINFO**, which is virtually the same except that it contains an offset to the start of the

Table 2.1—BITMAPFILEHEADER structure

Name	Data type	Description
bfType	UINT	Must be 0x4D42 which is "BM" in ASCII. Used as a file type identifier
bfSize	DWORD	File size in bytes.
bfReserved1	UINT	I have no clue.
bfReserved2	UINT	Ditto.
bfOffBits	DWORD	File offset to the beginning of the actual image data.

Table 2.2—BITMAPINFO structure

Name	Data type	Description
bmiHeader	BITMAPINFOHEADER	BITMAPINFOHEADER structure for the bitmap.
bmiColors	RGBQUAD	Beginning of *optional* bitmap color table.

color table. Table 2.2 shows the layout of a BITMAPINFO structure, while Table 2.3 shows the layout of a BITMAPINFOHEADER structure. Note that they both point to the same location in the bitmap.

BITMAPINFOHEADER

Seeing the values in the structures and reading their descriptions isn't the same thing as understanding how they're used. Let's take the structure members one at a time....

The **biSize** member has two uses. First, for a BITMAPINFOHEADER structure it's different than for a **BITMAPCOREHEADER**. A BITMAPCOREHEADER structure is found at the beginning of an OS/2 bitmap while a BITMAPINFOHEADER begins a Windows 3 format bitmap. You can use

Table 2.3—BITMAPINFOHEADER structure

Name	Data type	Description
biSize	DWORD	Size of the BITMAPINFOHEADER itself. Used to determine whether this is a Windows or OS/2 format bitmap. Also used in offset calculations.
biWidth	LONG	Image width in pixels.
biHeight	LONG	Image height in pixels (scan lines).
biPlanes	WORD	Number of color planes for display. *Must be 1.*
biBitCount	WORD	Number of color bits per pixel. See Table 2.4.
biCompression	DWORD	Coded image data compression mode. See Table 2.5.
biSizeImage	DWORD	Size of the image in bytes. This is *not* simply the image width times the image height. Refer to the ensuing description.
biXPelsPerMeter	LONG	Presumably the physical width of the image. Not used by Windows.
biYPelsPerMeter	LONG	Presumably the physical height of the image. Not used by Windows.
biClrUsed	DWORD	Number of colors in color table.
biClrImportant	DWORD	Number of colors in color table considered important when rendering the image.

the code fragment in Figure 2.9 to determine what type of bitmap you're dealing with.

The member is also used to compute the offset to the bitmap color table. There are three important pointers in the life of every bitmap: The pointer to the bitmap header (BITMAPINFOHEADER*); the pointer to the bitmap color table

(RGBQUAD*); and the pointer to the bitmap image data (BYTE*). The pointer to the color table is computed as follows:

```
LPBITMAPINFOHEADER        lpBI;
LPRGBQUAD        lpColorTable;
lpColorTable = (LPRGBQUAD)(HPBYTE)lpBI+(LONG)lpBI->biSize;
```

Figure 2.9—Bitmap type determination

```
LPBITMAPINFOHEADER        lpBI;
        if (lpBI->biSize == sizeof(BITMAPINFOHEADER))
        {
          here you've got a Windows 3 format bitmap.
        }
        else
        {
          here you've got an OS/2 format bitmap.
        }
```

What type is HPBYTE? Where did that come from? Typedef it as (BYTE huge*). Actually, it's not necessary here—LPBYTE would be sufficient—but pointer arithmetic is tricky.

You can ensure your pointer arithmetic** always **works if you cast pointers to huge and cast offsets to LONG.

The **biWidth** member is the width of the image, *not the image data*, in pixels. As was mentioned before, image data is stored as an array of image scan lines. To simplify data-handling, *each scan line is required to be a multiple of 32 bits (4 bytes)*. If you had a bitmap 1 pixel wide, and 2 pixels high, you must allocate 4 bytes for each scan line, 8 bytes total. Only the first byte of each scan line is used; the last three are useless padding. Use the formula in Figure 2.10 to determine scan line width.

Figure 2.10—Scan line width computation

$$slw = \frac{(biWidth \times biBitCount + 31) \& ^\wedge 31}{8}$$

The **biHeight** member is the height of the image in scan lines (pixels). A new feature is being introduced for expanded bitmap support: If the height value is positive, the bitmap is a "standard" Windows 3 upside-down image where the image data begins with the last scan line (lower left corner of the image). I know this is something we haven't spoken of yet; be patient. If the height is negative, the image data begins with the first scan line (upper left corner of the image).

The **biBitCount** member is the number of color bits per pixel in the image. This field is used to compute the number of colors in the color table. Indeed, it's used to determine if there even is a color table. If the value is 8 or less, there's a color table in the bitmap. Anything larger implies the image data is absolute color values. If the value is 8 or less, the number of colors in the color table is determined as shown in Table 2.4.

Table 2.4—Color bits per pixel

Bits	Total image colors
1	2
4	16
8	256
16	65,536
24	2^{24}
32	2^{32}
biClrUsed != 0	biClrUsed

The **biCompression** member contains one of the values in listed in Table 2.5. The image data for most Windows bitmaps is uncompressed. The run-length-encoded (RLE) data format is beyond the scope of this book, but

Table 2.5—Bitmap compression modes

Name	Description
BI_RGB	Uncompressed image data.
BI_RLE4	Run-length-encoded image data, 4 color bits per pixel.
BI_RLE8	Run-length-encoded-image data, 8 color bits per pixel.
BI_BITFIELDS	Bitmap is new format: 16 or 32 bits/pixel.

basically, compression is achieved by replacing groups of identical palette indices with a count and a single-color palette index value. A detailed explanation can be found in the *Programmer's Reference, Volume 3: Messages, Structures and Macros, Microsoft Windows SDK pp. 240-241.*

If the compression mode is BI_RGB, the **biSizeImage** member is often not used and may be set to 0. If, however, an RLE compression format is specified, this field contains the number of RLE-encoded bytes. If the compression mode is BI_BITFIELDS, the color table (bmiColors array) contains three **DWORD** values: the red bits mask, the green bits mask, and finally the blue bits mask. Logically, **or**-ing the three mask values produces a single DWORD which is the complete bits mask for a single pixel in the image.

The **biXPelsPerMeter** and **biYPelsPerMeter** members specify the horizontal and vertical resolution in pixels/meter for the target device of the bitmap. As far as I know, these fields aren't used by anyone for anything. At least not as far as I've seen.

The **biClrUsed** member is the number of entries in the color table if the maximum number of colors aren't used. If the image is 8 bits/pixel or less, normally all colors are used, the number of color table entries is determined from Table 2.4, and the **biClrUsed** member is 0. If fewer colors are used, this is the number of valid color table entries.

The **biClrImportant** member is the number of colors (in the color table) considered important to render the image properly. A value of 0 indicates all colors are equally important. Note that a nonzero value here implies the colors in the color table are arranged in order of importance.

Bitmap Color Table

The second member of the BITMAPINFO structure, **bmiColors**, is only present if:

- the image contains 8 bits/pixel or less

- the **biCompression** member of the **BITMAPINFOHEADER** structure has the value BI_BITFIELDS

If the image contains 8 bits/pixel or less, the color table consists of the number of entries found in Table 2.4. Each entry is an **RGBQUAD**, which is an RGBTRIPLE as shown in Figure 2.5—plus a null byte to make it mod 32 (long). Figure 2.11 shows the structure of an RGBQUAD.

Figure 2.11—RGB quad

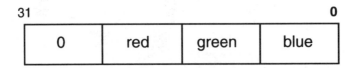

If you have an 8 bit/pixel image, there are 2^8 (256) RGBQUAD entries in the color table. If the biCompression member is BI_BITFIELDS, the color table is exactly three DWORDs in length, as described earlier.

Image Data

Remember, if there are 8 bits/pixel (256 or less colors) in the image, the image data is *not* actual RGB color values, but is indices into the color table. Anything more than 8 bits/pixel and the image data is actual RGB values, sized according to the **biBitsPixel** member.

One last thing to discuss when speaking of Windows bitmaps is the orientation of the image data. You wouldn't think this would cause any problems. However....

In both existing Windows 3 (old-style) and new-style bitmaps, the image data is physically placed in memory, as we have already discussed, as an array of scan lines. Each scan line is itself an array of pixel data. The difference is, in the older, existing Windows 3 bitmaps, the scan line order is physically reversed from what you would expect: The first scan line in memory is the bottom scan line of the image, while the last scan line in memory is the top scan line of the image, as shown in Figure 2.12. This was a holdover from OS/2 and Presentation Manager. In the newer, Win32-style bitmaps (those with a negative **biHeight** member in the **BITMAPINFOHEADER** structure), the image data is arranged such that the first scan line in memory is the top scan line of the image and the last scan line in memory is the bottom scan line of the image, as shown in Figure 2.13.

Figure 2.12—Image data (old style)

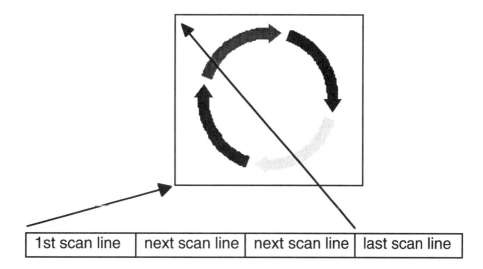

| 1st scan line | next scan line | next scan line | last scan line |

Note that new-style bitmaps probably won't work with most existing applications, particularly those released prior to a general awareness of Win32-style bitmap formats.

Figure 2.13—Image data (new style)

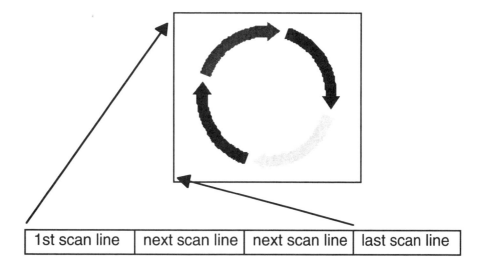

| 1st scan line | next scan line | next scan line | last scan line |

What We Haven't Talked About

We didn't cover two subjects: OS/2 bitmap format and the run-length-encoded (RLE) compressed format supported by Windows. These are beyond our discussion, but explanations for each can be found in the standard Microsoft documentation.

Waiting (for the Light?)

Windows provides the **WM_TIMER** message to those who must be patient. Internally, Windows maintains a number of global timers that are assigned to any application requiring them. Each timer is identified by its parent application and a user-assigned ID. Windows provides two functions for dealing with the timers, **SetTimer()** and **KillTimer()**.

SetTimer()

Executing this function causes Windows to generate a WM_TIMER message *every time* the specified time interval elapses. You can have multiple timers within your application simultaneously, but each time you create a timer you should verify that your request succeeded; don't forget there are other applications which are competing for the same resources.

SetTimer(HWND, UINT, UINT, TIMERPROC);

The HWND identifies the owner window. You can leave this NULL; the timer will simply be associated with your application.

The first UINT is a user-assigned ID value. If you have more than one timer going at a time, you identify them by the ID value.

The second UINT is the time interval, in milliseconds, before Windows generates a WM_TIMER message.

Finally, there is the TIMERPROC which is described below.

There are two basic methods through which a waiting mechanism can be handled:

- Standard message processing

- CALLBACK function (TIMERPROC)

When you create a timer, the last parameter can be left NULL or a CALLBACK function can be specified. If it is left NULL, when the time interval elapses and Windows generates a WM_TIMER message, that message is simply placed into the application's message queue and is processed by your **WndProc()** function in the same manner as any other function. Or, if a CALLBACK function is specified, instead of adding a WM_TIMER message to the application's message queue, Windows calls the user-specified TIMERPROC function. This is a normal CALLBACK function. You can specify different (or the same) CALLBACK functions for each timer you create.

KillTimer()

Once started, a timer is relentless: It will continue to generate WM_TIMER messages until stopped with the **KillTimer()** function. Identify the timer to be stopped by the ID specified when the timer was created.

Compiling an Application

To get a Windows application up and running you need to do the following:

- Create a source module which contains a **WinMain()** function and a Windows-message-processing function, usually called (but not required to be) **WndProc()**.

- Compile the source file(s) using **CL** to create .OBJ files.

- Create a .RC file.

- Run the resource compiler **RC** on the .RC file to create a .RES file.

- Create a .DEF file.

- Link the .OBJ files, a .DEF file and whatever Window's libraries are required using **LINK** to create a .EXE file.

- Run **RC** again to attach the .RES file to the .EXE file.

- Hold your breath and run the application (the .EXE file).

Compiling under Microsoft Visual Workbench

To compile the PIVR application under Visual Workbench, use the project file PIVR.MAK.

CHAPTER 3

THE APPLICATION

The Application

Let's continue the process of creating our application by repeating the iterative process of breaking each section component into less and less complex components. Note that each time this process is repeated, we have more statements describing the functional requirements of a component, but each describes, in more detail, a less functionally complex task.

The breakdown of a complex component is complete when we have a description consisting of a series of statements, each of which describes a single function.

Start Application

As previously stated, we need to initialize any global data and external subsystems and perform any application-specific initializations. So we can break down the **Start Application** component into three functions:

> **InitializeGlobalData();**
>
> **InitializeExternalSubsystems();**
>
> **InitializeApplication();**

InitializeGlobalData()

This function is where all data values are initialized. The key concept here is not what data is specifically initialized, but rather that the function is present. This way, as the application development progresses and new data items are found to be necessary, their initialization, if any, isn't scattered throughout the application code, but located in a single area. Bear in mind, you're going to require new data occasionally. Being able to know, without thinking, where to initialize it is one less thing to worry about.

Anything you can do to make your code more bulletproof can't possibly be wrong.

Many have a hard time understanding the previous statement goes beyond simple application execution performance, but extends to the code documentation as well. Maintaining code which is physically coherent and systematically laid out greatly reduces debugging and training time. I am constantly bemoaning the paucity of listing controls, such as page eject, subtitles and table of contents, available with current C and C++ compilers. Who takes listings any more? One way I attempt to bring order to a listing is to alphabetize functions wherever possible. Don't laugh, it's a small thing, but it helps.

InitializeExternalSubsystems()

Each application may or may not utilize external systems. In our example, we're treating the VR engine as a separate subsystem from the Windows portion of the application. So for us, call **vrBegin()** to initialize the VR engine satisfies the requirement of initializing external systems.

InitializeApplication()

For Windows, application-specific initializations means creating the window the user sees. This introduces a new concept, *window class*. Windows supports classes of windows, each with its own unique name. There are a number of pre-defined classes (called system global classes by Windows), i.e., "static," "edit," "button," etc. The quotes indicate the class name is literally the ASCII string **STATIC**. Each class has associated properties. There is no generic "I just want a basic window" class; you have to create your own using the **RegisterClass()** function as shown in Figure 3.1.

Figure 3.1—Registering a window class

```
WNDCLASS wc;                          // WNDCLASS structure

// Fill in WNDCLASS structure which describes the characteristics of the application
window we're creating...
        wc.style = CS_HREDRAW | CS_VREDRAW | CS_DBLCLKS | CS_BYTEALIGNCLIENT;
        wc.lpfnWndProc   = WndProc;
        wc.cbClsExtra    = 0;
        wc.cbWndExtra    = 0;
        wc.hInstance     = hInst;
        wc.hIcon = LoadIcon(hInst, MAKEINTRESOURCE(IDI_ICON1));
        wc.hCursor       = LoadCursor(NULL, IDC_ARROW);
        wc.hbrBackground= GetStockObject(BLACK_BRUSH);
        wc.lpszMenuName  = NULL;
        wc.lpszClassName= tClsName;

// Register window class. Exit with the return code from that function...
        if (RegisterClass(&wc)) return(TRUE);
        return(FALSE);
```

Fill in the fields of the **WNDCLASS** structure and pass it to the **RegisterClass()** function, which returns nonzero if successful, else returns zero. What do the various fields contain? Table 3.1 lists the field contents used by our application.

After **RegisterClass()**, we can create the actual window using **CreateWindow()**. The first parameter is the window class name **tClsName**, which we've just registered. Next is the window title "**Virtual Pinball**." Now our application is not going to display a title, because our window doesn't have a caption. This is required so that the Windows **ALT-TAB** task switching facility, which displays each application's icon and title, has something to show. Next is the window style value: **WS_POPUP | WS_CLIPCHILDREN | WS_VISIBLE**. Since we wish to utilize the entire screen, without showing a title or menu, we don't want the **WS_OVERLAPPED** style. **WS_CLIPCHILDREN** causes any child controls to be excluded from the paint update region when the window is invalidated, and **WS_VISIBLE** is just what it sounds like. Immediately following are four numeric values: start x, start y, width, and height. We always start at 0,0. Even with the prohibition against hard coded constants, that much we can guarantee. The size, however, is dynamic, and we rely on Windows to tell us exactly how large the screen is: **GetSystemMetrics(SM_CXSCREEN)** and **GetSystemMetrics(SM_CYSCREEN)**. Next, we have no parent, so specify **NULL**. We have no menu; specify **NULL**. Next is the handle to the application instance. Finally, we're not interested in passing a **CREATESTRUCT** to the **WM_CREATE** message handler function, so specify **NULL**. Figure 3.2 shows a code fragment which creates a window.

Figure 3.2—Window creation

```
hWnd = CreateWindow(tClsName,
        "Virtual Pinball",
        WS_POPUP | WS_CLIPCHILDREN | WS_VISIBLE,
        0,
        0,
        GetSystemMetrics(SM_CXSCREEN),
        GetSystemMetrics(SM_CYSCREEN),
        NULL,
        NULL,
        hInst,
        NULL);
return(hWnd);
```

Table 3.1—WNDCLASS structure contents

Field	Contents
style	CS_HREDRAW causes the entire window to be redrawn if the horizontal size changes. CS_VREDRAW causes the entire window to be redrawn if the vertical size changes. CS_BYTEALIGNCLIENT causes the client area of the window to be aligned on a byte boundary which provides better BitBlt performance. CS_DBLCLKS allows the window to receive the WM_xBUTTONDBLCLK message instead of a second WM_xBUTTONDOWN message. 0 if no special style requirements.
lpfnWndProc	This is the address of the function called by Windows (as a CALLBACK function) to process messages for the application. This is the **message processor** function from Figure 2.1. This field must not be NULL.
cbClsExtra	This is the number of extra bytes allocated for each instance of this class. 0 if no additional bytes required.
cbWndExtra	This is the number of extra bytes allocated for each instance of a window of this class. 0 if no additional bytes required.
hInstance	This is the handle of the application module and must not be NULL.
hIcon	This is the handle of the ICON associated with this class. Set to NULL if the application will draw its own icon.
hCursor	This is the handle to the CURSOR associated with all windows of this class. If NULL, the application is required to set the cursor each time it is moved into the window.
hbrBackground	This is the handle to the background brush used by Windows to color the background (client area) of a window of this class. If set to NULL, the application is responsible for erasing (drawing the background) of the window by processing the WM_ERASEBKGND message.
lpszMenuName	This is a pointer to the string which is the resource name of the default menu. If NULL, there is no default menu.
lpszClassName	This is a pointer to the string which is the class name. For example, "MyWindow."

So we can break down this function into simpler components, each of which actually performs a single, discrete function:

RegisterOurWindowClass()

CreateOurWindow()

Once this is done, application initialization is virtually complete. We need only display the window frame and paint the client area. Displaying the window frame is performed by the **ShowWindow()** function. On entry, Windows passes each application a code which is how the window should be displayed: normally, iconized, maximized. This value can, of course, be ignored; you can display your window frame however you wish. Finally, the **UpdateWindow()** function causes any **WM_PAINT** messages to be dequeued and processed immediately. This causes the client area to be painted.

In the meantime, we can have a little fun. That's what **DoStartup()** does. It also serves another purpose: demonstrating some of the bitmap processing methods available in Windows.

Display New View

Each time we detect a change in the controls, we pass that to the VR system. It in turn computes a new view in memory in the form of a Windows bitmap, and we, the Windows portion of PIVR, draw the bitmap on the display. Windows provides a number of methods for processing bitmaps, and it can get confusing because a number of factors come into play. Specifically, monitor specifications, video card color resolution, bitmap loading method, display method, palette control—it can leave you talking to yourself. The best way I know to develop an understanding is to go through each item, sometimes again and again. Well, here goes....

Monitor Specifications

We're going to make one assumption: you're not using a monochrome monitor. If you are, wherever we talk of colors, you need to think of shades of gray. All monitors have a physical size in terms of the glass CRT face size, number of pixels per scan line, and number of scan lines.

Video Card Color Resolution

Two things determine the capabilities (other than speed) of a video card: the technology of the hardware and the amount of memory. The hardware technology, especially now, is such that even the less expensive video cards are capable of fairly impressive performance, leaving the amount of memory to determine the card characteristics. Think of a sheet of rubber and how it can be stretched: You can make it wide and skinny or less wide and deeper. Think of the width as the number of pixels/scan line and the depth as the number of scan lines. Further, realize that, with any width we also need to specify a number of bits/pixel. As we increase that, we decrease the number of pixels/scan line. This rubber sheet we've been speaking of is the **video RAM** on the video card. The card is capable of performing, within limits, this stretching, thereby making available different display resolutions. For example, let's assume your display card contains 1MB of video RAM. Let's further assume you want true color (24 bits/pixel). How large an area can the card handle? At best:

$$\frac{1,048,576 / 24}{8} = 349,525$$

which is a 591 x 591 pixel square. If you wanted to handle a 1024 x 768 pixel display in 16M colors (24 bits/pixel) you'd require:

$$\frac{1024 \times 768 \times 24}{8} = 2,359,296$$

bytes of video RAM. Since video RAM is normally available in binary increments, this would require a card with 4MB.

Bear in mind that regardless of how many colors an image contains, the hardware has the final say. If it's set to display a maximum of 16 colors, that's all you're going to get!

Bitmap Loading Method

From here on out, we have some control over the final image. With the monitor and video card, all we could do was accept what was given. As we've discussed before, Windows provides two basic types of images: **device-dependent bitmap (DDB)** and **device-independent bitmap (DIB)**. A DIB carries its color definitions with it, while a DDB has no color information, but is a series of palette indices instead of actual colors. DDB images can be displayed *much* faster than DIB images. At this point you should pause and ask, what palette? Aha! The currently realized palette.

Which means DDB images are critically dependent on the current palette.

DDB images are displayed using the **BitBlt()** function, while DIB images can be displayed using either **SetDIBitsToDevice()** or **StretchDIBits()**, the latter being the runaway favorite.

There are four methods of loading a bitmap, depending on how it's stored: either as a resource in the executable file or as a bitmap image file.

No information is lost storing a bitmap as a resource. However, the **LoadResource()** function, the first method of loading an image, always loads a bitmap as a DDB. Unfortunately, Windows loads these images *using the system palette.* This means a maximum of 20 colors! Even if you store a true color image with thousands of colors, load it using **LoadResource()** and you'll see it reduced to the basic system palette colors.

The second method of loading an image is to open and load an image file from the application. This entails remembering or getting filenames, paths, etc., which, if this is a captive image, part of the application, is something you'd probably want to avoid. However, if you need to, refer to the **LoadDIB()** function in **bitmap.c** and replace the **LoadResource()** code with the code fragment found in Figure 3.3.

The third method is to load a DIB from the executable resource area, and that's what the **LoadDIB()** function in **bitmap.c** does. By loading the image as a DIB ourselves, we avoid Windows converting our image to a DDB referenced to the system palette.

However, as if there weren't enough, this brings up another problem. What do we do with a true color image if the display device is not capable of

Figure 3.3—Load DIB from file

```
// Open the file...
        hFile = OpenFile(szFilename, &ofs, OF_READ);
        if (hFile == HFILE_ERROR)
        {
          [process error]
          return;
        }

// Read file header to get size and image bits start. Make sure read is
// OK...
        wBytes = _lread(hFile, (LPBYTE)&BFH, sizeof(BFH));
        if (wBytes != sizeof(BFH))
        {
          [process error]
          _lclose(hFile);
          return;
        }

// We trying to read a bitmap?...

        if (BFH.bfType != 0x4D42)
        {
          [process error]
          _lclose(hFile);
          return;
        }
```

displaying true color? Come what may, we're never going to get more than the number of colors the hardware is capable of, period. If that's 256 colors (which it probably is), we've got to reduce the number of colors in the image somehow, and that is a whole other subject.

The principle involved is the computerized equivalent of stuffing 10 pounds into a five pound can. Basically, we need to find the 256 (or whatever number) colors which best represent the image when rendered. There are a number of techniques available by which the number of image colors can be reduced. Two of the most popular are known as **popularity** and **median cut**. Examples of both algorithms can be found in *Photorealism and Ray Tracing in C*, by Watkins, Coy and Finlay, M&T Books, 1992. More formal discussion of color reduction methods can be found in *Computer Graphics*, 2nd Ed., by Foley, van Dam, Feiner, Hughes, Addison-Wesley, 1990.

This presents another, more subtle problem. If we have palette images, we need to keep track of palettes now as well as pointers to DIBs, and prior to displaying an image, we need to ensure we're using the correct palette. This can very definitely slow down image display. There is, however, a partial solution: *use the same palette for all images*. Pause and think about that for a moment. As with all compromises, no one is completely satisfied, but neither are they going to jump off a bridge. This may work, you say, if the colors are chosen carefully, but how can they be, when we can never know what colors are required by any image? The result is itself another compromise, commonly called a **rainbow palette**. This palette consists of the 20 reserved Windows colors and groups of color sweeps of different hues and saturation. This gives us a system which has only one palette, to which all images are referenced. That sounds suspiciously like a DDB definition, which leads us to the fourth method of image processing.

Do what we just proposed, a combination of DIB and DDB. Load a resource as a DIB—this gives us access to all the image colors. Create a palette for each 256-color image and, if necessary, convert any high or true color bitmaps to 256-color, rainbow palette images.

Display Method

Two display methods are available to use, depending on whether we choose to use DIBs or DDBs. Displaying a DIB is much slower than displaying a DDB. So why not use DDBs exclusively? As mentioned before, a DDB has no actual color information, so it can't be passed from one application to another (which also excludes the clipboard), unless, of course, the applications have prearranged a common palette or something similar.

Palette Control

In all probability, you'll want more than 20 colors in your images, and 256-color images are more or less acceptable for most purposes, except where actual, accurate color information is required. So you're going to be using palettes a great deal. Might as well get used to them.

The **system palette** is actually the palette on the video card which is controlled by Windows. There's only one of them, so it gets pretty crowded with multiple applications, each wanting to display its own images with its own set of colors. This is handled in Windows through the use of the **SelectPalette()** and **RealizePalette()** functions.

Figure 3.4—Palette selection

```
// If there's a palette, select and realize it now...
        if (hPal != NULL)
        {
          SelectPalette(hdcMem, hPal, FALSE);
          hOld = SelectPalette(hDC, hPal, FALSE);
          RealizePalette(hDC);
        }

[Output the image...]

// If there's a palette, reselect the original and realize it now...

        if (hPal != NULL)
        {
          SelectPalette(hdcMem, hOld, FALSE);
          SelectPalette(hDC, hOld, FALSE);
          RealizePalette(hDC);
        }
```

You utilize the palette by maintaining a logical palette and selecting it, when required, into the actual hardware. **SelectPalette()** selects the specified logical palette into the device context in the same way that any other GDI object is selected using **SelectObject()**. **RealizePalette()** causes the selected palette values to be sent to the hardware itself, immediately causing the colors displayed on the monitor to be changed.

There are two basic approaches you can use when dealing with palettes, depending on whether or not the image already contains a palette. If the image already contains a palette, be thankful and use it. But it doesn't end there, because the palette contained in the .BMP isn't in palette index format, it's a series of RGB color values. You need to create an **identity palette**. *See MakeIndentityPalette() in bitmap.c.* An identity palette simply creates a logical palette from the RGB colors in the image color table, then creates a 1:1 map to be used with the DIB_PAL_COLORS uMode value in the selected blit function.

The other alternative rears its ugly head when the image doesn't contain a color table, which means it's high color or true color—in any event, there are more than 256 colors involved. If the current display driver handles more than 256 colors, that's all well and good. If not, you need to get involved. One way or another, you need to reduce the image to 256 colors or less. We've already talked about color remapping using sophisticated palette manipulation techniques such as popularity and median cut. What if all that is wanted is a quick approximation—a generic palette, if you will? In that case, try creating a palette with a selection of colors (something akin to a rainbow). *See*

MakeRainbowPalette() in *bitmap.c*. This solution, while by no means perfect, usually results in recognizable images.

In addition, Windows provides two messages:

WM_PALETTECHANGED

WM_QUERYNEWPALETTE

to support palette processing. WM_PALETTECHANGED is sent by Windows to all applications whenever the window with the input focus realizes (updates) its palette, causing the system palette (the actual hardware) to be changed, causing the displayed colors to be changed. Remember—there are a limited number of colors available in the palette! If the application which is currently realizing a palette uses all the colors, *all other applications will have their colors remapped by Windows to the newly realized colors.* WM_QUERYNEWPALETTE is sent by Windows to an application when it is about to receive the input focus. This gives the application time to realize its palette. The code fragment in Figure 3.5 shows how to process the two messages.

Figure 3.5—Palette message processing

```
        case WM_PALETTECHANGED:
            if (hWnd != (HWND) wParam) InvalidateRect (hWnd, NULL, FALSE);
            break;
// If we get the focus, make sure we are using our palette...

        case WM_QUERYNEWPALETTE:
          if (hPal)
          {
            hDC = GetDC (hWnd);
            hOldPal = SelectPalette (hDC, hPal, FALSE);
            cnt = RealizePalette (hDC);
            SelectPalette (hDC, hOldPal, FALSE);
            ReleaseDC (hWnd, hDC);
            if (cnt > 0) InvalidateRect (hWnd, NULL, FALSE);
            return(TRUE);
          }
          break;
```

The line **if (hWnd != wParam)** is included because Windows sends this message to all top-level windows and we don't want to process it if we're the window; we've already processed a palette to have caused this message in the first place.

When we get the focus, then select our palette and realize it. If there are any changes in the system palette (**cnt > 0**), then cause our client area to be updated.

Either of the methods in Figure 3.4 or Figure 3.5 can be used.

Wait for Navigation Control

Waiting in Windows can be a tricky thing.

One thing you must never do (in addition to spilling coffee in your computer) is to execute a code fragment like that shown in Figure 3.6 under Windows. You'll be there until your computer dies.

Figure 3.6—Waiting (forever)

```
do
{
  [do whatever]
} while (<wait for something to happen>);
```

Remember! *Windows 3 is not preemptive.* Unless you (your application) plays nice, there won't be any ball game. An application must frequently and voluntarily give up control so that Windows can give time to another application or process. Note we're not talking about real-time interrupt level stuff here, just standard application code.

So how do you wait? Modify the code fragment in Figure 3.6 slightly and give up control periodically; then you're OK. Figure 3.7 shows the updated code fragment.

The new code fragment now calls **PeekMessage()**, which returns immediately (with or without having retrieved a message), *after giving up control.*

Figure 3.7—Waiting (OK)

```
do
{
  while (PeekMessage(&Message, NULL, 0, 0, PM_REMOVE))
  {
    TranslateMessage(&Message);
    DispatchMessage(&Message);
  }
  [do whatever]
} while (<wait for something to happen>);
```

This allows Windows to execute other applications and *messages for your application continue to be processed*. Now **<wait for something to happen>** can actually happen!

Exit Application

Windows is most defenseless when an application exits. It depends almost entirely on the application to police itself when it terminates. One thing Windows can do is release allocated memory and GDI objects used by the application. But forget to release or delete a DC, and you're in trouble. Normally, when doing a **GetDC()**, which is only to be used temporarily, to prevent myself from forgetting the **ReleaseDC()**, I literally write:

```
GetDC()
ReleaseDC()
```

first, then back up and fill in the required code. Problems with unreleased resources have become almost nonexistent.

The application is told it's terminating when it receives a **WM_DESTROY** message. When this occurs, execute **PostQuitMessage()**. This causes the *Get message loop* in **WinMain()** to return FALSE from **GetMessage()**, which in turn causes the while loop to be terminated and **WinMain()** exits.

Something to bear in mind: The application and its windows are entirely separate things. Your application has an **HINSTANCE** which is an identifier for the application, and each window you create gets an **HWND** identifier.

CHAPTER 4

THE SOFTWARE

The Lesson Plan

There are a number of compile-time symbols that can be defined or left undefined which affect the behavior of the application. Define a symbol using the /D switch when compiling and the #ifdef, #ifndef, #else and #endif directives in the source code. The symbols allow the same code to be compiled in different ways. For example:

```
// Scroll the startup monologue. Leave out if in debug, makes me crazy waiting for
it...

#ifndef _DEBUG
        DoMonologue(hWnd);
#endif
```

The code between the **#ifndef** and **#endif** statements will be compiled *if the symbol* _DEBUG *(case-sensitive!) is **not** defined*.

There are a number of symbols which you can define that will alter the behavior of the application. Table 3.2 explains the various symbols. Note that some symbols can be defined in conjunction with others.

Table 3.2—Lesson symbols

Symbol	Defined
_DEBUG	Startup monologue is disabled.
_LESSON1	Load bitmaps as DIBs (device-independent bitmaps) with palettes. All processing done as DIBs. Opening scene bitmaps are 8 bit (256 color) images created with independent palettes. Do not define _LESSON2.
_LESSON2	Bitmaps are loaded as DDBs (device-dependent bitmaps) without palettes. All processing done as DDBs. PIVR image 24 bit (true color). Do not define _LESSON1.
_LESSON3	All images created with identical rainbow palette. Use with either _LESSON1 or _LESSON2.
_LESSON4	Delete automatic generation of rainbow palette for DIB images. Use with _LESSON1.
_LESSON5	Delete keyboard accelerators.
None	Bitmaps are loaded as DIBs, then converted to DDBs with palettes. All processing done as DDBs. Opening scene images 8 bit (256 color) images created with independent palettes. PIVR image created as 24 bit (true color) image and reduced to 8 bit image using median-cut algorithm.

If you are not thoroughly familiar with DIBs and DDBs and their differences, I strongly suggest you compile each of the different versions and see the results. For example, without any defines, note that there is a quick flash between the big red pushbutton image and the PIVR image. That comes from the palette processing, when the palette for the PIVR image is realized. For a few moments, the big red pushbutton image is still visible (haven't blit'ed the PIVR image yet) and it's suddenly being displayed with a totally wrong palette.

When _LESSON2 is defined, the PIVR image is horrible; it's been converted to 20 colors from its original 4000 or so.

barproc.c

This module contains the processing code for a child window which is viewed as the knob or bar portion of a "slider control." What we wish to accomplish is:

- detect the left button being pressed and dragged when on top of the bar bitmap

- move the bar bitmap image in response to the mouse being dragged

- stop moving when the left button is released

This module also demonstrates the use of the Get/SetWindowLong/Word functions. These functions allow us to make the function (**BarProc**) reentrant. When the BarProc window class is defined (in startup.c), note that 8 bytes are allocated in the **cbWndExtra** member of the **WNDCLASS** structure. These additional bytes are allocated for each instance of a BarProc window created and are accessed through the Get/SetWindowLong/Word functions by specifying a length (long or word) and an initial offset, in this case from 0 to 6. The offsets used for any particular data item are completely arbitrary.

By dragging the control left and right, we change a value which is used to control the rate-of-change of the azimuth and speed increments.

Note that the bitmap image is deleted when the window is destroyed.

```
// -------------------------------------------------------------------------------
                //
// "Plunging Into Virtual Reality", BARPROC.C
                //
// Copyright 1994, 1995 Russell J. Berube Jr. ALL RIGHTS RESERVED.              //
// This software is published, but is NOT public domain. It remains the exclusive    //
// property of Russell J. Berube Jr. and Brookside Systems, Inc. This software may not
                //
// be reproduced or integrated with other software without the prior written permission
                //
// of Russell J. Berube Jr. and Brookside Systems, Inc. It is provided herein for    //
```

```
// instructional purposes only.
        //
// --------------------------------------------------------------------------------
        //

#include "includes.h"          // include the world...
#include "bitmap.h"            // include bitmap functions definitions...
#include "vr.h"                // include VR definitions...

// ...BarProc...is the exported callback function used to process the messages sent to us by
// Windows...
//
// On entry we're passed:
//
// hWnd           A handle to our window instance.
//
// wMsg           A WORD containing the Windows message code we're being passed.
//
// wParam         A WORD containing a parameter specific to this message.
//
// lParam         A LONG containing a parameter specific to this message.

// BarProc's reason for living is to handle a slider bar control. This is going to require
// tracking the mouse and moving the entire window (slider bar) when we detect the user has
// clicked the mouse and is dragging us...

LRESULT CALLBACK BarProc(
         HWND      hWnd,        // handle to window instance
         WORD      wMsg,        // windows message code
         WPARAM    wParam,      // word parameter
         LPARAM    lParam)      // long parameter
{
HDC        hDC;                 // handle to display device context
int        x;                  // local junk
int        nPos;               // slider bar position
LPBAR      lpBar;              // far pointer to bar control
PAINTSTRUCT        ps;         // PAINTSTRUCT used by WM_PAINT
POINT      p;                  // mouse point
RECT       rect;               // client area rectangle

// This function must process the messages passed to it by Windows. The simplest way to
// handle them is with a switch (case) statement. However, there are more than 200 messages
// which can be sent by Windows that makes for a huge, unwieldy source file it we put all
// that code inline. Instead we'll try to make the source as readable as possible. One thing
// I've learned, which never fails to amaze me: I can live with a program and the source code
// for months, know it intimately, see the stuff in my sleep no less, then leave it for a few
// months/ and when I come back, I'm convinced I never wrote it in the first place.
Especially,
// especially, if it's not commented up to its eyeballs. Virtually every line. You wont
believe
// how easy it is to completely forget this stuff as soon as you leave it.

// It can't possibly be wrong (one of my favorite sayings) to heavily comment your code. DO
IT!!

// Note that the messages are case'd in alphabetical order. Simply one of my quirks, I'm fussy
// that way, consistency is important. When I come back and look at this stuff again, it helps
// get me realigned. All my code is the same way. Always structured the same, same sort of
// comments, parameter notation, module layout, etc. I suppose it's like traveling and finding
// a McDonalds off in outer space, it's reassuring. Also, it proves to me I wrote this and not
```

```
// my doppelganger...

        switch (wMsg)
        {
```

```
// ...WM_CREATE...this message is received when Windows is about to create the application
// window. It is generated as a direct result of the Create() function. We're passed a far
// pointer to a BAR structure which contains all the information we need to control a slide
// and bar window. Save the BAR structure pointer and initialize the bar's control increment
// to 1. Return 0, if OK, else return 1...

        case   WM_CREATE:
          lpBar = (LPBAR)((LPCREATESTRUCT)lParam)->lpCreateParams;
          SetWindowLong(hWnd, 0, (LONG)lpBar);
          SetWindowWord(hWnd, 4, 0);
          SetWindowWord(hWnd, 6, FALSE);
          *(lpBar->lpInc) = 1;
          return(0);
```

```
// ...WM_DESTROY...this message is received when Windows is about to destroy the application
// window. It is generated as a direct result of the DestroyWindow() function. Now's a good
// time to delete the bar bitmap. Return 0, if OK, else return 1...

        case   WM_DESTROY:
          lpBar = (LPBAR)GetWindowLong(hWnd, 0);
          DeleteObject(lpBar->lpBM->hBM);
          return(0);
```

```
// ...WM_LBUTTONDOWN...this message is received when Windows detects the left mouse button has
// been pressed when over the client area of the window which, in this case, is the actual
// "picture" of the bar (knob) control. Perform two functions: set the <mouse captured> flag
// (offset 6) true and actually capture the mouse. Now all mouse events, regardless of which
// window they occur in, are reported to this function...

        case   WM_LBUTTONDOWN:
          SetWindowWord(hWnd, 6, TRUE);
          SetCapture(hWnd);
          return(0);
```

```
// ...WM_LBUTTONUP...this message is received when Windows detects the left mouse button has
// been released. Note that doesn't have to occur "over" this window, but may happen anywhere.
// Reset the <mouse captured> flag and release the mouse capture...

        case   WM_LBUTTONUP:
          SetWindowWord(hWnd, 6, FALSE);
          ReleaseCapture();
          return(0);
```

```
// ...WM_MOUSEMOVE...this message is received when Windows detects the mouse being moved. When
// this happens, if our <mouse captured> flag is TRUE (the mouse button was pressed when on top
// of the bar image), then the user is attempting to drag the bar. Ignore if not. If so, only
// perform dragging if the mouse is actually over the bar image and not elsewhere. The few
// calculations below are done to ensure this and compute the new position of the image. Once
// that is accomplished, use the new information to move the window which is actually nothing
// more than our "bar" bitmap. This in effect, causes Windows to move the image for us, without
// us having to worry about erasing the existing image before drawing the new image...

        case   WM_MOUSEMOVE:
```

```
          if (!GetWindowWord(hWnd, 6)) break;
          p = MAKEPOINT(lParam);
          ClientToScreen(hWnd, &p);
          lpBar = (LPBAR)GetWindowLong(hWnd, 0);
          nPos = GetWindowWord(hWnd, 4);
          if (!PtInRect(&(lpBar->lpBM->rect), p)) break;
          GetClientRect(hWnd, &rect);
          x = (p.x-lpBar->lpBM->rect.left)/rect.right;
          if (nPos != x)
          {
            nPos = x;
            *(lpBar->lpInc) = x*lpBar->nInc;
            if (*(lpBar->lpInc) == 0) *(lpBar->lpInc) = 1;
            MoveWindow(hWnd,
                       lpBar->lpBM->rect.left+(x*rect.right),
                       lpBar->lpBM->rect.top,
                       rect.right,
                       rect.bottom,
                       TRUE);
          }
          SetWindowWord(hWnd, 4, nPos);
          return(0);

// ...WM_PAINT...this message is received whenever the window requires repainting. Display the
// current bar position...

       case  WM_PAINT:
          hDC = BeginPaint(hWnd, &ps);
          lpBar = (LPBAR)GetWindowLong(hWnd, 0);
          BlitDC(hDC, lpBar->lpBM->hBM, 0, 0, NULL);
          EndPaint(hWnd, &ps);
          return(0);
     }

// Any message we don't process, pass through to the Windows default message handler. Return
// whatever result it returns...

       return (DefWindowProc(hWnd, wMsg, wParam, lParam));
}
```

bitmap.c

The two palette creation functions, MakeRainbowPalette() and
MakeIdentityPalette() are only used if the current display driver is not in 256
color mode.

```
// ------------------------------------------------------------------------------
       //
// "Plunging Into Virtual Reality", BITMAP.C
       //
// Copyright 1994, 1995 Russell J. Berube Jr. ALL RIGHTS RESERVED.              //
```

```
// This software is published, but is NOT public domain. It remains the exclusive      //
// property of Russell J. Berube Jr. and Brookside Systems, Inc. This software may not
         //
// be reproduced or integrated with other software without the prior written permission
         //
// of Russell J. Berube Jr. and Brookside Systems, Inc. It is provided herein for       //
// instructional purposes only.
         //
// ----------------------------------------------------------------------------------
         //


#include "includes.h"           // include the world...
#include "funcs.h"              // include miscellaneous functions prototypes...
#include "resource.h"           // include the resource definitions...


// External data..

extern   HINSTANCE        ghInstance;       // handle to application instance
extern   int       gnX;        // x screen offset
extern   int       gnY;        // y screen offset

// ...BlitDC...is the function called to perform a BitBlt() to a specified device context.
// Always blit the entire bitmap...

void     WINAPI   BlitDC(
         HDC       hDC,               // handle to device context
         HBITMAP hBitmap, // handle to bitmap
         int       x,                 // x of display
         int       y,                 // y of display
         HPALETTE hPal)     // optional palette
{
BITMAP   bm;                           // BITMAP structure
HBITMAP  hbmOld;                       // handle to original bitmap
HDC      hdcMem;                       // handle to memory DC
HPALETTE hOld;                      // handle to original palette

// Create device context compatible to the display. This of course, can be done once and a
// global compatible DC referenced...

         hdcMem = CreateCompatibleDC(hDC);

// Get the image size, need that for the blit...

         GetObject(hBitmap, sizeof(bm), &bm);

// Select the bitmap into the newly created memory DC. We need someplace to hold the bitmap
// while it's copied to the display. Save handle to original bitmap. We'll replace it before
// destroying the temp DC...

         hbmOld = SelectObject(hdcMem, hBitmap);

// If there's a palette, select and realize it now. This is being done this way to facilitate
// the _LESSONx defines. If this were an optimized app with a single palette (which, once it
// gets going this is) it would be faster and more efficient to select and realize the palette
// ONCE when it was created/changed, then rely on the Windows palette messages
// WM_PALETTECHANGED and WM_QUERYNEWPALETTE to re-realize your application's palette after the
// system palette had been changed by another app..

         if (hPal != NULL)
         {
```

```
                SelectPalette(hdcMem, hPal, FALSE);
                hOld = SelectPalette(hDC, hPal, FALSE);
                RealizePalette(hDC);
            }
```

// Blit (copy) the bitmap image from the compatible (temporary) memory DC to the
// actual display at the window offset we specified: (x, y)...

```
            BitBlt(hDC, x, y, bm.bmWidth, bm.bmHeight, hdcMem, 0, 0, SRCCOPY);
```

// If there's a palette, reselect the original and realize it now. This also needn't be done if
// the _LESSONx defines weren't present. Once again, we'd set the palette once and not worry;
// knowing the Windows palette messages would protect us...

```
            if (hPal != NULL)
            {
              SelectPalette(hdcMem, hOld, FALSE);
              SelectPalette(hDC, hOld, FALSE);
              RealizePalette(hDC);
            }
```

// Reselect the original bitmap back into the temporary DC then destroy it. You never know
// what'll happen if the temp device context (DC) is deleted while there's a live bitmap
// selected into it...

```
            SelectObject(hdcMem, hbmOld);
            DeleteDC(hdcMem);
}
```

// ...Blit...is the function called to perform a BitBlt() to the display. Always blit the
// entire bitmap. This function is a simple shell around BlitDC. It simply does the GetDC()
// and ReleaseDC() for us...

```
void     WINAPI  Blit(
         HWND     hWnd,            // handle to window instance
         HBITMAP  hBitmap, // handle to bitmap
         int      x,               // x of display
         int      y,               // y of display
         HPALETTE hPal)    // optional palette
{
HDC      hDC;                      // handle to display device context

         hDC = GetDC(hWnd);
         BlitDC(hDC, hBitmap, x, y, hPal);
         ReleaseDC(hWnd, hDC);
}
```

// ...DeleteDIB...is the function used to delete (unlock and free) any allocated memory or
// objects associated with a DIB structure. I always wind up putting this function in after
// discovering somewhere, that I'd not correctly unlocked everything before trying to free
// it or that I'd forgotten to delete some object. This is more robust and requires far less
// thinking...

```
void     WINAPI  DeleteDIB(
         LPDIB    lpDIB)           // far pointer to DIB structure
{
```
// Keep unlocking until unlock count goes to 0, that way if we've missed to lock/unlock in
// sync somewhere we'll still recover...robust!

```
        while (GlobalUnlock(lpDIB->hBI));

// Remember the DIB itself is a resource. If it were a global memory object we'd use
// GlobalFree() instead...

        FreeResource(lpDIB->hBI);

// If there's a palette index area, nuke that...

        if (lpDIB->hPI != NULL)
        {
          while (GlobalUnlock(lpDIB->hPI));
          GlobalFree(lpDIB->hPI);
        }

// Let go the palette...

        if (lpDIB->hPal != NULL) DeleteObject(lpDIB->hPal);
}

// ...DrawDIB...is the function used to display a device-independent bitmap. Depending on
// whether or not the image requires a palette, we need to pass multiple parameters. They're
// all put together into a single nice structure for us by the LoadDIB() function. Thank you
// LoadDIB() function...

void    WINAPI   DrawDIB(
        HWND     hWnd,              // handle to application window
        LPDIB    lpDIB)            // pointer to DIB structure
{
HDC     hDC;                        // DC for display
HPALETTE hPal;                   // handle to original palette
HPBYTE   hpBits;                     // huge pointer to image bits
LPBITMAPINFO    lpBI;             // far pointer to BITMAPINFO structure
LPBITMAPINFO    lpPI;             // far pointer to palette index area

// We always need a pointer to the actual image...

        if ((lpBI = (LPBITMAPINFO)LockResource(lpDIB->hBI)) == NULL)
        {
          MBox(hWnd, IDS_ERRLGM, IDS_ERROR, MB_OK|MB_ICONEXCLAMATION);
          return;
        }

// And to the image bits. Again, note the pointer cast to huge to ensure the arithmetic
// works OK...

        hpBits = (HPBYTE)lpBI+lpBI->bmiHeader.biSize+lpDIB->dwTable;

// Get a handle to our device context...

        hDC = GetDC(hWnd);

// The display method we request depends on whether or not our image requires a palette or
// not. If the image is 256 colors or less, then a palette is required. If not, the image
// is at least HIGH COLOR (15+ bits/pixel) and could be TRUE COLOR (24 bits/pixel). So if
// the color table size is non-zero, we know there's a palette lurking around somewhere.
// Note that StretchDIBits is the blit function-of-choice, recommended by Microsoft...

        if (lpDIB->hPal)
        {
```

```
      hPal = SelectPalette(hDC, lpDIB->hPal, FALSE);
      RealizePalette(hDC);
      if (lpDIB->hPI != NULL)
      {
        if ((lpPI = (LPBITMAPINFO)GlobalLock(lpDIB->hPI)) == NULL)
        {
          MBox(hWnd, IDS_ERRLGM, IDS_ERROR, MB_OK|MB_ICONEXCLAMATION);
          return;
        }
      }
      else
        lpPI = lpBI;
      StretchDIBits(hDC,
                    gnX,
                    gnY,
                    (int)lpBI->bmiHeader.biWidth,
                    (int)lpBI->bmiHeader.biHeight,
                    0,
                    0,
                    (int)lpBI->bmiHeader.biWidth,
                    (int)lpBI->bmiHeader.biHeight,
                    hpBits,
                    lpPI,
                    DIB_PAL_COLORS,
                    SRCCOPY);
      GlobalUnlock(lpDIB->hPI);
      SelectPalette(hDC, hPal, FALSE);
   }
   else
   {
      StretchDIBits(hDC,
                    gnX,
                    gnY,
                    (int)lpBI->bmiHeader.biWidth,
                    (int)lpBI->bmiHeader.biHeight,
                    0,
                    0,
                    (int)lpBI->bmiHeader.biWidth,
                    (int)lpBI->bmiHeader.biHeight,
                    hpBits,
                    lpBI,
                    DIB_RGB_COLORS,
                    SRCCOPY);
   }

// Don't forget to release anything you do a GET on! (and unlock the image resource)...

      GlobalUnlock(lpDIB->hBI);
      ReleaseDC(hWnd, hDC);
}

// ...MakeRainbowPalette...is the function called to create a Windows palette using a
// standard array of colors. Always create a 256 color palette...

HPALETTE WINAPI   MakeRainbowPalette(
      HWND    hWnd)              // handle to window instance
{
BYTE    b;                       // blue value
BYTE    g;                       // green value
BYTE    r;                       // red value
```

```
int      i;                     // local junk
HLOCAL   hLocal;                // handle to temp area for logical palette
HPALETTE hPal;            // handle to new Windows palette
PLOGPALETTE      pPal;          // pointer to logical palette
```

```
// Allocate space for the new palette we're going to create (size of a LOGPALETTE structure +
// a palette entry for each color). With all memory allocations, make sure it works. Note we
// actually only need to allocate for (nColors-1) PALETTEENTRYs since the LOGPALETTE structure
// contains 1 PALETTEENTRY itself. This is another example where I believe the code is more
// readable, hence understandable, at the expense of a few bytes...
```

```
        hLocal = LocalAlloc(LPTR, sizeof(LOGPALETTE)+(sizeof(PALETTEENTRY)*PALSIZE));
```

```
// Get it? Complain if not...
```

```
        if (hLocal == NULL)
        {
          MBox(hWnd, IDS_ERRNOLM, IDS_ERROR, MB_OK|MB_ICONEXCLAMATION);
          return(NULL);
        }
```

```
// Now lock it down, check to ensure that worked also...
```

```
        if ((pPal = (PLOGPALETTE)LocalLock(hLocal)) == NULL)
        {
          MBox(hWnd, IDS_ERRLLM, IDS_ERROR, MB_OK|MB_ICONEXCLAMATION);
          LocalFree(hLocal);
          return(NULL);
        }
```

```
// If we've managed to get here, we've gotten a valid palette area. Initialize it. That means
// fill in the palette version, number of colors then transfer the actual colors from the
// image color table to the LOGPALETTE. That requires computing a pointer to the image color
// table from the pointer to the BITMAPINFO structure we're given. This is straightforward:
// the color table is immediately after the BITMAPINFOHEADER.
```

```
        pPal->palVersion = 0x0300;
        pPal->palNumEntries = PALSIZE;
```

```
// I never take advantage of the ability to define and initialize a var. I prefer extrinsic
// initialization. That way I can always see it happening, it goes with the flow of the code
// that I have in mind at the time I'm writing it. Also, it helps me maintain a constant
// programming style...
```

```
        r = 0;
        g = 0;
        b = 0;
```

```
// Fill in the palette entries, sliding through r, g, and b values in increments of 32 for r
// and g and 64 for b. Why? Because your eyeball is almost 10x more sensitive to r and g than
// b...
        for (i = 0; i < (int)pPal->palNumEntries; i++)
        {
          pPal->palPalEntry[i].peRed   = r;
          pPal->palPalEntry[i].peGreen = g;
          pPal->palPalEntry[i].peBlue  = b;
          pPal->palPalEntry[i].peFlags = 0;
          if (!(r += 32))
            if (!(g += 32))
              b += 64;
```

```
        }

// Have Windows create an actual palette for us then release the local memory used. Complain
if
// things didnt' work out OK...

        hPal = CreatePalette(pPal);
        LocalUnlock(hLocal);
        LocalFree(hLocal);
        if (hPal == NULL)
          MBox(hWnd, IDS_ERRPCF, IDS_ERROR, MB_OK|MB_ICONEXCLAMATION);
        return(hPal);
}

// ...MakeIdentityPalette...is the function called to create a Windows palette from a
// BITMAPINFO structure and number of colors. A palette is only required if the number of
// colors in the image is 256 or less. Don't fiddle with the system colors. Create the
// palette as a 1:1 match with the colors in the color table...

HPALETTE WINAPI   MakeIdentityPalette(
        HWND       hWnd,             // handle to window instance
        LPBITMAPINFO    lpBI,        // pointer to image BITMAPINFO structure
        int      nColors) // number of palette colors
{
int     i;                          // local junk
HLOCAL    hLocal;                   // handle to temp area for logical palette
HPALETTE hPal;                      // handle to new Windows palette
PLOGPALETTE       pPal;             // pointer to logical palette
LPRGBQUAD         lpRGBQ;           // pointer to RGBQUAD

// Allocate space for the new palette we're going to create (size of a LOGPALETTE structure +
// a palette entry for each color). With all memory allocations, make sure it works. Note we
// actually only need to allocate for (nColors-1) PALETTEENTRYs since the LOGPALETTE structure
// contains 1 PALETTEENTRY itself. This is another example where I believe the code is more
// readable, hence understandable, at the expense of a few bytes...

        hLocal = LocalAlloc(LPTR, sizeof(LOGPALETTE)+(sizeof(PALETTEENTRY)*nColors));

// Get it? Complain if not...

        if (hLocal == NULL)
        {
          MBox(hWnd, IDS_ERRNOLM, IDS_ERROR, MB_OK|MB_ICONEXCLAMATION);
          return(NULL);
        }

// Now lock it down, check to ensure that worked also...

        if ((pPal = (PLOGPALETTE)LocalLock(hLocal)) == NULL)
        {
          MBox(hWnd, IDS_ERRLLM, IDS_ERROR, MB_OK|MB_ICONEXCLAMATION);
          LocalFree(hLocal);
          return(NULL);
        }
```

// If we've managed to get here, we've gotten a valid palette area. Initialize it. That means
// fill in the palette version, number of colors then transfer the actual colors from the
// image color table to the LOGPALETTE. That requires computing a pointer to the image color
// table from the pointer to the BITMAPINFO structure we're given. This is straightforward:
// the color table is immediately after the BITMAPINFOHEADER.

```
            pPal->palVersion = 0x0300;
            pPal->palNumEntries = nColors;
```

```
// If this is a normal 256 (or less) color image, create an identity palette: a 1:1 match
// between the palette colors and the color indexes into the RGB color table.
```

```
// A subtle point here. Note the lpRGBQ address computation is base+offset: lpBI+offset.
// Don't get caught using sizeof(BITMAPINFOHEADER) here. You want this code to at least
// attempt to work if the size of the image header changes on you. Use the actual structure
// size instead: bmiHeader.biSize for the offset value. Note the pointer cast to huge to
// ensure pointer arithmetic works...
// Change the DIB color table to palette indexes. Create a 1:1 correspondence between the
// palette and indexes We know that'll work, we just created an identity palette from the
// color table. Note the cast to HPBYTE to ensure the pointer arithmetic works OK...
```

```
            lpRGBQ = (LPRGBQUAD)((HPBYTE)lpBI+(LONG)lpBI->bmiHeader.biSize);

            for (i = 0; i < (int)pPal->palNumEntries; i++)
            {
              pPal->palPalEntry[i].peRed = lpRGBQ[i].rgbRed;
              pPal->palPalEntry[i].peGreen = lpRGBQ[i].rgbGreen;
              pPal->palPalEntry[i].peBlue = lpRGBQ[i].rgbBlue;
              pPal->palPalEntry[i].peFlags = 0;
            }
```

```
// Have Windows create an actual palette for us then release the local memory used. Complain
if
// things didnt' work out OK...
```

```
            hPal = CreatePalette(pPal);
            LocalUnlock(hLocal);
            LocalFree(hLocal);
            if (hPal == NULL)
              MBox(hWnd, IDS_ERRPCF, IDS_ERROR, MB_OK|MB_ICONEXCLAMATION);
            return(hPal);
}
```

```
// ...NumDIBColors...is the function used to determine the number of colors actually used
// in a DIB. This information comes from the image bit count and colors used values in the
// bitmap header. Even here, things get a little snaky, not all conditions are defined and
// blow with the breeze as best you can and hope you don't run across any images not meeting
// our conditions. Really though, it shouldn't happen...
```

```
int     WINAPI   NumDIBColors(
        LPBITMAPINFO       lpBI)    // pointer to BITMAPINFO structure
{
LPBITMAPINFOHEADER        lpbi;    // pointer to BITMAPINFOHEADER structure
LPBITMAPCOREHEADER        lpbc;    // pointer to BITMAPCOREHEADER structure
int     nColors;        // number of colors
WORD    wBpP;                       // bits per pixel
```

```
// Could be a Windows 3.x or an OS/2 format bitmap, we'll know in a second, (hopefully
// sooner than that)...
```

```
            lpbi = &(lpBI->bmiHeader);
            lpbc = (LPBITMAPCOREHEADER)lpbi;
```

```
// Try to get the number of colors from the bits/pixel field...
```

```
            if (lpbi->biSize == sizeof(BITMAPINFOHEADER))
              wBpP = lpbi->biBitCount;
            else
              wBpP = lpbc->bcBitCount;
```

```
// Values of 8 (or less) imply a palette, since the actual number of colors (2^wBpP) is going
// to be 256 or less. Note that only values of 1, 4 and 8 are actually used for bitmaps with
// palettes. We do expect a value of 24, which is a TRUE COLOR image, return 0 for the number
// of colors to indicate no palette...
```

```
            switch(wBpP)
            {
              case   1:
                nColors=2;
                break;
              case   4:
                nColors=16;
                break;
              case   8:
                nColors=256;
                break;
              default:
                nColors=0;
                break;
            }
```

```
// If this is a Windows DIB, then color table length comes from biClrUsed field (possibly)...
```

```
            if (lpbi->biSize == sizeof(BITMAPINFOHEADER))
              if (lpbi->biClrUsed != 0)
                nColors = (int)lpbi->biClrUsed;
            return(nColors);
}
```

```
// ...LoadDIB...is the function used to load a DIB image resource from the .EXE file.
// A little scratching around in the Windows docs, and you'll find the format of a BITMAP
// resource is identical to that of the .BMP file, except the BITMAPFILEHEADER structure
// has been dropped. We return a handle to a global area containing a DIB structure. Note
// this is a structure we've made up and has nothing to do with Windows itself. Why you ask,
// actually waste global space by allocating the tiny DIB structure. Why not use local
// memory? You could if you don't want to move this function to a DLL, allowing all your
// apps to use it. If you do want to move it to a DLL, you'll have to pass an HINSTANCE,
// the handle to the calling application, containing the resources, as well. There's a lot
// of memory allocation going on here, watch carefully. Refer to the DoMonologue() function,
// there I've used goto's for common error exits, here we don't each is individual, decide
// for yourself which method you prefer...
```

```
BOOL     WINAPI    LoadDIB(
         HWND      hWnd,                // handle to window instance
         int       nID,                 // resource id
         LPDIB     lpDIB)               // far pointer to result DIB structure
{
#ifndef _LESSON4
BOOL     bPaletteDevice;               // display uses a palette flag
#endif
HDC      hDC;                          // handle to window display device context
HRSRC    hResource;                    // handle to bitmap resource
int      i;                            // local junk
int      nColors;          // number of image colors
LPBITMAPINFO      lpBI;                // far pointer to BITMAPINFO structure
```

```
LPWORD   lpPI;                        // far pointer to palette index area

// Initialize values...

        _fmemset(lpDIB, 0, sizeof(DIB));

// First, see if we can load the BITMAP image from .EXE resources. If that fails, nothing
// else matters...

        hResource = FindResource(ghInstance, MAKEINTRESOURCE(nID), RT_BITMAP);
        if (hResource == NULL) return(FALSE);

// Load the bitmap from the resource handle Windows returned to us...

        if ((lpDIB->hBI = LoadResource(ghInstance, hResource)) == NULL)
        {
          MBox(hWnd, IDS_ERRLGM, IDS_ERROR, MB_OK|MB_ICONEXCLAMATION);
          return(FALSE);
        }

// Lock it down, we need to fiddle a little. Make sure that works and complain if not.
// Take care to release everything...

        if ((lpBI = (LPBITMAPINFO)LockResource(lpDIB->hBI)) == NULL)
        {
          MBox(hWnd, IDS_ERRLGM, IDS_ERROR, MB_OK|MB_ICONEXCLAMATION);
          DeleteDIB(lpDIB);
          return(FALSE);
        }

// What we need to do now, is determine how many colors are contained in the image and if this
// is a palette device. That tells us whether we need to create a palette or not. Note that
// this code works with either an OS/2 or Windows 3.x format DIB. If this is a 24 bit/pixel
// image and we have a palette device we've also got problems. They (true color images), don't
// require palettes but the display driver does. Wonderful. There are a couple of solutions:
// you could analyze the colors in the image, reduce to the 256 most appropriate, remap the
// image to the new colors and create a temporary 8 bit/pixel image from the result. Or, much
// simpler, create a standard rainbow palette and force GDI to remap the 24 bit image colors
to
// the rainbow palette. If the display device does not require a palette, life is much
simpler.
// Make sure the global handle for the palette is NULL, we don't want to release an invalid
// area later. I know we requested GMEM_ZEROINIT (part of the GPTR definition) when the DIB
// structure memory was requested, but I never did trust computers...

#ifndef  _LESSON4
        hDC = GetDC(hWnd);
        bPaletteDevice = GetDeviceCaps(hDC, RASTERCAPS) & RC_PALETTE;
        ReleaseDC(hWnd, hDC);

        if ((bPaletteDevice) && (lpBI->bmiHeader.biBitCount == 24))
        {
          if ((lpDIB->hPal = MakeRainbowPalette(hWnd)) == NULL)
            lpDIB->hPal = (HPALETTE)-1;
        }
        else
#endif
            if ((nColors = NumDIBColors(lpBI)) > 0)
            {
              if ((lpDIB->hPal = MakeIdentityPalette(hWnd, lpBI, nColors)) == NULL)
```

```
            lpDIB->hPal = (HPALETTE)-1;
         lpDIB->dwTable = nColors*sizeof(RGBQUAD);
         lpDIB->hPI = GlobalAlloc(GPTR, lpBI->bmiHeader.biSize+(nColors*sizeof(WORD)));
         if (lpDIB->hPI == NULL)
         {
           MBox(hWnd, IDS_ERRNOGM, IDS_ERROR, MB_OK|MB_ICONEXCLAMATION);
           DeleteDIB(lpDIB);
           return(FALSE);
         }
         if ((lpPI = (LPWORD)GlobalLock(lpDIB->hPI)) == NULL)
         {
           MBox(hWnd, IDS_ERRLGM, IDS_ERROR, MB_OK|MB_ICONEXCLAMATION);
           DeleteDIB(lpDIB);
           return(FALSE);
         }
         _fmemcpy(lpPI, lpBI, (size_t)lpBI->bmiHeader.biSize);
         lpPI = (LPWORD)((HPBYTE)lpPI+(LONG)lpBI->bmiHeader.biSize);
         for (i = 0; i < nColors; i++) *lpPI++ = (WORD)i;
         GlobalUnlock(lpDIB->hPI);
       }

// Make sure to unlock the image resource...

         UnlockResource(lpDIB->hBI);

// Anything wrong ??

         if (lpDIB->hPal == -1)
         {
           lpDIB->hPal = NULL;
           DeleteDIB(lpDIB);
           return(FALSE);
         }

         return(TRUE);
}

// ...DrawDDB...is the function used to display a device-dependent bitmap...

void    WINAPI    DrawDDB(
        HWND      hWnd,             // handle to window instance
        HBITMAP hBitmap, // handle to DDB
        HPALETTE hPal)     // handle to optional palette
{
        Blit(hWnd, hBitmap, gnX, gnY, hPal);
}

// ...LoadDDB...is the function called to load a DIB then convert it to a DDB with a palette.
// This is used to show the differences between DDB with and without palettes. In order to do
// that some fiddling is required...

BOOL    WINAPI    LoadDDB(
        HWND      hWnd,             // handle to window instance
        int       nID,              // resource id
        LPDDB     lpDDB)            // far pointer to DDB structure
{
DIB     dib;                        // temp DIB structure
HDC     hDC;                        // handle to display device context
HPALETTE hOld;              // handle to original palette
HPBYTE  hpBits;                     // huge pointer to image bits
```

```
LPBITMAPINFO     lpBI;              // far pointer to BITMAPINFO structure

// Try to load the resource as a DIB first. If that fails, we go home...

        if (!LoadDIB(hWnd, nID, &dib)) return(FALSE);

// LoadDIB made a palette for us (probably). The only time it won't is if we've got a 24 bit
// image and the display driver is HIGH or TRUE color. (Not palettized). So that'll stop us
// also. In order to convert the DIB to a DDB, need to select and realize the new palette...

        if ((lpDDB->hPal = dib.hPal) == NULL) return(FALSE);

// We always need a pointer to the actual image...

        if ((lpBI = (LPBITMAPINFO)LockResource(dib.hBI)) == NULL)
        {
          MBox(hWnd, IDS_ERRLGM, IDS_ERROR, MB_OK|MB_ICONEXCLAMATION);
          DeleteObject(lpDDB->hPal);
          return(FALSE);
        }

// And to the image bits. Again, note the pointer cast to huge to ensure the arithmetic
// works OK. Once that's done, get the display DC, select in the new palette, realize it, then
// let CreateDIBitmap() do all the work. It returns a handle to a normal DDB. If that fails,
// dump the created palette, regardless, replace the old palette, dump the DIB image and come
// home to papa...

        hpBits = (HPBYTE)lpBI+lpBI->bmiHeader.biSize+dib.dwTable;
        hDC = GetDC(hWnd);
        hOld = SelectPalette(hDC, lpDDB->hPal, FALSE);
        RealizePalette(hDC);
        lpDDB->hBM = CreateDIBitmap(hDC, (LPBITMAPINFOHEADER)lpBI, CBM_INIT, hpBits, lpBI,
DIB_RGB_COLORS);
        SelectPalette(hDC, hOld, FALSE);
        RealizePalette(hDC);
        ReleaseDC(hWnd, hDC);
        if (lpDDB->hBM == NULL) DeleteObject(dib.hPal);
        UnlockResource(dib.hBI);
        FreeResource(dib.hBI);
        return(lpDDB->hBM != NULL);
}
```

dirproc.c

```
// --------------------------------------------------------------------------------
        //
// "Plunging Into Virtual Reality", DIRPROC.C
        //
// Copyright 1994, 1995 Russell J. Berube Jr. ALL RIGHTS RESERVED.                //
// This software is published, but is NOT public domain. It remains the exclusive  //
// property of Russell J. Berube Jr. and Brookside Systems, Inc. This software may not
        //
// be reproduced or integrated with other software without the prior written permission
        //
// of Russell J. Berube Jr. and Brookside Systems, Inc. It is provided herein for    //
```

```
// instructional purposes only.
        //
// --------------------------------------------------------------------------------
        //

#include "includes.h"          // include the world...
#include "vr.h"                // include VR definitions...

// External data...

extern   VR        gVR;                // VR structure

// Local data...

static   HBITMAP  hbmCompass;         // handle to compass bitmap
static   int      nPp10D;             // pixels/10 degrees
static   int      nHeight; // window height
static   int      nWidth;             // window width
static   RECT     rBitmap; // bitmap rectangle

// ...CreateCompassBitmap...is the function called to make a bitmap which is marked in 10
// degree increments from 0 - 350. On the actual display, I want to show 20 degrees, so if
// we're at 90 degrees exactly, the display will show part of 80 on the left, 90 in the
// middle and part of 100 on the right. Create a bitmap using the CreateBitmap() function.
// Once that's done, create a DC compatible to the display, select in your new, empty,
// bitmap, write on it, draw on it, whatever, then replace the old bitmap into the memory
// (compatible) DC, destroy that DC and your left with a handle to your bitmap...

void      CreateCompassBitmap(
          HWND      hWnd)              // handle to window instance
{
char     sz[4];                       // degrees value
HBITMAP  hbmOld;                      // handle to old bitmap
HDC      hDC;                         // handle to display device context
HDC      hdcMem;                      // handle to memory device context
HPEN     hpenOld;            // handle to old pen
HPEN     hPen;                        // line pen
int      center;                      // center of degree text
int      i;                           // local junk
int      offset;                      // local junk
RECT     rDraw;                       // drawing rectangle
RECT     rText;                       // text rectangle

// As usual, the final implementation turns out to be more complicated than originally
// anticipated. The actual width of the bitmap becomes crucial (see MakeBallAzimuth() in
// startup.c). To get things to work out correctly, the final approach used was to get the
// center of the window in even pixels (right-side/2), times 36 to get the final length of
// the resultant bitmap. Window width will be used to display 20 degrees, hence the previous
// calculation. Compute everything in terms of even pixel increments (nPp10D) to avoid
// display errors resulting from unequal delta pixels between 10 degree increments...

        GetClientRect(hWnd, &rBitmap);
        hDC = GetDC(hWnd);
        hdcMem = CreateCompatibleDC(hDC);
        nPp10D = rBitmap.right/2;
        rBitmap.right = nPp10D*36;
        hbmCompass = CreateBitmap(rBitmap.right,
                                  rBitmap.bottom,
                                  (BYTE)GetDeviceCaps(hDC, PLANES),
                                  (BYTE)GetDeviceCaps(hDC, BITSPIXEL),
```

```
                                        NULL);
        ReleaseDC(hWnd, hDC);
        hbmOld = SelectObject(hdcMem, hbmCompass);
        FillRect(hdcMem, &rBitmap, GetStockObject(WHITE_BRUSH));
        hPen = CreatePen(PS_SOLID, 2, COLOR_BLUE);
        hpenOld = SelectObject(hdcMem, hPen);
```

```
// Label the 10 degree increments. Find the actual position of each along the bitmap, compute
// the text rectangle size, then backup half the distance. This gets us the starting offset
// where the text output (degree value) is to begin. The DT_CALCRECT option is neat: it
// returns the actual height or width (you supply the other) of a text string. We used RED
// and BLACK for the marker indicators every 90 degrees. You can of course rise superior to
// my poor talents and use different fonts, styles, shading, etc. Have fun!
```

```
        for (i = 0; i < 36; i++)
        {
          itoa(i*10, sz, 10);
          SetRect(&rText, 0, 0, rBitmap.bottom, 0);
          DrawText(hdcMem, sz, strlen(sz), &rText, DT_SINGLELINE | DT_VCENTER | DT_CALCRECT);
          center = nPp10D*i;
          offset = center-rText.right/2;
          SetRect(&rDraw, offset, 0, offset+rText.right, rBitmap.bottom);
          SelectObject(hdcMem, hPen);
          MoveTo(hdcMem, center+nPp10D/2, rBitmap.bottom/4);
          LineTo(hdcMem, center+nPp10D/2, rBitmap.bottom-rBitmap.bottom/4);
          if (i%9 == 0)
            SetTextColor(hdcMem, COLOR_RED);
          else
            SetTextColor(hdcMem, COLOR_BLACK);
          DrawText(hdcMem, sz, strlen(sz), &rDraw, DT_SINGLELINE | DT_VCENTER);
          if (i == 0)
          {
            SetRect(&rDraw, rBitmap.right-rText.right/2, 0, rBitmap.right, rBitmap.bottom);
            DrawText(hdcMem, sz, strlen(sz), &rDraw, DT_SINGLELINE | DT_VCENTER);
          }
        }
```

```
// Reselect the original objects back into the memory dc before deleting it...
```

```
        SelectObject(hdcMem, hpenOld);
        SelectObject(hdcMem, hbmOld);
        DeleteObject(hPen);
        DeleteDC(hdcMem);
}
```

```
// ...DirProc...is the exported callback function used to process the messages sent to us by
// Windows...
//
// On entry we're passed:
//
// hWnd          A handle to our window instance.
//
// wMsg          A WORD containing the Windows message code we're being passed.
//
// wParam        A WORD containing a parameter specific to this message.
//
// lParam        A LONG containing a parameter specific to this message.
```

```
// DirProc's reason for living is to show the current ball direction. We're going to pretend
// we're looking at a compass, in which the direction is displayed as a number of degrees on
```

```
// the perimeter. A little thought and you realize you don't want to do this by actually
// writing the degrees value to the window: since this is a circular compass and we're reading
// around the edge, there may be multiple degree values partially displayed. Picture instead a
// long thin bitmap, like a ruler. If we can figure out where to start it, just bliting it to
// the screen should be fastest. Plus, we can do fancy things, like different size fonts and
// marker lines along the compass. The thought of creating the bitmap by hand is very
depressing
// so we'll do it at run-time. Now let's see...

LRESULT CALLBACK DirProc(
            HWND      hWnd,           // handle to window instance
            WORD      wMsg,           // windows message code
            WPARAM    wParam,         // word parameter
            LPARAM    lParam)         // long parameter
{
HBITMAP hbmOld;                       // handle to original bitmap
HDC     hDC;                          // handle to display device context
HDC     hdcMem;                       // handle to memory device context
int     degree;                       // starting degrees
int     diff;                         // width remainder
int     dx;                           // x offset in compass bitmap
int     w;                            // blit width
int     x;                            // starting offset in window
PAINTSTRUCT     ps;                   // PAINTSTRUCT used by WM_PAINT

// This function must process the messages passed to it by Windows. The simplest way to
// handle them is with a switch (case) statement. However, there are more than 200 messages
// which can be sent by Windows that makes for a huge, unwieldy source file it we put all
// that code inline. Instead we'll try to make the source as readable as possible. One thing
// I've learned, which never fails to amaze me: I can live with a program and the source code
// for months, know it intimately, see the stuff in my sleep no less, then leave it for a few
// months/ and when I come back, I'm convinced I never wrote it in the first place.
Especially,
// especially, if it's not commented up to its eyeballs. Virtually every line. You wont
believe
// how easy it is to completely forget this stuff as soon as you leave it.

// It can't possibly be wrong (one of my favorite sayings) to heavily comment your code. DO
IT!!

// Note that the messages are case'd in alphabetical order. Simply one of my quirks, I'm fussy
// that way, consistency is important. When I come back and look at this stuff again, it helps
// get me realigned. All my code is the same way. Always structured the same, same sort of
// comments, parameter notation, module layout, etc. I suppose it's like traveling and finding
// a McDonalds off in outer space, it's reassuring. Also, it proves to me I wrote this and not
// my doppelganger...

        switch (wMsg)
        {

// ...WM_CREATE...this message is received when Windows is about to create the application
// window. It is generated as a direct result of the Create() function. Use this time to do
// any global initialization required. Return 0, if OK, else return 1...

        case   WM_CREATE:
            CreateCompassBitmap(hWnd);
            return(0);

// ...WM_DESTROY...this message is received when Windows is about to destroy the application
// window. It is generated as a direct result of the DestroyWindow() function. Use this time
```

```
// to do any final window cleanup. Here, we delete the compass bitmap. Return 0, if OK, else
// return 1...

            case   WM_DESTROY:
               DeleteObject(hbmCompass);
               return(0);

// ...WM_PAINT...this message is received whenever the window requires repainting. Display the
// current ball azimuth. The calculations are again based on the same 10 degree increment
value
// as used to create the bitmap (nPp10D), create the basic 10 degree offset, then extrapolate
// the rest of the way. Note that we may have to perform 2 blits if we've wrapped around
either
// end of the bitmap...

            case   WM_PAINT:
               hDC = BeginPaint(hWnd, &ps);
               degree = gVR.nDirection-10;
               if (degree < 0) degree += 360;
               x = nWidth/2-nPp10D;
               w - degree/10;
               dx = nPp10D*w+nPp10D*(degree-(w*10))/10;
               w = min(nWidth, rBitmap.right-dx);
               hdcMem = CreateCompatibleDC(hDC);
               hbmOld = SelectObject(hdcMem, hbmCompass);
               BitBlt(hDC, x, 0, w, nHeight, hdcMem, dx, 0, SRCCOPY);
               if (w < 2*nPp10D)
               {
                 diff = 2*nPp10D-w;
                 BitBlt(hDC, x+w, 0, diff, nHeight, hdcMem, 0, 0, SRCCOPY);
               }
               SelectObject(hdcMem, hbmOld);
               DeleteDC(hdcMem);
               EndPaint(hWnd, &ps);
               return(0);

// ...WM_SIZE...this message is received when Windows is changing the size of the window. This
// includes creating, resizing and moving. Note that, once again, although we know the actual
// size of the window (from the CreateView() function), don't use it. If we use those values
// here, if the size is changed, this code will have to be modified. This way, again, the code
// is more robust...

            case   WM_SIZE:
               nWidth = LOWORD(lParam);
               nHeight = HIWORD(lParam);
               return(0);
         }

// Any message we don't process, pass through to the Windows default message handler. Return
// whatever result it returns...

         return (DefWindowProc(hWnd, wMsg, wParam, lParam));
}
```

funcs.c

```
// ------------------------------------------------------------------------------
        //
// "Plunging Into Virtual Reality", FUNCS.C
        //
// Copyright 1994, 1995 Russell J. Berube Jr. ALL RIGHTS RESERVED.           //
// This software is published, but is NOT public domain. It remains the exclusive   //
// property of Russell J. Berube Jr. and Brookside Systems, Inc. This software may not
        //
// be reproduced or integrated with other software without the prior written permission
        //
// of Russell J. Berube Jr. and Brookside Systems, Inc. It is provided herein for    //
// instructional purposes only.
        //
// ------------------------------------------------------------------------------
        //

#include "includes.h"            // include the world...
#include "bitmap.h"              // include bitmap functions prototypes...
#include "funcs.h"               // include functions prototypes...
#include "resource.h"            // include resource definitions...
#include "vr.h"                  // include VR definitions...

// External data...

extern   BOOL      gbLeft;                   // left mouse button down flag
extern   BOOL      gbDFR;                    // display frame rate flag
extern   enum      CONTROLMODE    geMode;    // control mode
extern   HFONT     ghfView;          // handle to view azimuth font
extern   HINSTANCE       ghInstance;      // handle to application instance
extern   HPALETTE  ghPalette;     // handle to vr window palette
extern   HWND      ghwndDir;                 // handle to ball direction (azimuth) window
extern   HWND      ghwndSpd;                 // handle to ball speed window
extern   HWND      ghwndView;                // handle to view window
extern   HWND      ghwndView;                // handle to view window
extern   int       gnAzX;                    // view azimuth X start
extern   int       gnAzY;                    // view azimuth Y start
extern   int       gnPaintMode;              // current paint mode
extern   int       gnHeight;                 // client area height
extern   int       gnWidth;         // client area width
extern   int       gnViewW;         // view window width
extern   int       gnViewX;         // view window X start
extern   int       gnViewY;         // view window Y start
extern   POINT     gMousePoint;              // mouse point
extern   RECT      grFrameRate;              // frame rate text rectangle
extern   VR        gVR;                      // VR structure

// Local data...

DWORD    dwLast;                             // time of last frame

// ...Draw3DBorder...is the function called to draw a border around the client area of the
// specified window to give the appearance of depth. Conform to the existing Windows light
// source orientation: upper left...

void     WINAPI    Draw3DBorder(
         HWND      hWnd,           // handle to window
         HDC       hDC)            // handle to window device context
```

```
{
HPEN     hOldPen;          // handle to original pen
HPEN     hGray;                   // handle to gray pen
HPEN     hWhite;                  // handle to white pen
```

```
// Create white and gray pens, we'll use these for our borders. Regardless of the border width
// we want, create 1 pixel wide pens. That's the only way we can accurately draw beveled edges
// for a border > 1 pixel...
```

```
        hWhite = CreatePen(PS_SOLID, 1, COLOR_WHITE);
        hGray = CreatePen(PS_SOLID, 1, COLOR_DKGRAY);
```

```
// Save old pen, select in the white pen and draw all the white lines around the perimeter of
// the client area and the perimeter of the view window...
```

```
        hOldPen = SelectObject(hDC, hWhite);
        MoveTo(hDC, 0, gnHeight-1);
        LineTo(hDC, 0, 0);
        LineTo(hDC, gnWidth-1, 0);
        MoveTo(hDC, 1, gnHeight-2);
        LineTo(hDC, 1, 1);
        LineTo(hDC, gnWidth-2, 1);
        MoveTo(hDC, gnViewX, gnViewY+VWHEIGHT);
        LineTo(hDC, gnViewX+gnViewW, gnViewY+VWHEIGHT);
        LineTo(hDC, gnViewX+gnViewW, gnViewY-2);
        MoveTo(hDC, gnViewX-1, gnViewY+VWHEIGHT+1);
        LineTo(hDC, gnViewX+gnViewW+1, gnViewY+VWHEIGHT+1);
        LineTo(hDC, gnViewX+gnViewW+1, gnViewY-3);
```

```
// Select in the gray pen and draw all the gray lines. Note when drawing in a rectangle the
// pen actually draws to the right and below a pixel position which is why you see -1 and -2
// appended to the position values...
```

```
        SelectObject(hDC, hGray);
        MoveTo(hDC, gnWidth-1, 0);
        LineTo(hDC, gnWidth-1, gnHeight-1);
        LineTo(hDC, 0, gnHeight-1);
        MoveTo(hDC, gnWidth-2, 1);
        LineTo(hDC, gnWidth-2, gnHeight-2);
        LineTo(hDC, 1, gnHeight-2);
        MoveTo(hDC, gnViewX-2, gnViewY+VWHEIGHT+1);
        LineTo(hDC, gnViewX-2, gnViewY-2);
        LineTo(hDC, gnViewX+gnViewW+1, gnViewY-2);
        MoveTo(hDC, gnViewX-1, gnViewY+VWHEIGHT);
        LineTo(hDC, gnViewX-1, gnViewY-1);
        LineTo(hDC, gnViewX+gnViewW, gnViewY-1);
```

```
// Reselect original pen and delete the one's we made...
```

```
        SelectObject(hDC, hOldPen);
        DeleteObject(hWhite);
        DeleteObject(hGray);
}
```

```
// ...MBox...is the function used to display a message box. On entry we're passed resource
// ID's for the message text and dialog box title, display and return result...
```

```
int     WINAPI  MBox(
        HWND    hWnd,           // handle to window instance
        int     nText,          // resource id of text string
```

```
          int       nTitle,          // resource id of title string
          UINT      uStyle)          // messagebox style
{
char      szText[256];              // text goes here
char      szTitle[64];              // title goes here
```

```
// Load the message box title string and append the actual resource ID number to it. This can
// be used as an easy reference to an error list in an online help system. Leave room for the
// " [xxx]" we append to the title text.
```

```
// Note that you must explicitly typecast any wsprintf() string parameters to (LPSTR).
Strictly
// speaking (LPCSTR) is better. The point however, is that you MUST force the compiler to push
// a 32-bit address on the stack which is what wsprintf() expects...
```

```
          LoadString(ghInstance, nTitle, szText, sizeof(szTitle)-7);
          wsprintf(szTitle, "%s [%03d]", (LPCSTR)szText, nText);
```

```
// Load the message box text string...
```

```
          LoadString(ghInstance, nText, szText, sizeof(szText)-1);
```

```
// Then put up the actual dialog box. Return message box result...
```

```
          return(MessageBox(hWnd, szText, szTitle, uStyle));
}
```

```
// ...UpdatePalette...is the function called to change the global palette for the virtual view
// window if required. This is indicated by the MF_PALETTE bit in the uMode member of the VR
// structure being set by the VR routines...
```

```
void      WINAPI   UpdatePalette()
{
// Reset <palette action required> flag MF_PALETTE, then update current logical palette...
```

```
          gVR.uMode &= ~MF_PALETTE;
          SetPaletteEntries(ghPalette, gVR.uPalStart, gVR.uPalEntries, gVR.lpPal);
}
```

```
// ...UpdateView...is the function called to update the view window after the VR engine has
// danced...
```

```
void      WINAPI   UpdateView(
          HWND      hWnd)            // handle to window instance
{
char      sz[32];                   // local junk
BOOL      bOK;                      // OK flag
DWORD     dwNow;                    // current time (msecs)
DWORD     dwTime;                   // frame delay time
HDC       hDC;                      // handle to display DC
```

```
// Let the VR engine process the last change. If it returns TRUE, the new image is different
// from the previous so show it by invalidating the window. That causes the view window
// processor ViewProc() to receive a WM_PAINT message which will get the job done. Do the
// same for the ball speed and direction windows. If there's no update we're done...
```

```
          bOK = vrUpdate(hWnd, &gVR);
```

```
// Update the frame rate. Do this by getting the current time (after showing the last frame)
// and subtracting the time for the previous frame. This gives us the elapsed time since the
```

```
// previous frame. Display the result as text on the main window...

// Get handle to display device context. Then compute frame rate. Use difference between last
// time and now, convert to microseconds and divide by 1000 to go back to milliseconds. Use
// GetTimerResolution(); GetTickCount() doesn't return actual milliseconds. Avoid floating
// point by premultiplying by 1,000,000 then dividing by 1,000. Note we only do this if the
// frame rate update flag is set...

        if (gbDFR)
        {
          dwNow = GetTickCount();
          if ((dwTime = dwNow-dwLast) > 0)
          {
            dwLast = dwNow;
            dwTime = 1000000000L/(dwTime*GetTimerResolution());
            wsprintf(sz, "%lu.%lu frames/sec", dwTime/1000, dwTime%1000);
            hDC = GetDC(hWnd);
            SetBkColor(hDC, COLOR_FRAME);
            ExtTextOut(hDC, 4, 4, ETO_OPAQUE, &grFrameRate, sz, lstrlen(sz), NULL);
            ReleaseDC(hWnd, hDC);
          }
        }

// Update palette if required...

        if (gVR.uMode & MF_PALETTE) UpdatePalette();

// Finally, if vrUpdate returned TRUE, it's changed the virtual world so we need to update
// the appropriate windows...

        if (bOK)
        {
          InvalidateRect(ghwndView, NULL, FALSE);
          InvalidateRect(ghwndDir, NULL, FALSE);
          InvalidateRect(ghwndSpd, NULL, FALSE);
        }
}

// ...UpdateAzimuth...is the function called to change the viewer azimuth and update the
// display...

void    WINAPI  UpdateAzimuth(
        HWND    hWnd,           // handle to window instance
        int     delta)          // azimuth delta
{
char    sz[8];                  // text area
HDC     hDC;                    // handle to device context
HFONT   hFont;                  // handle to old font

// Update the azimuth value and clip it into the range 0-360...

        gVR.nAzimuth += delta;
        if (gVR.nAzimuth < 0) gVR.nAzimuth += 360;
        if (gVR.nAzimuth >= 360) gVR.nAzimuth -= 360;

// Update the virtual view...

        UpdateView(hWnd);

// Now show user the new azimuth value. Since we're using a proportional font, the width of
```

```
// the output text changes each time. Padding the output ("%3d  ") with trailing spaces is a
// quick and dirty way (read computationally fast) way to ensure the previous output is
// erased...

        wsprintf(sz, "%3d  ", gVR.nAzimuth);
        hDC = GetDC(hWnd);
        hFont = SelectObject(hDC, ghfView);
        SetTextColor(hDC, RGB(0,0,255));
        SetBkColor(hDC, COLOR_FRAME);
        TextOut(hDC, gnAzX, gnAzY, sz, 5);
        SelectObject(hDC, hFont);
        ReleaseDC(hWnd, hDC);
}

// ...UpdateControlMode...is the function called to update the current control mode and
// display the results...

void    WINAPI  UpdateControlMode(
        HWND    hWnd,           // handle to window instance
        int     mode)           // control mode
{
// Update the control mode...

        geMode = mode;

// Change the button text...

        SendMessage(GetDlgItem(hWnd, IDC_MODE),
                    WM_SETTEXT,
                    0,
                    (LPARAM)(LPCSTR)((geMode==eVIEWER)?"> &Ball":"> &Viewer"));
}

// ...UpdateDirection...is the function called to change the ball direction. Note this only
// works in manual mode so call vrUpdate() only if auto-update is on...

void    WINAPI  UpdateDirection(
        HWND    hWnd,           // handle to window instance
        int     delta)          // azimuth delta
{
// Update the direction value and clip it into the range 0-360...

        gVR.nDirection += delta;
        if (gVR.nDirection < 0) gVR.nDirection += 360;
        if (gVR.nDirection >= 360) gVR.nDirection -= 360;

// Update if required...

        if (gVR.uMode & MF_UPDATE) UpdateView(hWnd);

// Now force the direction window to show us the new value. Note that we use the global
// window handle directly. An alternate approach is used in UpdateSpeed()...

        InvalidateRect(ghwndDir, NULL, TRUE);
        UpdateWindow(ghwndDir);
}

// ...UpdateElevation...is the function called to change the viewer height and update the
// display...
```

```
void    WINAPI  UpdateElevation(
        HWND    hWnd,           // handle to window instance
        int     delta,          // azimuth delta
        BOOL    bAbsolute)      // absolute change flag
{
// Update the height value and clip it into the range 0-MAXELEVATION. Then show the results on
// the scroll bar. Remember it's inverted...

        if (bAbsolute)
          gVR.nElevation = delta;
        else
          gVR.nElevation += delta;

// Clip it...

        gVR.nElevation = max(0, min(gVR.nElevation, MAXELEVATION));

// Update the virtual view...

        UpdateView(hWnd);

// Now show the new position...

        SetScrollPos(ghwndView, SB_VERT, MAXELEVATION-gVR.nElevation, TRUE);
}

// ...UpdateSpeed...is the function called to change the ball speed and update the display.
// Like UpdateDirection(), this only works in manual mode, so no UpdateView(). Unless the
// auto-update flag is set, then of course, we call UpdateView()...

void    WINAPI  UpdateSpeed(
        HWND    hWnd,           // handle to window instance
        int     delta)          // azimuth delta
{
HWND    hwnd;                   // handle to ball direction window

// Update the speed value and clip it into the range -MAXSPEED to MAXSPEED...

        gVR.nSpeed += delta;
        gVR.nSpeed = max(-MAXSPEED, min(gVR.nSpeed, MAXSPEED));

// Update if required...

        if (gVR.uMode & MF_UPDATE) UpdateView(hWnd);

// Now force the speed window to show us the new value. Here we use GetDlgItem() to
// get the handle to the ball speed window. UpdateDirection() uses an alternate
// approach...

        hwnd = GetDlgItem(hWnd, IDC_SPEED);
        InvalidateRect(hwnd, NULL, TRUE);
        UpdateWindow(hwnd);
}

// ...WaitFor...is the function used to wait here, releasing control to Windows between
// messages, while waiting for the paint mode to change from whatever...

void    WINAPI  WaitFor(
        enum    PAINTMODE       mode)    // paint mode
{
```

```
MSG     Msg;                        // Windows MSG structure

        do
          while (PeekMessage(&Msg, NULL, 0, 0, PM_REMOVE))
          {
            TranslateMessage(&Msg);
            DispatchMessage(&Msg);
          }
          while (gnPaintMode == mode);
}

// ...WaitForLeftMouseDown...is the function used to wait here, releasing control to Windows
// between messages, while waiting for the left mouse button to be pressed. Return with the
// mouse click position...

POINT   WINAPI  WaitForLeftButtonDown()
{
MSG     Msg;                        // Windows MSG structure

        do
          while (PeekMessage(&Msg, NULL, 0, 0, PM_REMOVE))
          {
            TranslateMessage(&Msg);
            DispatchMessage(&Msg);
          }
          while (!gbLeft);

        return(gMousePoint);
}

// ...WaitForLeftMouseUp...is the function used to wait here, releasing control to Windows
// between messages, while waiting for the left mouse button to be released. Return with the
// mouse click position...

POINT   WINAPI  WaitForLeftButtonUp()
{
MSG     Msg;                        // Windows MSG structure

        do
          while (PeekMessage(&Msg, NULL, 0, 0, PM_REMOVE))
          {
            TranslateMessage(&Msg);
            DispatchMessage(&Msg);
          }
          while (gbLeft);

        return(gMousePoint);
}

// ...WaitForManual...is the function used to wait here, releasing control to Windows between
// messages, while waiting for the VR mode to be NOT auto (autopilot off)...

void    WINAPI  WaitForManual()
{
MSG     Msg;                        // Windows MSG structure

        do
          while (PeekMessage(&Msg, NULL, 0, 0, PM_REMOVE))
            {
              TranslateMessage(&Msg);
```

```
        DispatchMessage(&Msg);
    }
    while (gVR.uMode & MF_AUTO);
}
```

includes.c

includes.c contains a single "active" line #include "includes.h" which causes the include file "includes.h" to be processed. The special processing occurs in the .MAK file which contains the compiler switch /Yuincludes.h. The include file is built once; then the resultant **.pch** file is compiled with the remaining source files. **.pch** indicates a precompiled header which compiles much more quickly than recompiling the same include files over and over....

```
// ----------------------------------------------------------------------------------
//                                                                               //
// "Plunging Into Virtual Reality", INCLUDES.C
//                                                                               //
// Copyright 1994, 1995 Russell J. Berube Jr. ALL RIGHTS RESERVED.              //
// This software is published, but is NOT public domain. It remains the exclusive   //
// property of Russell J. Berube Jr. and Brookside Systems, Inc. This software may not
//                                                                               //
// be reproduced or integrated with other software without the prior written permission
//                                                                               //
// of Russell J. Berube Jr. and Brookside Systems, Inc. It is provided herein for   //
// instructional purposes only.
//                                                                               //
// ----------------------------------------------------------------------------------
//                                                                               //

#include "includes.h"              // include application definitions
```

message.c

```
// ----------------------------------------------------------------------------------
//                                                                               //
// "Plunging Into Virtual Reality", MESSAGE.C
//                                                                               //
// Copyright 1994, 1995 Russell J. Berube Jr. ALL RIGHTS RESERVED.              //
// This software is published, but is NOT public domain. It remains the exclusive   //
// property of Russell J. Berube Jr. and Brookside Systems, Inc. This software may not
//                                                                               //
// be reproduced or integrated with other software without the prior written permission
//                                                                               //
```

```
// of Russell J. Berube Jr. and Brookside Systems, Inc. It is provided herein for     //
// instructional purposes only.
//            //
// -----------------------------------------------------------------------------
//            //

#include "includes.h"           // include the world...
#include "bitmap.h"             // include bitmap functions prototypes...
#include "funcs.h"              // include miscellaneous functions prototypes...
#include "resource.h"           // include resource definitions...
#include "startup.h"            // include startup functions prototypes...
#include "vr.h"                 // include VR definitions...

// External data...

extern    BM        gDir;                       // direction bitmap BM structure
extern    BM        gDirBar;        // direction slide bar bitmap BM structure
extern    BM        gDirSlide;              // direction slide bitmap BM structure
extern    BM        gSpd;                   // speed bitmap BM structure
extern    BM        gSpdBar;        // speed slide bar bitmap BM structure
extern    BM        gSpdSlide;              // speed slide bitmap BM structure
#ifdef _LESSON1
extern    DIB       gDIB1;                      // DIB for "up pushbutton" image
extern    DIB       gDIB2;                      // DIB for "down pushbutton" image
extern    DIB       gDIB3;                      // DIB for "plunging into virtual reality" image
#else
#ifdef _LESSON2
extern    HBITMAP   ghDDB1;                      // handle to DDBitmap for "up pushbutton" image
extern    HBITMAP   ghDDB2;                      // handle to DDBitmap for "down pushbutton" image
extern    HBITMAP   ghDDB3;                      // handle to DDBitmap for "plunging into virtual
reality" image
#else
extern    DDB       gDDB1;                       // DDB structure for "up pushbutton" image
extern    DDB       gDDB2;                       // DDB structure for "down pushbutton" image
extern    DDB       gDDB3;                       // DDB structure for "plunging into virtual
reality" image
#endif
#endif
extern    BUTTON    gAuto;                       // autopilot owner-draw BUTTON structure
extern    BUTTON    gVLA;                        // left arrow owner-draw BUTTON structures
extern    BUTTON    gVRA;                        // right arrow owner-draw BUTTON structures
extern    enum      CONTROLMODE      geMode;     // control mode
extern    HBRUSH    ghbrBkgnd;                   // handle to background brush
extern    HDC       ghdcMem;         // handle to compatible DC containing monologue
extern    HFONT     ghfView;         // handle to view angle font
extern    HINSTANCE          ghInstance;         // handle to application instance
extern    LPSTR     gpszMono;                    // pointer to monologue text
extern    int       gnPaintMode;                 // current paint mode
extern    int       gnRepeat;                    // key repeat time
extern    int       gnScrollInc;                 // monologue scroll increment
extern    int       gnWidth;         // client area width
extern    int       gnViewW;         // view window width
extern    int       gnMonoHeight;                // monologue text height
extern    RECT      grFrameRate;                 // frame rate text output rectangle
extern    RECT      grMono;                      // monologue rectangle
extern    VR        gVR;                         // VR structure

// Global data...

BOOL      gbLeft;                       // left mouse button down flag
```

```
BOOL    gbDFR;                  // display frame rate flag
int     gnUpdate;               // autopilot update rate
POINT   gMousePoint;            // mouse point

// Local data...

static  HMENU   hPopup;         // handle to popup menu
static  int     napu[]  =       {1, 2, 5, 10, 100};        // autopilot update divisor

// ...MsgCommand...is the function called to process the WM_COMMAND message. We receive this
// message whenever a menu item is selected, or one of our child window controls burps. Since
// we don't have a menu, that pretty much narrows it down...

void    WINAPI  MsgCommand(
        HWND    hWnd,           // handle to window instance
        WPARAM  wParam,         // WORD parameter
        LPARAM  lParam)         // LONG parameter
{
// Switch on command ID. Don't forget to return the input focus back to the main window...

        switch (wParam)
        {

// ...IDC_3D...invert the 3D-image (anaglyph) flag. Then force a VR update...

        case IDC_3D:
          gVR.uMode ^= MF_3D;
          UpdateView(hWnd);
          break;

// ...IDC_AUTO...invert the auto-update-in-manual flag...

        case IDC_AUTO:
          gVR.uMode ^= MF_UPDATE;
          break;

// ...IDC_EXIT...time to go. DestroyWindow() will generate a WM_DESTROY message which
// we'll process in turn...

        case IDC_EXIT:
          DestroyWindow(hWnd);
          break;

// ...IDC_FRAME...invert the display-frame-rate flag. If we turn it off, invalidate that
// area so it will be repainted...

        case IDC_FRAME:
          if (gbDFR)
          {
            gbDFR = FALSE;
            InvalidateRect(hWnd, &grFrameRate, TRUE);
          }
          else
            gbDFR = TRUE;
          break;

// ...MODE button...update control mode, change button text. Disallow a change to BALL mode
// if we're in AUTOPILOT...

        case IDC_MODE:
```

```
            if ((geMode == eVIEWER) && (gVR.uMode & MF_AUTO)) break;
            UpdateControlMode(hWnd, (geMode==eBALL)?eVIEWER:eBALL);
            break;

// ...UPDATE button...force manual VR update...

        case IDC_UPDATE:
          UpdateView(hWnd);
          break;

// ...IDC_X1-IDC_FAST...change the autopilot update rate. Restart the timer if currently
// running...

        case IDC_X1:
        case IDC_X2:
        case IDC_X5:
        case IDC_X10:
        case IDC_FAST:
          gnUpdate = UPDATEx1/napu[wParam-IDC_X1];
          if (gVR.uMode & MF_AUTO)
          {
            KillTimer(hWnd, IDB_AUTOON);
            SetTimer(hWnd, IDB_AUTOON, gnUpdate, NULL);
          }
          break;
      }
      SetFocus(hWnd);
}

// ...MsgCreate...is the function called to process the WM_CREATE message. This occurs when
// the window is created. Initialize all global data and create the popup menu...

void    WINAPI  MsgCreate(
        HWND    hWnd)              // handle to window instance
{
char    sz[32];                   // menu text area
int     i;                        // local junk

        GlobalInit(hWnd);
        hPopup = CreatePopupMenu();

// Create the menu items...

        for (i = IDC_X1; i <= IDC_FAST; i++)
        {
          LoadString(ghInstance, i, sz, sizeof(sz));
          AppendMenu(hPopup, MF_ENABLED, i, sz);
        }

// Then add a separator and the final menu item...

        AppendMenu(hPopup, MF_SEPARATOR, 0, NULL);
        LoadString(ghInstance, IDC_AUTO, sz, sizeof(sz));
        AppendMenu(hPopup, MF_ENABLED, IDC_AUTO, sz);

// It was decided to add 3D images, so we've got a new final menu item. Let's separate it
// from the auto-update in manual also...

        AppendMenu(hPopup, MF_SEPARATOR, 0, NULL);
        LoadString(ghInstance, IDC_3D, sz, sizeof(sz));
```

```
            AppendMenu(hPopup, MF_ENABLED, IDC_3D, sz);

// It was (also) decided an indication of the current frame rate would be nice, so add that.
// Separate it from the 3D flag...

            AppendMenu(hPopup, MF_SEPARATOR, 0, NULL);
            LoadString(ghInstance, IDC_FRAME, sz, sizeof(sz));
            AppendMenu(hPopup, MF_ENABLED, IDC_FRAME, sz);

// And lastly, we need a menu method to exit...

            AppendMenu(hPopup, MF_SEPARATOR, 0, NULL);
            LoadString(ghInstance, IDC_EXIT, sz, sizeof(sz));
            AppendMenu(hPopup, MF_ENABLED, IDC_EXIT, sz);

}


// ...MsgDestroy...is the function called to process the WM_DESTROY message. We receive this
// message when we're shutting down. The window is being destroyed. This is it, the last (or
// almost the last) message we'll receive. Get rid of (release) everything we used then do
// PostQuitMessage(). This causes us to send ourselves the WM_QUIT message. Which, if you'll
// remember, we test for in the main message loop: GetMessage() returns FALSE if the message
// it is returning is WM_QUIT. Don't forget to shutdown the VR system and lose the popup menu
// we created...

void    WINAPI  MsgDestroy(
        HWND    hWnd)               // handle to window instance
{
        vrEnd(hWnd, &gVR);
        if (ghfView != NULL) DeleteObject(ghfView);
        if (gAuto.hbmUp != NULL) DeleteObject(gAuto.hbmUp);
        if (gAuto.hbmDown != NULL) DeleteObject(gAuto.hbmDown);
        if (gVLA.hbmUp != NULL) DeleteObject(gVLA.hbmUp);
        if (gVLA.hbmDown != NULL) DeleteObject(gVLA.hbmDown);
        if (gVRA.hbmDown != NULL) DeleteObject(gVRA.hbmUp);
        if (gVRA.hbmDown != NULL) DeleteObject(gVRA.hbmDown);
        if (gDir.hBM != NULL) DeleteObject(gDir.hBM);
        if (gDirSlide.hBM != NULL) DeleteObject(gDirSlide.hBM);
        if (gSpd.hBM != NULL) DeleteObject(gSpd.hBM);
        if (gSpdSlide.hBM != NULL) DeleteObject(gSpdSlide.hBM);
        DestroyMenu(hPopup);
        PostQuitMessage(0);
}

// ...MsgDrawItem...is the function called to process the WM_DRAWITEM message. We receive this
// message whenever Windows is about to draw a control. See if the control is one of our owner
// draw buttons. Draw it here if so and return TRUE, otherwise return FALSE...

BOOL    WINAPI  MsgDrawItem(
        HWND    hWnd,              // handle to window instance
        int     nID,              // control ID
        LPDRAWITEMSTRUCT lpDIS)   // far pointer to DRAWITEMSTRUCT structure
{
HBITMAP hBM;                       // handle to bitmap
LPBUTTON lpBtn;            // far pointer to BUTTON structure

// If we're here, the drawing of the control belongs to us. See what itemAction and
// itemState are. They determine what we draw. After drawing, process the control itself.
// Start the repeat key timer. If we're no longer selected, kill the timer and return the
// keyboard focus to the main window...
```

```
          switch (nID)
          {
            case IDB_LAU:
            case IDB_RAU:
              if (nID == IDB_LAU) lpBtn = &gVLA;
              if (nID == IDB_RAU) lpBtn = &gVRA;
              if (lpDIS->itemAction & (ODA_DRAWENTIRE|ODA_SELECT))
              {
                if (gnRepeat == 0)
                {
                  hBM = lpBtn->hbmUp;
                  if (lpDIS->itemState & ODS_SELECTED) hBM = lpBtn->hbmDown;
                  BlitDC(lpDIS->hDC, hBM, lpDIS->rcItem.left, lpDIS->rcItem.top, NULL);
                }
                if (lpDIS->itemState & ODS_SELECTED)
                {
                  UpdateAzimuth(hWnd, (nID==IDB_LAU)? AZINC:-AZINC);
                  gnRepeat = KEYREPEAT;
                  SetTimer(hWnd, nID, KEYREPEAT, NULL);
                }
                else
                {
                  gnRepeat = 0;
                  SetFocus(hWnd);
                  KillTimer(hWnd, nID);
                }
              }
              return(TRUE);
```

```
// If the AUTOPILOT button is clicked, see if we're currently in autopilot mode (MF_AUTO flag)
// and invert it if we're now selected, redraw new image (BlitDC()) and turn on/off the UPDATE
// button. We don't want the user to be able to force a manual update when we're doing it
// automatically, so disable the window which is the UPDATE button. That causes the text to be
// grayed: Window's way of telling you the button is unavailable. We also don't want the user
// trying to switch to, (or be in) BALL mode if we go into autopilot, so force a change to
// VIEWER mode. Note this time the mode button isn't grayed, but it doesn't work either (as
// long as we're in autopilot). So that's two different approachs to controlling controls...
```

```
            case IDB_AUTOON:
              if (lpDIS->itemAction & (ODA_DRAWENTIRE|ODA_SELECT))
              {
                hBM = gAuto.hbmUp;
                if (gVR.uMode & MF_AUTO) hBM = gAuto.hbmDown;
                BlitDC(lpDIS->hDC, hBM, lpDIS->rcItem.left, lpDIS->rcItem.top, NULL);
              }
              if (lpDIS->itemState & ODS_SELECTED) gVR.uMode ^= MF_AUTO;
              EnableWindow(GetDlgItem(hWnd, IDC_UPDATE), !(gVR.uMode & MF_AUTO));
              if (gVR.uMode & MF_AUTO)
              {
                SetTimer(hWnd, IDB_AUTOON, gnUpdate, NULL);
                UpdateControlMode(hWnd, eVIEWER);
              }
              else
                KillTimer(hWnd, IDB_AUTOON);
              return(TRUE);
          }

          return(FALSE);
}
```

```
// ...MsgInitMenuPopup...is the function called to process the WM_INITMENUPOPUP message. This
// message is received when the floating popup (or any other popup) is about to be displayed.
// Check the menu item which is the currently selected autopilot update rate and uncheck any
// other...

void     WINAPI  MsgInitMenuPopup(
         HWND    hWnd,                  // handle to window instance
         HMENU   hMenu)                 // handle to popup menu instance
{
char     sz[32];                        // menu text area
int      i;                             // local junk
int      check;                         // local junk

         for (i = IDC_X1; i <= IDC_FAST; i++)
         {
            GetMenuString(hMenu, i, sz, sizeof(sz), MF_BYCOMMAND);
            check = (UPDATEx1/gnUpdate == napu[i-IDC_X1])? MF_CHECKED:MF_UNCHECKED;
            ModifyMenu(hMenu,
                      i,
                      MF_BYCOMMAND | check,
                      i,
                      sz);
         }

// Handle manual auto-update separately...

         GetMenuString(hMenu, IDC_AUTO, sz, sizeof(sz), MF_BYCOMMAND);
         check = (gVR.uMode & MF_UPDATE)? MF_CHECKED:MF_UNCHECKED;
         ModifyMenu(hMenu,
                   IDC_AUTO,
                   MF_BYCOMMAND | check,
                   IDC_AUTO,
                   sz);

// Handle 3D-images separately. However, notice that this code lends itself quite nicely to
// being table-driven and if I come up with another VR flag/menu item combination, it will be
// better to change over. For now, leave things, it only took 30 seconds to copy the previous
// lines and modify them from IDC_AUTO/MF_UPDATE to IDC_3D/MF_3D

         GetMenuString(hMenu, IDC_3D, sz, sizeof(sz), MF_BYCOMMAND);
         check = (gVR.uMode & MF_3D)? MF_CHECKED:MF_UNCHECKED;
         ModifyMenu(hMenu,
                   IDC_3D,
                   MF_BYCOMMAND | check,
                   IDC_3D,
                   sz);

// Well, I'vr got another but I'm leaving things as they are. The reason? Same as before, it
// only took 30 seconds to copy the previous lines and modify them...

         GetMenuString(hMenu, IDC_FRAME, sz, sizeof(sz), MF_BYCOMMAND);
         check = (gbDFR)? MF_CHECKED:MF_UNCHECKED;
         ModifyMenu(hMenu,
                   IDC_FRAME,
                   MF_BYCOMMAND | check,
                   IDC_FRAME,
                   sz);
}
```

```
// ...MsgKeyDown...is the function called to process the WM_KEYDOWN message. On entry we're
// passed a virtual keycode. Process some, ignore most. Return TRUE if we process a key, else
// return FALSE:

//      B               switch to BALL mode
//      U               update view
//      V               switch to VIEWER mode
//      DOWN ARROW      decrease viewer elevation
//      UP ARROW increase viewer elevation
//      END             change viewer direction 180 degrees
//      ESC             kill speed
//      HOME            ball mode: 0 direction.
//                      viewer mode: 0 azimuth
//      LEFT ARROW      ball mode: incearse direction
//                      viewer mode: increase azimuth
//      RIGHT ARROW     ball mode: decearse direction
//                      viewer mode: decrease azimuth
//      PAGE UP         ball mode: max speed
//                      viewer mode: max elevation
//      PAGE DOWN       ball mode: zero speed
//                      viewer mode: zero elevation
//      F1              HELP!

BOOL    WINAPI  MsgKeyDown(
        HWND    hWnd,               // handle to window instance
        UINT    uKey)               // virtual key code
{
        switch (uKey)
        {
          case  'B':
            if (geMode != eBALL)
              if (!(gVR.uMode & MF_AUTO))
                UpdateControlMode(hWnd, eBALL);
            return(TRUE);
          case  'U':
            if (!(gVR.uMode & MF_AUTO))
              UpdateView(hWnd);
            return(TRUE);
          case  'V':
            if (geMode != eVIEWER)
              UpdateControlMode(hWnd, eVIEWER);
            return(TRUE);
          case  VK_DOWN:
            if (geMode == eVIEWER)
              UpdateElevation(hWnd, -HGTINC, FALSE);
            else
              if (!(gVR.uMode & MF_AUTO))
                UpdateSpeed(hWnd, -gVR.nSpdInc);
            return(TRUE);
          case  VK_END:
            if (geMode == eBALL)
              if (!(gVR.uMode & MF_AUTO))
                UpdateDirection(hWnd, 180);
            return(TRUE);
          case  VK_ESCAPE:
            UpdateSpeed(hWnd, -gVR.nSpeed);
            return(TRUE);
          case  VK_HOME:
            if (geMode == eVIEWER)
              UpdateAzimuth(hWnd, -gVR.nAzimuth);
```

```
                 else
                   if (!(gVR.uMode & MF_AUTO))
                     UpdateDirection(hWnd, -gVR.nDirection);
                 return(TRUE);
             case  VK_LEFT:
                 if (geMode == eVIEWER)
                   UpdateAzimuth(hWnd, AZINC);
                 else
                   if (!(gVR.uMode & MF_AUTO))
                     UpdateDirection(hWnd, gVR.nDirInc);
                 return(TRUE);
             case  VK_NEXT:
                 if (geMode == eVIEWER)
                   UpdateElevation(hWnd, 0, TRUE);
                 else
                   if (!(gVR.uMode & MF_AUTO))
                     UpdateSpeed(hWnd, -MAXSPEED-gVR.nSpeed);
                 return(TRUE);
             case  VK_PRIOR:
                 if (geMode == eVIEWER)
                   UpdateElevation(hWnd, MAXELEVATION, TRUE);
                 else
                   if (!(gVR.uMode & MF_AUTO))
                     UpdateSpeed(hWnd, MAXSPEED-gVR.nSpeed);
                 return(TRUE);
             case  VK_RIGHT:
                 if (geMode == eVIEWER)
                   UpdateAzimuth(hWnd, -AZINC);
                 else
                   if (!(gVR.uMode & MF_AUTO))
                     UpdateDirection(hWnd, -gVR.nDirInc);
                 return(TRUE);
             case  VK_UP:
                 if (geMode == eVIEWER)
                   UpdateElevation(hWnd, HGTINC, FALSE);
                 else
                   if (!(gVR.uMode & MF_AUTO))
                     UpdateSpeed(hWnd, gVR.nSpdInc);
                 return(TRUE);
             case  VK_F1:
                 WinHelp(hWnd, "pivr.hlp", HELP_CONTENTS, 0L);
                 return(TRUE);
         }

         return(FALSE);
}


// ...MsgLeftButtonDown...is the function called when the user has clicked the left mouse
// button. Set the left mouse button flag and capture the mouse. Then save the position of
// the mouse...

void     WINAPI  MsgLeftButtonDown(
         HWND     hWnd,           // handle to window instance
         POINT    point)          // mouse down point
{
// Indicate the mouse has been captured and the left button is down then capture the mouse...

         gbLeft = TRUE;
         gMousePoint = point;
         SetCapture(hWnd);
```

```
        }

// ...MsgLeftButtonUp...is the function called to process the WM_LBUTTONUP message. The
// user has released the mouse button. Reset the left mouse button flag and release the mouse
// capture. Finally, save the mouse point...

void     WINAPI   MsgLeftButtonUp(
         HWND      hWnd,              // handle to window instance
         POINT     point)            // mouse down point
{
// Indicate the mouse has been released and the left button is up then release the mouse
// capture, finally save the mouse position...

         gbLeft = FALSE;
         gMousePoint = point;
         ReleaseCapture();
}

// ...MsgPaint...is the function called to process a WM_PAINT message. This is received
// whenever our client area needs brushing up. What gets painted depends on the current
// paint mode...

void     WINAPI   MsgPaint(
         HWND      hWnd,              // handle to window instance
         HDC       hDC,              // handle to display device context
         LPPAINTSTRUCT    lpps)      // far pointer to PAINTSTRUCT
{
RECT     rect;                       // local junk

         switch (gnPaintMode)
         {
           case eMONO:
             BitBlt(hDC, 0, grMono.top, gnWidth, gnMonoHeight, ghdcMem, 0, 0, SRCCOPY);
             break;
           case eBRP1:
#ifdef   _LESSON1
             DrawDIB(hWnd, &gDIB1);
#else
#ifdef   _LESSON2
             DrawDDB(hWnd, ghDDB1, NULL);
#else
             DrawDDB(hWnd, gDDB1.hBM, gDDB1.hPal);
#endif
#endif
             break;
           case eBRP2:
#ifdef   _LESSON1
             DrawDIB(hWnd, &gDIB2);
#else
#ifdef   _LESSON2
             DrawDDB(hWnd, ghDDB2, NULL);
#else
             DrawDDB(hWnd, gDDB2.hBM, gDDB2.hPal);
#endif
#endif
             break;
           case ePIVR:
#ifdef   _LESSON1
             DrawDIB(hWnd, &gDIB3);
#else
```

```
#ifdef  _LESSON2
          DrawDDB(hWnd, ghDDB3, NULL);
#else
          DrawDDB(hWnd, gDDB3.hBM, gDDB3.hPal);
#endif
#endif
          break;
        case eNORMAL:
          Draw3DBorder(hWnd, hDC);
          BlitDC(hDC, gDir.hBM, gDir.rect.left, gDir.rect.top, NULL);
          BlitDC(hDC, gDirSlide.hBM, gDirSlide.rect.left, gDirSlide.rect.top, NULL);
          BlitDC(hDC, gSpd.hBM, gSpd.rect.left, gSpd.rect.top, NULL);
          BlitDC(hDC, gSpdSlide.hBM, gSpdSlide.rect.left, gSpdSlide.rect.top, NULL);
          SetBkColor(hDC, COLOR_FRAME);
          CopyRect(&rect, &gDir.rect);
          OffsetRect(&rect, 0, -24);
          DrawText(hDC, "Direction", 9, &rect, DT_SINGLELINE|DT_CENTER);
          CopyRect(&rect, &gSpd.rect);
          OffsetRect(&rect, 0, -24);
          DrawText(hDC, "R - Speed - F", 13, &rect, DT_SINGLELINE|DT_CENTER);
          break;
        }
}

// ...MsgRightButtonDown...is the function called when the user has clicked the right mouse
// button. Put up the popup menu we created when the window was new...

void    WINAPI  MsgRightButtonDown(
        HWND    hWnd,              // handle to window instance
        POINT   point)             // mouse down point
{
// Convert mouse point from client area relative to screen relative...

        ClientToScreen(hWnd, &point);
        TrackPopupMenu(hPopup, TPM_LEFTALIGN, point.x, point.y, 0, hWnd, NULL);
}

// ...MsgTimer...is the function called to process a WM_TIMER message. This message is
// received whenever a timer count expires and we haven't specified a callback function to
// process the timer. Use the timer ID (from SetTimer()) to identify timer source and
// therefore what function we're to perform...

void    WINAPI  MsgTimer(
        HWND    hWnd,              // handle to window instance
        UINT    uID)              // timer ID
{
        switch (uID)
        {
          case  eMONO:
            if (grMono.bottom < 0)
            {
              KillTimer(hWnd, eMONO);
              gnPaintMode = eUNKNOWN;
            }
            else
            {
              InvalidateRect(hWnd, &grMono, FALSE);
              grMono.top -= gnScrollInc;
              grMono.bottom -= gnScrollInc;
            }
```

```
            return;
        case   eBRP1:
        case   ePIVR:
          MBox(hWnd, IDS_STUCK, IDS_QUERY, MB_OK|MB_ICONQUESTION);
          KillTimer(hWnd, uID);
          return;
        case   IDB_LAU:
        case   IDB_RAU:
          if (gnRepeat > KEYFAST)
          {
            gnRepeat -= KEYACCEL;
            KillTimer(hWnd, uID);
            SetTimer(hWnd, uID, gnRepeat, NULL);
          }
          UpdateAzimuth(hWnd, (uID==IDB_LAU)?AZINC:-AZINC);
          return;
        case   IDB_AUTOON:
          UpdateView(hWnd);
          return;
    }
}

// ...MsgVScroll...is the function called to process a WM_VSCROLL message. This message is
// received whenever any vertical scroll which is a child of hWnd is activated...

void     WINAPI  MSGVScroll(
         HWND     hWnd,            // handle to window instance
         UINT     uCode,           // scroll code
         int      nPos,            // scroll position
         HWND     hwndCtrl)        // handle to control window instance
{
BOOL     bAbsolute;               // absolute value flag
int      scroll;                  // scroll amount

// What we do, depends on the scroll code, in all cases we're going to modify the scroll bar
// so it stays in the range 0-MAXELEVATION. Ignore the ENDSCROLL code, or rather don't ignore
// it, but don't do UpdateElevation() when it occurs. Assume change is relative...

        bAbsolute = FALSE;

        switch (uCode)
        {
          case   SB_TOP:
            scroll = 0;
            bAbsolute = TRUE;
            break;
          case   SB_LINEDOWN:
            scroll = -1;
            break;
          case   SB_LINEUP:
            scroll = 1;
            break;
          case   SB_BOTTOM:
            scroll = MAXELEVATION;
            bAbsolute = TRUE;
            break;
          case   SB_PAGEUP:
            scroll = MAXELEVATION/3;
            break;
          case   SB_PAGEDOWN:
```

```
            scroll = -MAXELEVATION/3;
            break;
        case   SB_THUMBPOSITION:
            scroll = nPos;
            bAbsolute = TRUE;
            break;
        default:
            return;
    }

// Update elevation with new scroll position...

        UpdateElevation(hWnd, scroll, bAbsolute);
        return;
}
```

spdproc.c

spdproc.c is the window handler (similar to WndProc) which handles the messages for the ball speed window. Even though the entire window is a single bitmap, it still gets a message processor.

```
// -------------------------------------------------------------------------------
        //
// "Plunging Into Virtual Reality", SPDPROC.C
        //
// Copyright 1994, 1995 Russell J. Berube Jr. ALL RIGHTS RESERVED.              //
// This software is published, but is NOT public domain. It remains the exclusive  //
// property of Russell J. Berube Jr. and Brookside Systems, Inc. This software may not
        //
// be reproduced or integrated with other software without the prior written permission
        //
// of Russell J. Berube Jr. and Brookside Systems, Inc. It is provided herein for   //
// instructional purposes only.
        //
// -------------------------------------------------------------------------------
        //

#include "includes.h"          // include the world...
#include "vr.h"                 // include VR definitions...

// External data...

extern   VR       gVR;          // VR structure

// Local data...

static   BOOL     bLeft;          // left mouse button flag
static   int      nHeight; // window height
static   int      nWidth;         // window width
```

```
// ...SpdProc...is the exported callback function used to process the messages sent to us by
// Windows...
//
// On entry we're passed:
//
// hWnd          A handle to our window instance.
//
// wMsg          A WORD containing the Windows message code we're being passed.
//
// wParam        A WORD containing a parameter specific to this message.
//
// lParam        A LONG containing a parameter specific to this message.
//
// SpdProc's reason for living is to display and allow the user to change the pinball speed
// and direction. A bonus! We do this by dragging the mouse across the face of the gauge. The
// further to the left, the faster we're going backwards while the further to the right, the
// faster we're going forwards. In the middle is dead stop. Just for fun, (why else are we
// doing this?) let's change the color of the bar from green to yellow to red as we approach
// 100% speed. Now what's 100%? That's as far as the bar can be dragged to either side. The
// speed value we pass to the VR engine is a value from -MAXSPEED to +MAXSPEED...

LRESULT CALLBACK SpdProc(
          HWND      hWnd,          // handle to window instance
          WORD      wMsg,          // windows message code
          WPARAM    wParam,        // word parameter
          LPARAM    lParam)        // long parameter
{
COLORREF rgb;              // brush color
HBRUSH   hBrush;                   // habdle to gauge bar brush
HDC      hDC;                      // handle to display device context
int      begin;                   // begining offset
int      width;                   // gauge bar width
PAINTSTRUCT       ps;             // PAINTSTRUCT used by WM_PAINT
POINT    p;                        // mouse point
RECT     rect;                     // gauge rectangle

// This function must process the messages passed to it by Windows. The simplest way to
// handle them is with a switch (case) statement. However, there are more than 200 messages
// which can be sent by Windows that makes for a huge, unwieldy source file it we put all
// that code inline. Instead we'll try to make the source as readable as possible. One thing
// I've learned, which never fails to amaze me: I can live with a program and the source code
// for months, know it intimately, see the stuff in my sleep no less, then leave it for a few
// months/ and when I come back, I'm convinced I never wrote it in the first place.
Especially,
// especially, if it's not commented up to its eyeballs. Virtually every line. You wont
believe
// how easy it is to completely forget this stuff as soon as you leave it.

// It can't possibly be wrong (one of my favorite sayings) to heavily comment your code. DO
IT!!

// Note that the messages are case'd in alphabetical order. Simply one of my quirks, I'm fussy
// that way, consistency is important. When I come back and look at this stuff again, it helps
// get me realigned. All my code is the same way. Always structured the same, same sort of
// comments, parameter notation, module layout, etc. I suppose it's like traveling and finding
// a McDonalds off in outer space, it's reassuring. Also, it proves to me I wrote this and not
// my doppelganger...

          switch (wMsg)
          {
```

```
// ...WM_CREATE...this message is received when Windows is about to create the application
// window. It is generated as a direct result of the Create() function. Use this time to do
// any global initialization required. Return 0, if OK, else return 1...

          case    WM_CREATE:
            bLeft = FALSE;
            return(0);

// ...WM_LBUTTONDOWN...this message is received when Windows detects the left mouse button
// has been pressed WHEN OVER OUR CLIENT AREA. If we're not in auto mode, remember the
// mouse button (bLeft) and capture the mouse. Mouse capture ensures all mouse messages,
// normally only sent to the window over which the mouse is positioned, are sent to us.
// Depending on where the user has clicked the mouse button over us, determines the new
// ball speed. Then redraw so the speed bar correctly reflects the new speed...

          case    WM_LBUTTONDOWN:
            if (gVR.uMode & MF_AUTO) break;
            bLeft = TRUE;
            SetCapture(hWnd);
            p = MAKEPOINT(lParam);
            begin = nWidth/2;
            gVR.nSpeed = (p.x-begin)*MAXSPEED/begin;
            InvalidateRect(hWnd, NULL, TRUE);
            UpdateWindow(hWnd);
            return(0);

// ...WM_LBUTTONUP...this message is received when Windows detects the left mouse button has
// been released. Reset the mouse flag and release the mouse capture so other applications
// can process it...

          case    WM_LBUTTONUP:
            bLeft = FALSE;
            ReleaseCapture();
            return(0);

// ...WM_MOUSEMOVE...this message is received when Windows detects the mouse moving over our
// window (or, if captured, moving anywhere). We need to know if this is movement with or
// without the mouse button being down (dragging), hence the bLeft flag. If so, calculate the
// new speed and cause the window to be redrawn. If we do it correctly, it'll appear as if
// the speed bar is magically following the mouse pointer as it's dragged...

          case    WM_MOUSEMOVE:
            if (!bLeft) break;
            p = MAKEPOINT(lParam);
            SetRect(&rect, 0, 0, nWidth, nHeight);
            if (!PtInRect(&rect, p)) break;
            begin = nWidth/2;
            gVR.nSpeed = (p.x-begin)*MAXSPEED/begin;
            InvalidateRect(hWnd, NULL, TRUE);
            UpdateWindow(hWnd);
            return(0);

// ...WM_PAINT...this message is received when Windows is telling us the window needs to be
// painted. Either because it was covered or it's been changed (invalidated). Compute a
// rectangle from the current speed and display it. We added a tiny fancy touch by changing
// the color of the rectangle as we hit 80% or 90% of max speed...

          case    WM_PAINT:
            hDC = BeginPaint(hWnd, &ps);
```

```
            begin = nWidth/2;
            width = begin*gVR.nSpeed/MAXSPEED;
            if (width < 0) begin += width;
            SetRect(&rect, begin, 0, begin+abs(width), nHeight);
            rgb = COLOR_GREEN;
            if ((abs(gVR.nSpeed) >= MAXSPEED/10*8) && (abs(gVR.nSpeed) < MAXSPEED/10*9)) rgb
= COLOR_YELLOW;
            if (abs(gVR.nSpeed) >= MAXSPEED/10*9) rgb = COLOR_RED;
            hBrush = CreateSolidBrush(rgb);
            FillRect(hDC, &rect, hBrush);
            DeleteObject(hBrush);
            if (gVR.nSpeed != 0)
            {
              MoveTo(hDC, rect.left, rect.top);
              LineTo(hDC, rect.right-1, rect.top);
              LineTo(hDC, rect.right-1, rect.bottom-1);
              LineTo(hDC, rect.left, rect.bottom-1);
              LineTo(hDC, rect.left, rect.top);
            }
            EndPaint(hWnd, &ps);
            return(0);

// ...WM_SIZE...this message is received when Windows is changing the size of the window. This
// includes creating, resizing and moving. Note that, once again, although we know the actual
// size of the window (from the CreateView() function), don't use it. If we use those values
// here, if the size is changed, this code will have to be modified. This way, again, the code
// is more robust...

        case    WM_SIZE:
            nWidth = LOWORD(lParam);
            nHeight = HIWORD(lParam);
            return(0);
    }

// Any message we don't process, pass through to the Windows default message handler. Return
// whatever result it returns...

        return (DefWindowProc(hWnd, wMsg, wParam, lParam));
}
```


startup.c

startup.c contains all the software which is used once, then no longer required. Why bother separating it? Because Windows can discard segments (and we've been careful to separate all our code into separate segments: each source module is compiled and linked as a separate module) when they're not in use. This enables memory to be recovered. Your applications should always behave!

```
// -----------------------------------------------------------------------------
    //
```

```
// "Plunging Into Virtual Reality", STARTUP.C
        //
// Copyright 1994, 1995 Russell J. Berube Jr. ALL RIGHTS RESERVED.              //
// This software is published, but is NOT public domain. It remains the exclusive  //
// property of Russell J. Berube Jr. and Brookside Systems, Inc. This software may not
        //
// be reproduced or integrated with other software without the prior written permission
        //
// of Russell J. Berube Jr. and Brookside Systems, Inc. It is provided herein for  //
// instructional purposes only.
        //
// --------------------------------------------------------------------------------
        //

#include "includes.h"           // include the world...
#include "bitmap.h"             // include bitmap functions prototypes...
#include "funcs.h"              // include miscellaneous functions prototypes...
#include "resource.h"           // include resource definitions...
#include "vr.h"                 // include virtual reality definitions...

// Function prototypes...

LRESULT CALLBACK BarProc(// Slide bar window processor
        HWND    hWnd,           // handle to window instance
        UINT    nMessage,       // message
        WPARAM  wParam,         // word parameter
        LPARAM  lParam); // long parameter

LRESULT CALLBACK DirProc(// Direction window processor
        HWND    hWnd,           // handle to window instance
        UINT    nMessage,       // message
        WPARAM  wParam,         // word parameter
        LPARAM  lParam); // long parameter

LRESULT CALLBACK SpdProc(// Speed window processor
        HWND    hWnd,           // handle to window instance
        UINT    nMessage,       // message
        WPARAM  wParam,         // word parameter
        LPARAM  lParam); // long parameter

LRESULT CALLBACK ViewProc(      // View window processor
        HWND    hWnd,           // handle to window instance
        UINT    nMessage,       // message
        WPARAM  wParam,         // word parameter
        LPARAM  lParam); // long parameter

LRESULT CALLBACK WndProc(// Main window processor
        HWND    hWnd,           // handle to window instance
        UINT    nMessage,       // message
        WPARAM  wParam,         // word parameter
        LPARAM  lParam); // long parameter

// External data..

extern  BOOL    gbLeft;         // left mouse button down flag
extern  HINSTANCE       ghInstance;     // handle to application instance
extern  int     gnHeight;       // client area height
extern  int     gnUpdate;       // autopilot update
extern  int     gnWidth; // client area width
```

```
// Global data...

BM      gDir;                       // direction BM structure
BM      gSpd;                       // speed BM structure
BM      gDirBar;            // direction slide bar BM structure
BM      gDirSlide;              // direction slide BM structure
BM      gSpdBar;        // speed slide bar BM structure
BM      gSpdSlide;              // speed slide BM structure
BUTTON  gAuto;                      // Autopilot BUTTON structure
BUTTON  gVLA;                       // view left arrow BUTTON structure
BUTTON  gVRA;                       // view right arrow BUTTON structure
enum    CONTROLMODE     geMode; // control mode
#ifdef  _LESSON1
DIB     gDIB1;                      // DIB for "up pushbutton" image
DIB     gDIB2;                      // DIB for "down pushbutton" image
DIB     gDIB3;                      // DIB for "plunging into virtual reality" image
#else
#ifdef  _LESSON2
HBITMAP ghDDB1;                     // handle to DDBitmap for "up pushbutton" image
HBITMAP ghDDB2;                     // handle to DDBitmap for "down pushbutton" image
HBITMAP ghDDB3;                     // handle to DDBitmap for "plunging into virtual reality"
image
#else
DDB     gDDB1;                      // DDB structure for "up pushbutton" image
DDB     gDDB2;                      // DDB structure for "down pushbutton" image
DDB     gDDB3;                      // DDB structure for "plunging into virtual reality" image
#endif
#endif
HDC     ghdcMem;            // handle to compatible device context
HFONT   ghfView;            // handle to view angle font
HWND    ghwndDir;                   // handle to ball speed window
HWND    ghwndSpd;                   // handle to ball direction window
HWND    ghwndView;                  // handle to view window
int     gnAzX;                      // view azimuth x offset
int     gnAzY;                      // view azimuth y offset
int     gnMonoHeight;               // monologue text height
int     gnPaintMode;                // paint mode
int     gnScrollInc;                // scroll increment
int     gnX;                        // x screen offset
int     gnY;                        // y screen offset
int     gnViewW;            // view window width
int     gnViewX;            // view window x screen offset
int     gnViewY;            // view window y screen offset
RECT    grFrameRate;                // frame rate text rectangle
RECT    grMono;                     // monologue rectangle
VR      gVR;                        // VRE structure

// Local data...

static  LOGFONT lf =                // title logical font
        {
        0,                          // height
        0,                          // width
        0,                          // escapement
        0,                          // orientation
        FW_BOLD,        // weight
        0,                          // italic
        0,                      // underline
        0,                          // strikethrough
        ANSI_CHARSET,               // character set
```

```
            OUT_TT_PRECIS,              // match precision
            CLIP_DEFAULT_PRECIS,        // clip precision
            PROOF_QUALITY,              // font quality
            VARIABLE_PITCH | FF_ROMAN,// pitch and family
            "Arial"};

static   LOGFONT lfv =                  // view angle display logical font
            {
            0,                          // height
            0,                          // width
            0,                          // escapement
            0,                          // orientation
            FW_BOLD,           // weight
            0,                          // italic
            0,                     // underline
            0,                          // strikethrough
            ANSI_CHARSET,               // character set
            OUT_TT_PRECIS,              // match precision
            CLIP_DEFAULT_PRECIS,        // clip precision
            PROOF_QUALITY,              // font quality
            VARIADLE_PITCII | FF_ROMAN,// pitch and family
            "Arial"};
static   LPSTR   lpszMono;        // pointer to opening monologue text
```

```
// ...STARTUP...is the module which contains the one-time initialization code used by the
// application. There is nothing special about the module other than the fact that all the
// functions here are disposable once the application is started...

// ...CreateMainWindow...is the one-time startup function used to create the main window and
// get resultant handle. Use the classname we registered with the RegisterWindowClasses()
// function. Supply a window title, even though we're creating a popup window without a title,
// the Windows <ALT><TAB> system which cycles through the available applications, uses the
// application icon and window title to indicate an available application. Without a title
// here, there's no title there. WS_CLIPCHILDREN causes any child windows we create to be left
// out when the window is redrawn and WS_VISIBLE is required to make the window visible.

// We create our window as a POPUP instead of an OVERLAPPED because we don't want a title or
// menu and since we want the entire screen, get the system "metrics" for the entire screen
// and use those for our size values. Position us at 0,0...

// Out: HWND    window creation succeeded
//      0       window creation failed

HWND    WINAPI   CreateMainWindow()
{
HWND    hWnd;                     // handle to resultant window

// The window is about to be created. This will send a WM_CREATE message to the WndProc for
// this window. The window title will be "Virtual Pinball" (which won't be visible) and the
// window will be positioned at 0, 0 and cover the entire screen...

        hWnd = CreateWindow(tAppName,
                        "Virtual Pinball",
                        WS_POPUP | WS_CLIPCHILDREN | WS_VISIBLE,
                        0,
                        0,
                        GetSystemMetrics(SM_CXSCREEN),
                        GetSystemMetrics(SM_CYSCREEN),
                        NULL,
                        NULL,
```

```
                                      ghInstance,
                                      NULL);
                return(hWnd);
        }


// ...MakeViewWindow...is the function called to create the view child window. Compute its
// position and do it. Note we've already registered the class for this new child. Return
// TRUE if OK, else return FALSE...

BOOL    WINAPI  MakeViewWindow(
        HWND    hWnd)             // handle to parent window
{
        ghwndView = CreateWindow(tViewName,
                                  NULL,
                                  WS_CHILD | WS_VSCROLL | WS_VISIBLE,
                                  gnViewX,
                                  gnViewY,
                                  gnViewW,
                                  VWHEIGHT,
                                  hWnd,
                                  NULL,
                                  ghInstance,
                                  NULL);
                return(ghwndView != NULL);
        }


// ...MakeLeftArrow...is the function called to create the window for the viewer azimuth
// left arrow child window. Compute its position and do it. Note we've already registered
// the class for this new child. Return TRUE if OK, else return FALSE...

BOOL    WINAPI  MakeLeftArrow(
        HWND    hWnd)             // handle to parent window
{
BITMAP  bm;                       // BITMAP structure
int     cx;                       // control x position
int     cy;                       // control y position

// Load left arrow bitmaps, exit on error...

        if ((gVLA.hbmUp = LoadBitmap(ghInstance, MAKEINTRESOURCE(IDB_LAU))) == NULL)
          return(FALSE);
        if ((gVLA.hbmDown = LoadBitmap(ghInstance, MAKEINTRESOURCE(IDB_LAD))) == NULL)
          return(FALSE);

// Get arrows bitmap size, either one will do, they're identical...

        GetObject(gVLA.hbmUp, sizeof(bm), &bm);

// Figure out where to put it: align left edge with left edge of view window. Leave a 16
// pixel gap from the bottom of the view window to the top of our buttons...

        cx = gnViewX;
        cy = gnViewY+VWHEIGHT+16;

// Now create child window...

        gVLA.hWnd = CreateWindow("button",
                                  NULL,
                                  WS_CHILD | WS_VISIBLE | BS_OWNERDRAW,
                                  cx,
```

```
                                        cy,
                                        bm.bmWidth,
                                        bm.bmHeight,
                                        hWnd,
                                        IDB_LAU,
                                        ghInstance,
                                        NULL);
            return(gVLA.hWnd != NULL);
}

// ...MakeRightArrow...is the function called to create the window for the viewer azimuth
// right arrow child window. Compute its position and do it. Note we've already registered
// the class for this new child. Return TRUE if OK, else return FALSE...

BOOL    WINAPI  MakeRightArrow(
        HWND    hWnd)                   // handle to parent window
{
BITMAP  bm;                             // BITMAP structure
int     cx;                             // control x position
int     cy;                             // control y position

// Load right arrow bitmaps, exit on error...

        if ((gVRA.hbmUp = LoadBitmap(ghInstance, MAKEINTRESOURCE(IDB_RAU))) == NULL)
          return(FALSE);
        if ((gVRA.hbmDown = LoadBitmap(ghInstance, MAKEINTRESOURCE(IDB_RAD))) == NULL)
          return(FALSE);

// Get arrows bitmap size, either one will do, they're identical...

        GetObject(gVRA.hbmUp, sizeof(bm), &bm);

// Figure out where to put it: align right edge with right edge of view window. Leave a 16
// pixel gap from the bottom of the view window to the top of our buttons...

        cx = gnViewX+VWWIDTH-bm.bmWidth;
        cy = gnViewY+VWHEIGHT+16;

// Now create button...

        gVRA.hWnd = CreateWindow("button",
                                NULL,
                                WS_CHILD | WS_VISIBLE | BS_OWNERDRAW,
                                cx,
                                cy,
                                bm.bmWidth,
                                bm.bmHeight,
                                hWnd,
                                IDB_RAU,
                                ghInstance,
                                NULL);
            return(gVRA.hWnd != NULL);
}

// ...MakeAutoButton...is the function called to create the window for the autopilot child
// window. Compute its position and do it. Note we've already registered the class for this
// new child. Return TRUE if OK, else return FALSE...

BOOL    WINAPI  MakeAutoButton(
        HWND    hWnd)                   // handle to parent window
```

```
{
BITMAP     bm;                       // BITMAP structure
HDC        hDC;                      // handle to device context
HFONT      hFont;                    // handle to old font
int        cx;                       // control x position
int        cy;                       // control y position
TEXTMETRIC         tm;               // TEXTMETRIC structure

// Load auto button bitmaps, exit on error...

        if ((gAuto.hbmUp = LoadBitmap(ghInstance, MAKEINTRESOURCE(IDB_AUTOOFF))) == NULL)
          return(FALSE);
        if ((gAuto.hbmDown = LoadBitmap(ghInstance, MAKEINTRESOURCE(IDB_AUTOON))) == NULL)
          return(FALSE);

// Use the following code to properly size a font on your screen. Fonts are sized in points
// which are 1/72's of an inch (.013888..."). So we need to know the number of logical
// pixels per vertical inch and get the ratio of the font size/72 times pixels per inch.
// That gives us the physical size we want (note the minus sign), that informs Windows the
// height specification is a physical number of pixels...

        hDC = GetDC(hWnd);
        lfv.lfHeight = MulDiv(-14, GetDeviceCaps(hDC, LOGPIXELSY), 72);
        ghfView = CreateFontIndirect(&lfv);
        hFont = SelectObject(hDC, ghfView);
        GetTextMetrics(hDC, &tm);
        gnAzX = (gnWidth-3*tm.tmAveCharWidth)/2;
        gnAzY = gnViewY+VWHEIGHT+16;
        SelectObject(hDC, hFont);
        ReleaseDC(hWnd, hDC);

// Get AUTO bitmap size...

        GetObject(gAuto.hbmUp, sizeof(bm), &bm);

// Create child control (button window) for AUTOBITMAP. Figure out where to put it: let's
// center it horizontally  and leave a 64 pixel gap from the bottom of the view window to the
// top...

        cx = gnViewX+(VWWIDTH-bm.bmWidth)/2;
        cy = gnViewY+VWHEIGHT+64;

// Now create button...

        gAuto.hWnd = CreateWindow("button",
                            NULL,
                            WS_CHILD | WS_VISIBLE | BS_OWNERDRAW,
                            cx,
                            cy,
                            bm.bmWidth,
                            bm.bmHeight,
                            hWnd,
                            IDB_AUTOON,
                            ghInstance,
                            NULL);
        return(gAuto.hWnd != NULL);
}

// ...MakeModeButton...is the function called to create the window for the mode button child
// window. Compute its position and do it. Since this is a standard button, there's no special
```

```
// class to register. Return TRUE if OK, else return FALSE...

BOOL      WINAPI   MakeModeButton(
          HWND     hWnd)                    // handle to parent window
{
HWND      hwnd;                             // handle to result window
int       cx;                              // control x position
int       cy;                              // control y position
RECT      rect;                            // autopilot window rectangle

// Figure out where to put it...

          GetWindowRect(gAuto.hWnd, &rect);
          cx = rect.left-64-16;
          cy = rect.top+(rect.bottom-rect.top)/2-16;

// Now create button...

          hwnd = CreateWindow("button",
                              "> &Ball",
                              WS_CHILD | WS_VISIBLE | BS_PUSHBUTTON,
                              cx,
                              cy,
                              64,
                              32,
                              hWnd,
                              IDC_MODE,
                              ghInstance,
                              NULL);
          return(hwnd != NULL);
}

// ...MakeUpdateButton...is the function called to create the window for the update button
// child window. Compute its position and do it. Since this is a standard button, there's no
// special class to register. Return TRUE if OK, else return FALSE...

BOOL      WINAPI   MakeUpdateButton(
          HWND     hWnd)                    // handle to parent window
{
HWND      hwnd;                             // handle to result window
int       cx;                              // control x position
int       cy;                              // control y position
RECT      rect;                            // autopilot window rectangle

// Figure out where to put it...

          GetWindowRect(gAuto.hWnd, &rect);
          cx = rect.right+16;
          cy = rect.top+(rect.bottom-rect.top)/2-16;

// Now create button...

          hwnd = CreateWindow("button",
                              "&Update",
                              WS_CHILD | WS_VISIBLE | BS_PUSHBUTTON,
                              cx,
                              cy,
                              64,
                              32,
                              hWnd,
```

```
                                        IDC_UPDATE,
                                        ghInstance,
                                        NULL);
                return(hwnd != NULL);
}
```

```
// ...MakeBallDirection...is the function called to create the window for the ball direction
// child window. Compute its position and do it. This is definitely a special window, it has
// its own Proc() function (as do all registered windows). Return TRUE if OK, else return
// FALSE...
```

```
BOOL    WINAPI  MakeBallDirection(
        HWND    hWnd)                   // handle to parent window
{
static  BAR     bar;                    // BAR structure
BITMAP  bm1;                            // BITMAP structure
BITMAP  bm2;                            // BITMAP structure
BITMAP  bm3;                            // BITMAP structure
HWND    hwnd;                           // temp window handle
int     cx;                             // control x position
int     cy;                             // control y position
```

```
// Now load gauge and slide bitmaps, we use these for the ball direction. Exit if we fail...
```

```
        if ((gDir.hBM = LoadBitmap(ghInstance, MAKEINTRESOURCE(IDB_GAUGE1))) == NULL)
          return(FALSE);
        if ((gDirSlide.hBM = LoadBitmap(ghInstance, MAKEINTRESOURCE(IDB_SLIDE))) == NULL)
          return(FALSE);
        if ((gDirBar.hBM = LoadBitmap(ghInstance, MAKEINTRESOURCE(IDB_KNOB))) == NULL)
          return(FALSE);
```

```
// Get bitmap sizes, we'll use that to size the ball direction window...
```

```
        GetObject(gDir.hBM, sizeof(bm1), &bm1);
        GetObject(gDirSlide.hBM, sizeof(bm2), &bm2);
        GetObject(gDirBar.hBM, sizeof(bm3), &bm3);
```

```
// Now create ball direction window. I think I'll put it on top of the view window, aligned on
// the left side, with an 12 pixel border, then the slider control, then the actual gauge 4
// pixels above that. This is just a little tricky: the gauge and slider bitmaps are actually
// part of the parent window so the direction window only needs to worry about the
// direction display. So create the direction window "inside" the bitmap. If you look
// carefully, you'll see there's a 3 pixel border around the white area, except where the red
// arrows are, there, the border is 7 pixels, so imagine a rectangle the size of the bitmap
// reduced -3, -7, -3, -7. The slider control is the same sort of thing, the slider bar is a
// separate window by itself. The fiddling we're doing with the slider bar is to align it with
// the left edge and index lines along the slider bitmap...
```

```
        cx = gnViewX;
        cy = gnViewY-bm1.bmHeight-bm2.bmHeight-4-12;
        SetRect(&gDir.rect, cx, cy, cx+bm1.bmWidth, cy+bm1.bmHeight);
        SetRect(&gDirSlide.rect, cx, cy+bm1.bmHeight+4, cx+bm1.bmWidth,
cy+bm1.bmHeight+4+bm2.bmHeight);
        CopyRect(&gDirBar.rect, &gDirSlide.rect);
        gDirBar.rect.left += 1;
        gDirBar.rect.bottom += 4;
        gDirBar.rect.top = gDirBar.rect.bottom-bm3.bmHeight;
        gDirBar.rect.right -= 1;
```

```
// Now create direction window...
```

```
                ghwndDir = CreateWindow(tDirName,
                                        NULL,
                                        WS_CHILD | WS_VISIBLE,
                                        cx+3,
                                        cy+7,
                                        bm1.bmWidth-6,
                                        bm1.bmHeight-14,
                                        hWnd,
                                        IDC_DIRECTION,
                                        ghInstance,
                                        NULL);
            if (ghwndDir == NULL) return(FALSE);

// Now create direction slider bar window. Build BAR structure which contains pointer to bar
// bitmap, direction increment/position change and the direction increment address...

                bar.lpBM = &gDirBar;
                bar.nInc = DIRINCMAX/((gDirBar.rect.right-gDirBar.rect.left)/bm3.bmWidth);
                bar.lpInc = &gVR.nDirInc;
                hwnd = CreateWindow(tBarName,
                                        NULL,
                                        WS_CHILD | WS_VISIBLE,
                                        gDirBar.rect.left,
                                        gDirBar.rect.top,
                                        bm3.bmWidth,
                                        bm3.bmHeight,
                                        hWnd,
                                        0,
                                        ghInstance,
                                        &bar);
            return(hwnd != NULL);
}

// ...MakeBallSpeed...is the function called to create the window for the ball speed child
// window. Compute its position and do it. This is definitely a special window, it has its
// own Proc() function (as do all registered windows). Return TRUE if OK, else return FALSE...

BOOL    WINAPI  MakeBallSpeed(
        HWND    hWnd)               // handle to parent window
{
static  BAR     bar;               // BAR structure
BITMAP  bm1;                        // BITMAP structure
BITMAP  bm2;                        // BITMAP structure
BITMAP  bm3;                        // BITMAP structure
HWND    hwnd;                       // temp window handle
int     cx;                         // control x position
int     cy;                         // control y position

// Now load gauge and slide bitmaps, we use these for the ball speed. Exit if we fail...

            if ((gSpd.hBM = LoadBitmap(ghInstance, MAKEINTRESOURCE(IDB_GAUGE1))) == NULL)
                return(FALSE);
            if ((gSpdSlide.hBM = LoadBitmap(ghInstance, MAKEINTRESOURCE(IDB_SLIDE))) == NULL)
                return(FALSE);
            if ((gSpdBar.hBM = LoadBitmap(ghInstance, MAKEINTRESOURCE(IDB_KNOB))) == NULL)
                return(FALSE);

// Get bitmap sizes, we'll use that to size the ball direction window...
```

```
        GetObject(gSpd.hBM, sizeof(bm1), &bm1);
        GetObject(gSpdSlide.hBM, sizeof(bm2), &bm2);
        GetObject(gSpdBar.hBM, sizeof(bm3), &bm3);
```

```
// Now create ball speed window. That'll go on top of the view window also, aligned on the
// right side, with the standard 16 pixel border. This is the same as the direction window...
```

```
        cx = gnViewX+VWWIDTH-bm1.bmWidth;
        cy = gnViewY-bm1.bmHeight-bm2.bmHeight-4-12;
        SetRect(&gSpd.rect, cx, cy, cx+bm1.bmWidth, cy+bm1.bmHeight);
        SetRect(&gSpdSlide.rect, cx, cy+bm1.bmHeight+4, cx+bm1.bmWidth,
cy+bm1.bmHeight+4+bm2.bmHeight);
        CopyRect(&gSpdBar.rect, &gSpdSlide.rect);
        gSpdBar.rect.left += 1;
        gSpdBar.rect.bottom += 4;
        gSpdBar.rect.top = gSpdBar.rect.bottom-bm3.bmHeight;
        gSpdBar.rect.right -= 1;
```

```
// Now create speed window...
```

```
        ghwndSpd = CreateWindow(tSpdName,
                                NULL,
                                WS_CHILD | WS_VISIBLE,
                                cx+5,
                                cy+7,
                                bm1.bmWidth-8,
                                bm1.bmHeight-14,
                                hWnd,
                                IDC_SPEED,
                                ghInstance,
                                NULL);
        if (ghwndSpd == NULL) return(FALSE);
```

```
// Now create speed slider bar window. Build BAR structure which contains pointer to bar
// bitmap, direction increment/position change and the direction increment address...
```

```
        bar.lpBM = &gSpdBar;
        bar.nInc = SPDINCMAX/((gSpdBar.rect.right-gSpdBar.rect.left)/bm3.bmWidth);
        bar.lpInc = &gVR.nSpdInc;
        hwnd = CreateWindow(tBarName,
                            NULL,
                            WS_CHILD | WS_VISIBLE,
                            gSpdBar.rect.left,
                            gSpdBar.rect.top,
                            bm3.bmWidth,
                            bm3.bmHeight,
                            hWnd,
                            0,
                            ghInstance,
                            &bar);
        return(hwnd != NULL);
}
```

```
// ...CreateView...is the function called to create the view child window. Compute its
// position and do it. Note we've already registered the class for this new child. Return
// TRUE if OK, else return FALSE...
```

```
BOOL    WINAPI  CreateView(
        HWND    hWnd)           // handle to parent window
{
```

```
// Compute start point of view window. Put the horizontal centerline down 20% and the vertical
// centerline over 50%. Don't linger if we failed. Notice that we make the X starting offset

        gnViewW = VWWIDTH+GetSystemMetrics(SM_CXVSCROLL);
        gnViewX = (gnWidth-gnViewW)/2;
        gnViewY = gnHeight/10*2;

// Make the VR view window...

        if (!MakeViewWindow(hWnd)) return(FALSE);

// This is a perfect example of what I was talking about re DEBUGGING. When I first ran the
// program. The height scroll bar wasn't being set properly. At the time I had better things
// to do, so I wrote it down and promptly forgot about it. When I ran the debugging kernel,
// it complained immediately. 10 seconds investigation and I found the problem, I was trying
// to initialize the scroll bar position in the WM_CREATE function of ViewProc(), but
// UpdateHeight() uses ghwndView, since that's who the scroll bar belongs to. Well, in the
// WM_CREATE function, ghwndView is still invalid (we haven't gotton back from CreateWindow()
// so how could it be?). The answer of course, is to initialize the height here with
// UpdateHeight(), where we know the window handle is valid. It can't possibly be wrong to run
// your application through the debugging kernel again and again and again...

// After all that, turns out that's wrong as well. Once again, I ame exposed as a clam in the
// oysterbed of knowledge. UpdateHeight() calls vrUpdate() which we can't do yet. So, just
// set the #*(^! scroll bar where it's supposed to be now...

        SetScrollPos(ghwndView, SB_VERT, MAXELEVATION, TRUE);

// Now, create view position controls: turn left, turn right and DOM (direction of motion)
// lock. Note that the view move up and view move down are controlled by the vertical
// scroll bar we created. I want to place the two turn controls (left arrow and a right
// arrow) as well as the current view azimuth display underneath the view window at the far
// left, far right and center. Some of these buttons are going to be owner-draw, (so we have
// something else to talk about), create a BUTTON structure for each.

// Create viewer azimuth left arrow button...

        if (!MakeLeftArrow(hWnd)) return(FALSE);

// Create viewer azimuth right arrow button...

        if (!MakeRightArrow(hWnd)) return(FALSE);

// Do VIEW ANGLE DISPLAY next. Figure out where to put it: center it underneath the view
// window. Leave a 16 pixel gap from the bottom of the view window to the top. Use the same
// cy as the arrows, BUT! COMPUTE IT don't assume it's still there. I just spent 15 minutes
// trying to figure out why I no longer saw the viewer azimuth after adding the AUTOPILOT
// code. What I'd done was insert the AUTOPILOT code in front of this code, that destroyed
// the value in cy and therefore the line (commented out) gnAzY = cy; was wrong. What I should
// have done was what I'm doing now: gnAzY = gnViewY+VWHEIGHT+16; recompute it each time it's
// needed. Always treat each logical section of code as if it is a standalone entity: another
// reason for converting this into a series of separate calls rather than stringing it out the
// way it is. The cy problem wouldn't have happened then. So now, that's what I've done...

        if (!MakeAutoButton(hWnd)) return(FALSE);

// Now create mode control button: viewer or ball. This button controls which set of
// controls the keyboard affects. I think I'll put it to the right of the view window.
// Again, leave a 16 pixel border...
```

```
// Well, that didn't work out so well. When I ran this code on a 640x480 display (its being
// developed on a 1024x780 17" screen), the mode and update buttons we're barely clipped off
// the right edge, so I think we'll put'm either side of the AUTO button...

        if (!MakeModeButton(hWnd)) return(FALSE);

// Now create update button. This button, when clicked causes us to move once in the VR world.
// I think I'll put it underneath the mode button. Note we left 16 pixels between buttons...
// Wrong again...

        if (!MakeUpdateButton(hWnd)) return(FALSE);

// Make the ball direction window. (Don't confuse this with the viewer direction!).

        if (!MakeBallDirection(hWnd)) return(FALSE);

// Finally, make the ball speed window...

        return(MakeBallSpeed(hWnd));
}

// ...LoadMonologue...is the function used to load the monologue text from the .EXE resource
// stringtable. It's stored as a group of individual strings. Our job here is to load all of
// the strings and concatenate them into one loonnngggg string. Put the result into the static
// string lpszMono. Keep the last line separate...

HLOCAL    WINAPI    LoadMonologue(
          HWND      hWnd,               // handle to window instance
          LPSTR     lpsz)               // caller provided string area
{
HLOCAL    hMono;                        // handle to monologue text area
int       count;                        // number of characters
int       i;                            // local junk
int       j;                            // local junk

// So the first thing we do, since this function is so simple, is sit down and type away. What
// could be simpler ??
//
// Allocate an area for and get the opening monologue text. Complain if no memory. Request at
// least BIGNUMBER bytes, more than enough for the monologue text. Something that bound to be
// safe, Right? Wrong...
//
//        hMono = LocalAlloc(LPTR, BIGNUMBER);
//
//        if ((hMono == NULL) || ((lpszMono = (LPSTR)LocalLock(hMono)) == NULL))
//        {
//           if (hMono) LocalFree(hMono);
//           MBox(hWnd, IDS_ERRNOLM, IDS_ERROR, MB_OK|MB_ICONEXCLAMATION);
//           return;
//        }
//
//        LoadString(ghInstance, IDS_MONO1, lpsz, 255);
//        strcpy(lpszMono, lpsz);
//        LoadString(ghInstance, IDS_MONO2, lpsz, 255);
//        strcat(lpszMono, lpsz);
//        LoadString(ghInstance, IDS_MONO3, lpsz, 255);
//        strcat(lpszMono, lpsz);
//        return(hLocal);
//
// This works right away, couldn't be easier, couldn't be worse code either. STOP. THINK.
```

```
// Before you write anything, ask yourself not only does this code meet the design
// requirements established for it, but can it cope with continginces?? Suppose someone else
// is writing the monologue script and they decide to write a small novel? What happens if
// they exceed 3 lines (IDS_MONO1-IDS_MONO3)? Or worse yet, they exceed BIGNUMBER bytes,
// wouldn't that be special? Sure would be nice if we had an autoloading string function...
// Envision a function which loads strings and concatenates them as long as the last character
// in the string is a (pick something) "+"? Now we don't care how many strings they string
// (small pun) together. Well, we still have one problem, how much memory do we need? Simple
// enough to figure out, count it! The only restriction we place on the monologue text is that
// no one string be longer than 255 characters, which shouldn't be a problem...

// Scan through the strings, count up all the characters. Scan strings until we don't have the
// magic "+" anymore. There is of course, a price to be paid: this code is far more complex,
// (relative to the other) and therefore requires a greater investment in time to implement
// properly. Once done though, we sleep much better at night, knowing our little program is
// wandering, alone, somewhere in the big world. We did our best to protect it...

          count = 0;
          i = IDS_MONO1;

          do
          {
            count += LoadString(ghInstance, i++, lpsz, 255)-1;
          } while (lpsz[strlen(lpsz)-1] == '+');

// There is the possibility that count == 0 now, indicating there is no monologue text, check
// for this condition and leave gracefully...

          if (count == 0) return(NULL);

// Otherwise, allocate what we need (+1 for the count algorithm, +1 for a null byte), go back
// and build the actual text string...

          hMono = LocalAlloc(LPTR, count+2);

// Always, always, check to ensure thate memory allocations work!

          if ((hMono == NULL) || ((lpszMono = (LPSTR)LocalLock(hMono)) == NULL))
          {
            if (hMono) LocalFree(hMono);
            MBox(hWnd, IDS_ERRNOLM, IDS_ERROR, MB_OK|MB_ICONEXCLAMATION);
            return(NULL);
          }

// Remember, we want to load the last line, but not append it to the monologue text...

          i = IDS_MONO1;

          do
          {
            LoadString(ghInstance, i++, lpsz, 255);
            j = strlen(lpsz)-1;
            if (lpsz[j] == '+')
            {
              lpsz[j] = 0;
              if (i == IDS_MONO1)
                strcpy(lpszMono, lpsz);
              else
                strcat(lpszMono, lpsz);
            }
```

```
         else
           break;
      } while(TRUE);
```

```
// If we're here, we're done. hMono is the handle to the local area containing the monologue
// text and lpsz contains the last line...
```

```
      return(hMono);
}
```

```
// ...DoBigRedPushButton...is the function called to display the red pushbutton image(s) and
// wait for the user to click the mouse where we want it. Return TRUE if OK, else return
// FALSE...
```

```
BOOL    WINAPI  DoBigRedPushButton(
        HWND    hWnd)             // handle to window instance
{
#ifdef   _LESSON1
LPBITMAPINFO    lpBI;             // far pointer to image BITMAPINFO structure
#else
BITMAP  bm;                       // BITMAP structure
#endif
POINT   p;                        // mouse click point
RECT    rect;                     // window rectangle
```

```
// No paint mode for a moment or two...
```

```
      gnPaintMode = eUNKNOWN;
```

```
// Start the "are you stuck?" timer...
```

```
      SetTimer(hWnd, eBRP1, STUCKTIME, NULL);
```

```
// Load the two "start button" images at the same time, that way, when we switch from the
first
// image to the second, we won't encounter the image loading delay which would happen if we
// loaded the second image only when required. As always, there's a penalty: more memory is
// used for a while...
```

```
// We want the images to be centered on the screen. So the first step is to get the size of
the
// bitmaps. Now we know these images are 640x480, but never hard code values, it'll always
come
// back to bite you. The proper way, is to perform the required calculations. That requires
// loading an image then,
```

```
#ifdef   _LESSON1
// extracting the size info from the image header since what we've loaded is a Device-
// Independent Bitmap (DIB), which is what you get calling the Pinball LoadDIB() function.
// Complain and exit if there's a problem loading the DIB, otherwise continue. The size
// information we need is in the image header...
```

```
      if (!LoadDIB(hWnd, IDB_BITMAP1, &gDIB1))
      {
        MBox(hWnd, IDS_ERRDIB1, IDS_ERROR, MB_OK|MB_ICONEXCLAMATION);
        KillTimer(hWnd, eBRP1);
        return(FALSE);
      }
```

```
// Now lock the global handle to the actual image data and ask Windows to convert the handle
```

```
// to a pointer to a memory area. Programmer-lingo for this is "dereference". Used in a
// sentence we can say "Johnny dereferenced the global handle DIB1.hBI to the pointer lpBI."
// Impressed? Note that this can fail also! Many times I've seen code where only the actual
// request to Windows to actually allocate the global memory is checked for failure.

        if ((lpBI = (LPBITMAPINFO)LockResource(gDIB1.hBI)) == NULL)
        {
          MBox(hWnd, IDS_ERRLGM, IDS_ERROR, MB_OK|MB_ICONEXCLAMATION);
          DeleteDIB(&gDIB1);
          KillTimer(hWnd, eBRP1);
          return(FALSE);
        }
#else
// asking Windows for information regarding the object which in this case, is a Device-
// Dependent Bitmap (DDB), which is what you get calling the Windows LoadBitmap() function.
// Complain and exit if there's a problem loading the DDB, otherwise continue.
// We need the size of the DDB, this is returned by the Windows GetObject() function...

#ifdef  _LESSON2
        if ((ghDDB1 = LoadBitmap(ghInstance, MAKEINTRESOURCE(IDB_BITMAP1))) == NULL)
        {
          MBox(hWnd, IDS_ERRDDB1, IDS_ERROR, MB_OK|MB_ICONEXCLAMATION);
          KillTimer(hWnd, eBRP1);
          return(FALSE);
        }

        GetObject(ghDDB1, sizeof(bm), &bm);
#else
        if (!LoadDDB(hWnd, IDB_BITMAP1, &gDDB1))
        {
          MBox(hWnd, IDS_ERRDDB1, IDS_ERROR, MB_OK|MB_ICONEXCLAMATION);
          KillTimer(hWnd, eBRP1);
          return(FALSE);
        }

        GetObject(gDDB1.hBM, sizeof(bm), &bm);
#endif
#endif

// To center the image, subtract the size of the image from the size of the window and go
// halfway. Again, note that we don't directly use the size of the screen, even though we know
// that's what was used by the CreateMainWindow() function. It's better to get the actual
// Window size now and use that. That way, if the CreateMainWindow() function changes, they'll
// be no effect here. gnHeight and gnWidth we're set by the WM_SIZE message processed when we
// created the main window...

#ifdef  _LESSON1
// The size of the image is contained in the DIB BITMAPINFO structure, part of the image
// header. Note we cast the size values to (int), they're actually (DWORD). Unlock the image
// area as soon as we're done. We've got enough memory locked down as it is, don't need any
// more confusing things...

        gnX = (gnWidth-(int)lpBI->bmiHeader.biWidth)/2;
        gnY = (gnHeight-(int)lpBI->bmiHeader.biHeight)/2;
        UnlockResource(gDIB1.hBI);
#else
// The size information is contained in the BITMAP structure...

        gnX = (gnWidth-bm.bmWidth)/2;
        gnY = (gnHeight-bm.bmHeight)/2;
```

```
#endif

// Once we've successfully loaded the 1st image and computed the starting coordinates on our
// window, load the 2nd image so we have both resident at the same time, this reduces the time
// it takes to put up the 2nd image, making our "animation" look smoother...

        gnPaintMode = eBRP1;

#ifdef   _LESSON1
        if (!LoadDIB(hWnd, IDB_BITMAP2, &gDIB2))
        {
          MBox(hWnd, IDS_ERRDIB2, IDS_ERROR, MB_OK|MB_ICONEXCLAMATION);
          DeleteDIB(&gDIB1);
          KillTimer(hWnd, eBRP1);
          return(FALSE);
        }

// Now draw 1st image. Paint mode is set also...

        DrawDIB(hWnd, &gDIB1);
#else
#ifdef   _LESSON2
        if ((ghDDB2 = LoadBitmap(ghInstance, MAKEINTRESOURCE(IDB_BITMAP2))) == NULL)
        {
          MBox(hWnd, IDS_ERRDDB2, IDS_ERROR, MB_OK|MB_ICONEXCLAMATION);
          DeleteObject(ghDDB1);
          KillTimer(hWnd, eBRP1);
          return(FALSE);
        }

// Now draw 1st image. Paint mode is set also...

        DrawDDB(hWnd, ghDDB1, NULL);
#else
        if (!LoadDDB(hWnd, IDB_BITMAP2, &gDDB2))
        {
          MBox(hWnd, IDS_ERRDDB2, IDS_ERROR, MB_OK|MB_ICONEXCLAMATION);
          DeleteObject(gDDB1.hBM);
          DeleteObject(gDDB1.hPal);
          KillTimer(hWnd, eBRP1);
          return(FALSE);
        }

// Now draw 1st image. Paint mode is set also...

        DrawDDB(hWnd, gDDB1.hBM, gDDB1.hPal);
#endif
#endif

// Our scenario calls for the user to click the left mouse button on the red "button" part
// of the image that's being displayed now. So we want to wait here until:
//
// 1)    the left mouse button is clicked AND
// 2)    it's clicked where we want it to be clicked
//
// How do we know where, physically on the image we expecting a mouse hit? As far as I know,
// there's no other method than actually knowing the coordinates of the image rectangle
// beforehand. Once this is known, we can at least make it relative to the starting point
// of the image. The numbers you see: x+264, y+126, etc. I actually measured sometime in the
// dim past...
```

```
            SetRect(&rect, gnX+264, gnY+126, gnX+382, gnY+220);

            do
            {
              p = WaitForLeftButtonDown();
              if (PtInRect(&rect, p)) break;
            } while (TRUE);
```

```
// If we've gotten here, the user's clicked the left mouse button smack where we wanted'm to.
// His reward is another picture. Use the same x, y values. One thing I am sure of, both
// images are the same size, whatever it is. Though, with a little thought, you soon realize
// they need not be the same size at all. Only part of the 2nd image differs from the first,
// so why not display a smaller rectangle offset somewhere within the first? Sounds like a
// segue to another book...

            gnPaintMode = eBRP2;
#ifdef    _LESSON1
            DrawDIB(hWnd, &gDIB2);
#else
#ifdef    _LESSON2
            DrawDDB(hWnd, ghDDB2, NULL);
#else
            DrawDDB(hWnd, gDDB2.hBM, gDDB2.hPal);
#endif
#endif
```

```
// Finally, leave the second image (button pushed down) displayed until he let's go, then
// pop the button back up and time to go...

            WaitForLeftButtonUp();
            gnPaintMode = eBRP1;
#ifdef    _LESSON1
            DrawDIB(hWnd, &gDIB1);
```

```
// Make sure to release whatever we used. We specifically requested the memory for the DIBs
// so unlock and free it...

            DeleteDIB(&gDIB2);
            DeleteDIB(&gDIB1);
#else
```

```
// Make sure to release whatever we used. Since Windows loaded these objects for us,
// let Windows dispose of them...

#ifdef    _LESSON2
            DrawDDB(hWnd, ghDDB1, NULL);
            DeleteObject(ghDDB1);
            DeleteObject(ghDDB2);
#else
            DrawDDB(hWnd, gDDB1.hBM, gDDB1.hPal);
            DeleteObject(gDDB1.hBM);
            DeleteObject(gDDB1.hPal);
            DeleteObject(gDDB2.hBM);
            DeleteObject(gDDB2.hPal);
#endif
#endif
```

```
// Don't forget to kill the timer...
```

```
        KillTimer(hWnd, eBRP1);
        return(TRUE);
}


// ...DoMonologue...is the function used to scroll the startup monologue on the screen. We
// implement this function using the ScrollWindow() function and a timer...

void    WINAPI  DoMonologue(
        HWND    hWnd)                   // handle to main window instance
{
char    sz[256];        // local junk
HBITMAP hbmOld;                         // handle to original bitmap
HBITMAP hBitmap;        // handle to temp bitmap
HDC     hDC;                            // handle to our device context
HFONT   hFont1;                         // handle to monologue font
HFONT   hFont2;                         // handle to monologue font
HFONT   hOrigFont;                      // handle to original font
HLOCAL  hMono;                          // handle to monologue text
RECT    rect;                           // local junk

// Get the text strings which comprise the opening monologue, concatenate them to make one
// large string. All except for the last line which we'll treat as special. Leave if there is
// no monologue text to do...

        if ((hMono = LoadMonologue(hWnd, sz)) == NULL) return;

// Compute number of scroll lines as text height + client area height. Also, create font for
// monologue text. Set the font height to 24 point. Do this by:
// font_height = (point_size*logical_pixels_per_y_display_inch)/72.
// There are 72 points per inch. Since we decided to do some fancy text output, with multiple
// fonts and colors, we've got to compute the total height of the output bitmap as two
separate
// operations. Do the first set of calculations for the basic monologue text...

        SetRect(&grMono, 0, 0, gnWidth, 0);
        hDC = GetDC(hWnd);
        ghdcMem = CreateCompatibleDC(hDC);
        lf.lfHeight = MulDiv(-24, GetDeviceCaps(ghdcMem, LOGPIXELSY), 72);
        hFont1 = CreateFontIndirect(&lf);
        hOrigFont = SelectObject(ghdcMem, hFont1);
        DrawText(ghdcMem, lpszMono, -1, &grMono, DT_CALCRECT|DT_WORDBREAK);

// We need to wind up with a rectangle which contains the width and height of all the text we
// wish to display in the opening monologue. Start by setting the rectangle width to the width
// of the client area and the height to 0, creating the font to be used with the first part of
// the monologue text, then call DrawText() on the opening monologue using DT_CALCRECT. This
// will compute the height of the text. After that, make the font for the second part of the
// text and compute that height in a separate rectangle. Add'm together and you have it...

        lf.lfHeight = MulDiv(-48, GetDeviceCaps(ghdcMem, LOGPIXELSY), 72);
        lf.lfItalic = TRUE;
        hFont2 = CreateFontIndirect(&lf);
        SelectObject(ghdcMem, hFont2);
        SetRect(&rect, 0, 0, gnWidth, 0);
        DrawText(ghdcMem, sz, -1, &rect, DT_CALCRECT|DT_WORDBREAK);
        rect.top = grMono.bottom;
        grMono.bottom += rect.bottom;
        grMono.bottom += gnScrollInc;
        gnMonoHeight = grMono.bottom;
        rect.bottom = grMono.bottom;
```

```
// Now that we have to total text height in grMono, create a color bitmap the size of the
// computed text area and select it into the memory DC...

        hBitmap = CreateBitmap(gnWidth,
                               gnMonoHeight,
                               (BYTE)GetDeviceCaps(hDC, PLANES),
                               (BYTE)GetDeviceCaps(hDC, BITSPIXEL),
                               NULL);
        ReleaseDC(hWnd, hDC);
        hbmOld = SelectObject(ghdcMem, hBitmap);

// Fill the memory DC with black, the created bitmap isn't initialized and there's junk in it,
// so paint it the color of our background...

        FillRect(ghdcMem, &grMono, GetStockObject(BLACK_BRUSH));

// Now draw the 1st part of the monologue text on the bitmap in the memory DC using the right
// font and colors...

        SelectObject(ghdcMem, hFont1);
        SetBkColor(ghdcMem, RGB(0,0,0));
        SetTextColor(ghdcMem, RGB(255,255,255));
        DrawText(ghdcMem, lpszMono, -1, &grMono, DT_WORDBREAK);

// Now do it again for the 2nd part of the monologue text, and change the text color. Today I
// like bright red...

        SelectObject(ghdcMem, hFont2);
        SetTextColor(ghdcMem, RGB(255,0,0));
        DrawText(ghdcMem, sz, -1, &rect, DT_WORDBREAK|DT_CENTER);

// Fiddle the monologue rectangle: translate it down to the bottom of the screen. We want to
// scroll the display so our monologue text appears at the bottom of the window and scrolls off
// the top...

        grMono.top += gnHeight;
        grMono.bottom += gnHeight;

// Now start timer which gets us going...

        gnPaintMode = eMONO;
        SetTimer(hWnd, gnPaintMode, 10, NULL);

// Wait for monologue to complete...

        WaitFor(eMONO);

// Now release memory we used and destroy the stuff we created...

        LocalUnlock(hMono);
        LocalFree(hMono);
        SelectObject(ghdcMem, hbmOld);
        SelectObject(ghdcMem, hOrigFont);
        DeleteObject(hFont1);
        DeleteObject(hFont2);
        DeleteObject(hBitmap);
        DeleteDC(ghdcMem);
}
```

```
// ...DoPlunge...is the function called to display the "Plunging into Virtual Reality" image.
// Then wait til the user clicks on the hatch opening...

BOOL    WINAPI  DoPlunge(
        HWND    hWnd)                   // handle to main window instance
{
POINT   p;                              // mouse click point
RECT    rect;                           // window rectangle

// No paint mode for a moment or two...

        gnPaintMode = eUNKNOWN;

// Start the "are you stuck?" timer...

        SetTimer(hWnd, ePIVR, STUCKTIME, NULL);

#ifdef  _LESSON1
// Complain and exit if there's a problem loading the DIB, otherwise display the picture at
// the specified coordinates...

        if (!LoadDIB(hWnd, IDB_BITMAP3, &gDIB3))
        {
          MBox(hWnd, IDS_ERRDIB3, IDS_ERROR, MB_OK|MB_ICONEXCLAMATION);
          KillTimer(hWnd, ePIVR);
          return(FALSE);
        }

        gnPaintMode = ePIVR;
        DrawDIB(hWnd, &gDIB3);
#else
// Complain and exit if there's a problem loading the DDB, otherwise continue. We need the
// size of the DDB, this is returned by the Windows GetObject() function. Then put up the
// image immediately, no fooling around with fading in...
#ifdef  _LESSON2
        if ((ghDDB3 = LoadBitmap(ghInstance, MAKEINTRESOURCE(IDB_BITMAP3))) == NULL)
        {
          MBox(hWnd, IDS_ERRDDB3, IDS_ERROR, MB_OK|MB_ICONEXCLAMATION);
          KillTimer(hWnd, ePIVR);
          return(FALSE);
        }

        gnPaintMode = ePIVR;
        DrawDDB(hWnd, ghDDB3, NULL);
#else
        if (!LoadDDB(hWnd, IDB_BITMAP3, &gDDB3))
        {
          MBox(hWnd, IDS_ERRDDB3, IDS_ERROR, MB_OK|MB_ICONEXCLAMATION);
          KillTimer(hWnd, ePIVR);
          return(FALSE);
        }

        gnPaintMode = ePIVR;
        DrawDDB(hWnd, gDDB3.hBM, gDDB3.hPal);
#endif
#endif

// Our scenario calls for the user to click the left mouse button on the red "button" part
// of the image that's being displayed now. So we want to wait here until:
```

```
//
// 1)    the left mouse button is clicked AND
// 2)    it's clicked where we want it to be clicked

        SetRect(&rect, gnX+225, gnY+74, gnX+255, gnY+104);

        do
        {
          p = WaitForLeftButtonDown();
          if (PtInRect(&rect, p)) break;
        } while (TRUE);
```

```
// If we've gotten here, the user's clicked the left mouse button smack where we wanted'm to.
// His reward is ours too. We're done with this function...
```

```
#ifdef   _LESSON1
// Make sure to release whatever we allocated. That means the global area for the actual DIB
// image and, if used, the image palette...

        DeleteDIB(&gDIB3);
#else
// Make sure to release whatever we used. Since Windows loaded these objects for us, let
// Windows dispose of them. If we've done a conversion from a DIB to a DDB, we'll need to
// dump the palette as well...

#ifdef   _LESSON2
        DeleteObject(ghDDB3);
#else
        DeleteObject(gDDB3.hBM);
        DeleteObject(gDDB3.hPal);
#endif
#endif

// Don't forget to dump the timer...

        KillTimer(hWnd, ePIVR);
        return(TRUE);
}
```

```
// ...SetupNormalMode...is the function called to switch us from the startup sequence to the
// "normal" mode: gray 3D background, bunch of controls and a viewing window. Return TRUE if
// OK, else return FALSE...

BOOL     SetupNormalMode(
         HWND      hWnd)               // handle to window instance
{
// Our last act of startup, set the new paint mode to normal, change the background brush
// and force the entire window to be repainted...

        gnPaintMode = eNORMAL;
        SetClassWord(hWnd, GCW_HBRBACKGROUND, CreateSolidBrush(COLOR_FRAME));
```

```
// Begin the process of computing view window and control locations. Note that since we've
// chosen to appear as a popup window covering the entire desktop, we don't have to worry
// about WM_SIZE messages. Though if we were a normal overlapped window, all we'd need do for
// a WM_SIZE message would be to recompute the positions (possibly) of the child windows...

// We're going to create a view window on top of the main window. The view window is what
// we're going to paint the virtual world on. We want to allow the user to specify a size for
// the view window, within limits. The window size is defined by two constants: VWWIDTH and
```

```
// VWHEIGHT. Since these values are compile-time not run-time, we assume (probably a bad thing
// to do) the programmer will view the result and ensure that the specified values are OK...
// We're going to put the view window centerline about 40% of the way down. That gives us more
// room for the controls. Note the layout is strictly arbitrary, any control can be put where
// you want it...

// Create the view window and associated controls (child windows)...

        if (CreateView(hWnd) == NULL) return(FALSE);
        InvalidateRect(hWnd, NULL, TRUE);
        return(TRUE);
}

// ...DoStartup...is the function used to do the application startup sequence. Exit TRUE if
// all OK, else exit FALSE. All one time startup processes are performed here...

BOOL    WINAPI   DoStartup(
        HWND     hWnd,             // handle to main window instance
        LPCSTR   lpszCmd) // far pointer to command line
{
BOOL    bOK;                       // vr result flag

// Scroll the startup monologue. Leave out if in debug, makes me crazy waiting for it...

#ifndef _DEBUG
//      DoMonologue(hWnd);
#endif

// Do the pushbutton...

        if (!DoBigRedPushButton(hWnd)) return(FALSE);

// Now, let's go to the "plunging" picture and have some fun with that...

        if (!DoPlunge(hWnd)) return(FALSE);

// Setup for the normal mode of operation...

        if (!SetupNormalMode(hWnd)) return(FALSE);

// I promise, this is it, nothing else need be done here; initialize the VR engine, pass it
// a pointer to the VRE structure and give it the command line we got, it'll use that to parse
// the virtual world system. The function will return TRUE if all OK, else return FALSE. If
the
// VR system starts OK, setup the palette it wants to use...

        bOK = vrBegin(hWnd, &gVR, lpszCmd, VWWIDTH, VWHEIGHT);
        if (gVR.uMode & MF_PALETTE) UpdatePalette();
        return(bOK);
}

// ...GlobalInit...is the one-time startup function used to initialize and setup any global
// data required by the PINBALL application. This is one of the standard functions I use over
// and over, regardless of whether or not there's any global data. This method cuts down the
// time-to-startup dramatically for a Windows application...

void    WINAPI   GlobalInit(
        HWND     hWnd)             // handle to window instance
{
HDC     hDC;                       // handle to device context
```

```
TEXTMETRIC      tm;                    // TEXTMETRIC structure

// Initialize paint mode to nothing. Don't want to paint while we've got nothing to paint...

        gnPaintMode = eUNKNOWN;

// This is the number of pixels to increment per monologue scroll. Decrease to make a slower
// but smoother scroll, increase to do the opposite...

        gnScrollInc = 4;

// Set the auto-update in manual rate to the slowest value we have...

        gnUpdate = UPDATEx1;

// Initialize the control mode to viewer vs. ball...

        geMode = eVIEWER;

// Turn on 3D images to start with. Note this clears all other flags as well...

        gVR.uMode = MF_3D;

// Dynamically initialize the frame rate text output rectangle. Once again, notice everything
// should be done to be as dynamically robust as possible. The more you anticipate these
// situations, the less support calls you get...

// Get handle to display device context...

        hDC = GetDC(hWnd);
        GetTextMetrics(hDC, &tm);
        SetRect(&grFrameRate, 4, 4, 4+tm.tmMaxCharWidth*20,
4+tm.tmHeight+tm.tmExternalLeading);
        ReleaseDC(hWnd, hDC);
}

// ...Register...is the function used to perform the actual window registration...

// On exit:      TRUE     register window class succeeded
//               FALSE    register window class failed

BOOL    WINAPI  Register(
        UINT    style,          // window style
        WNDPROC wndproc, // far pointer to WndProc function
        int     nIcon,          // icon ID
        int     nBrush,         // brush ID
        LPCSTR  lpszName,       // far pointer to class name
        int     nExtra)         // extra bytes/window
{
WNDCLASS wc;                    // WNDCLASS structure

// Now why didn't we do what the basic MicroSoft Windows texts show? That is, allocate and
// lock a local area of memory the size of a WNDCLASS structure? Well, if that allocation
// fails, (though I don't see how it could), there's gonna be a GP fault, because they never
// check to see if it worked in the first place. Granted, the probability of it failing is
// tiny, but at least creating the structure on the stack (frame) guarantees that we're OK,
// can't overflow the stack, we aren't in deep enough...

// Fill in WNDCLASS structure which describes the characteristics of the application window
// we'll create...
```

```
            wc.style = style;
            wc.lpfnWndProc   = wndproc;
            wc.cbClsExtra    = 0;
            wc.cbWndExtra    = nExtra;
            wc.hInstance     = ghInstance;
            if (nIcon != 0)
              wc.hIcon       = LoadIcon(ghInstance, MAKEINTRESOURCE(IDI_ICON1));
            else
              wc.hIcon       = NULL;
            wc.hCursor       = LoadCursor(NULL, IDC_ARROW);
            wc.hbrBackground= GetStockObject(nBrush);
            wc.lpszMenuName  = NULL;
            wc.lpszClassName= lpszName;

// Register window class. Exit with the return code from that function...

            return(RegisterClass(&wc));
}


// ...RegisterWindowClasses...is the one-time startup function used to register the window
// classes used by the PINBALL application. Some comments on the class style: CS_DBLCLKS
// allows us to receive mouse double-clicks. CS_BYTEALIGNWINDOW speeds up bitblitting. There
// are two window classes we need to define: the basic application window and a child window
// which is the view window that we're going to paint the virtual world on...

// On exit:     TRUE    register window class succeeded
//              FALSE   register window class failed

BOOL    WINAPI  RegisterWindowClasses()
{
// Application window...

            if (!Register(CS_DBLCLKS, WndProc, IDI_ICON1, BLACK_BRUSH, tAppName, 0))
              return(FALSE);

// Ball direction window...

            if (!Register(CS_BYTEALIGNCLIENT, DirProc, 0, WHITE_BRUSH, tDirName, 0))
              return(FALSE);

// Slider bar window...

            if (!Register(CS_BYTEALIGNCLIENT, BarProc, 0, LTGRAY_BRUSH, tBarName, 8))
              return(FALSE);

// Ball speed window...

            if (!Register(CS_BYTEALIGNCLIENT, SpdProc, 0, WHITE_BRUSH, tSpdName, 0))
              return(FALSE);

// VR view window...

            return(Register(CS_BYTEALIGNCLIENT, ViewProc, 0, BLACK_BRUSH, tViewName, 0));
}
```

viewproc.c

```
// --------------------------------------------------------------------------------
//      //
// "Plunging Into Virtual Reality", VIEWPROC.C
//      //
// Copyright 1994, 1995 Russell J. Berube Jr. ALL RIGHTS RESERVED.                  //
// This software is published, but is NOT public domain. It remains the exclusive   //
// property of Russell J. Berube Jr. and Brookside Systems, Inc. This software may not
//      //
// be reproduced or integrated with other software without the prior written permission
//      //
// of Russell J. Berube Jr. and Brookside Systems, Inc. It is provided herein for   //
// instructional purposes only.
//      //
// --------------------------------------------------------------------------------
//      //


#include "includes.h"            // include the world...
#include "bitmap.h"              // include bitmap functions prototypes...
#include "message.h"             // include Windows message functions prototypes...
#include "funcs.h"               // include miscellaneous functions prototypes...
#include "vr.h"                  // include VR definitions...


// External data...

extern   HINSTANCE       ghInstance;        // handle to application instance
extern   VR        gVR;              // VR structure

// Global data...

HPALETTE ghPalette;         // handle to VR window palette

// ...ViewProc...is the exported callback function used to process the messages sent to us by
// Windows...
//
// On entry we're passed:
//
// hWnd          A handle to our window instance.
//
// wMsg          A WORD containing the Windows message code we're being passed.
//
// wParam        A WORD containing a parameter specific to this message.
//
// lParam        A LONG containing a parameter specific to this message.

LRESULT CALLBACK ViewProc(
        HWND      hWnd,              // handle to window instance
        WORD      wMsg,              // windows message code
        WPARAM    wParam,            // word parameter
        LPARAM    lParam)            // long parameter
{
HDC      hDC;                        // handle to display device context
PAINTSTRUCT        ps;               // PAINTSTRUCT used by WM_PAINT

// This function must process the messages passed to it by Windows. The simplest way to
// handle them is with a switch (case) statement. However, there are more than 200 messages
// which can be sent by Windows that makes for a huge, unwieldy source file it we put all
// that code inline. Instead we'll try to make the source as readable as possible. One thing
```

```
// I've learned, which never fails to amaze me: I can live with a program and the source code
// for months, know it intimately, see the stuff in my sleep no less, then leave it for a few
// months/ and when I come back, I'm convinced I never wrote it in the first place.
Especially,
// especially, if it's not commented up to its eyeballs. Virtually every line. You wont
believe
// how easy it is to completely forget this stuff as soon as you leave it.

// It can't possibly be wrong (one of my favorite sayings) to heavily comment your code. DO
IT!!

// Note that the messages are case'd in alphabetical order. Simply one of my quirks, I'm fussy
// that way, consistency is important. When I come back and look at this stuff again, it helps
// get me realigned. All my code is the same way. Always structured the same, same sort of
// comments, parameter notation, module layout, etc. I suppose it's like traveling and finding
// a McDonalds off in outer space, it's reassuring. Also, it proves to me I wrote this and not
// my doppelganger...

        switch (wMsg)
        {

// ...WM_CREATE...this message is received when Windows is about to create the application
// window. It is generated as a direct result of the Create() function. Use this time to do
// any global initialization required. Return 0, if OK, else return 1. Start by creating a
// rainbow palette as the default...

            case   WM_CREATE:
              SetScrollRange(hWnd, SB_VERT, 0, MAXELEVATION, FALSE);
              ghPalette = MakeRainbowPalette(hWnd);
              return(0);

// ...WM_DESTROY...this message is received when Windows is about to destroy the application
// window. It is generated as a direct result of the DestroyWindow() function. Use this time
// to do any final application cleanup. Here, we delete the class name for our application
// window with the UnregisterClass() function. Send ourselves the WM_QUIT message with the
// PostQuitMessage() function. That'll finally end us (see the WinMain module). Return 0, if
// OK, else return 1...

            case   WM_DESTROY:
              DeleteObject(ghPalette);
              return(0);

// ...WM_PAINT...this message is received when we need to update the display. Normally, the
// only time we get here is if there's been a change in the VR world. However, we can also
// get here if another window was covering us and has been moved to re-expose this window...

            case   WM_PAINT:
              hDC = BeginPaint(hWnd, &ps);
              BlitDC(hDC, gVR.hBitmap, 0, 0, NULL);
              EndPaint(hWnd, &ps);
              return(0);

// ...WM_VSCROLL...this message is received whenever the vertical scroll bar is activated.
// Note that we (this window) NOT the parent window belonging to the PINBALL application "own"
// the vertical scroll bar, so we're the one getting the message from Windows...

            case   WM_VSCROLL:
              MsgVScroll(hWnd, wParam, LOWORD(lParam), (HWND)HIWORD(lParam));
              return(0);
        }
```

```
// Any message we don't process, pass through to the Windows default message handler. Return
// whatever result it returns...

        return (DefWindowProc(hWnd, wMsg, wParam, lParam));
}
```

vr.c

vr.c is the module which contains the interface code between the Windows software and the virtual engine. The different parts of the application were written separately (about 1600 miles apart). This method can be used (all data passed within a single structure VR and a limited number of functions) quite successfully for other projects as well.

```
// ------------------------------------------------------------------------------
        //
// "Plunging Into Virtual Reality", VR.C                                     //
// Copyright 1994, 1995 Russell J. Berube Jr. ALL RIGHTS RESERVED.          //
// This software is published, but is NOT public domain. It remains the exclusive  //
// property of Russell J. Berube Jr. and Brookside Systems, Inc. This software may not
        //
// be reproduced or integrated with other software without the prior written permission
        //
// of Russell J. Berube Jr. and Brookside Systems, Inc. It is provided herein for   //
// instructional purposes only.
        //
// Portions copyright Chris Laurel.
// ------------------------------------------------------------------------------
        //

#include "includes.h"          // include the world...
#include "funcs.h"             // include functions prototypes...
#include "resource.h"          // include the resource definitions...
#include "vr.h"                // include VR definitions...

#include "graphics.h"

// ...vrBegin...is the function called by the Windows interface to start up the VR system.
// Return TRUE if everything OK, else return FALSE. Check to ensure we're in 256x8 bpp mode,
// then create the bitmap which is the area the VR engine will be changing...

BOOL    WINAPI  vrBegin(
        HWND    hWnd,           // handle to window instance
        LPVR    lpVR,           // far pointer to VR structure
        LPCSTR  lpszCmd, // far pointer to command line
        int     nWidth,         // view window width
        int     nHeight) // view window height
{
BITMAP  bm;                     // BITMAP structure
```

```
HDC       hDC;                        // handle to display device context
extern wtWorld ReadWorldFile(char *filename, wtPalette *GamePalette);
wtPalette GamePalette;

// Get handle to display device context, it contains the color information we need to create
// a compatible bitmap...

        hDC = GetDC(hWnd);

// Don't make a move until we see if we're in 8bpp x 1plane color mode. We need a palette to
// operate and that ends that discussion...

        if (
            (!(GetDeviceCaps(hDC, RASTERCAPS) & RC_PALETTE)) ||
            (GetDeviceCaps(hDC, BITSPIXEL) != 8) ||
            (GetDeviceCaps(hDC, PLANES) != 1)
          )
        {
          MBox(hWnd, IDS_NOT256, IDS_ERROR, MB_OK|MB_ICONHAND);
          ReleaseDC(hWnd, hDC);
          return(FALSE);
        }

// Don't forget this! If you do a GetSomething(), you must do a ReleaseSomething()...

        ReleaseDC(hWnd, hDC);

// Create a bitmap, the size of our view window. Allocate and lock down an area for the
// bits. Don't wan't to mess around locking and unlocking that while we're in the heat of
// battle. Use the size we're given, presumably this is the same size as the view window
// the bitmap will be displayed in...

        bm.bmType = 0;
        bm.bmPlanes = 1;
        bm.bmBitsPixel = 8;
        lpVR->nWidth = nWidth;
        lpVR->nHeight = nHeight;
        bm.bmWidth = lpVR->nWidth;
        bm.bmHeight = lpVR->nHeight;
        lpVR->nScan = (bm.bmWidth*bm.bmBitsPixel+15)/16*2;
        bm.bmWidthBytes = lpVR->nScan;
        lpVR->dwSize = (DWORD)bm.bmWidthBytes*(DWORD)bm.bmHeight;
        lpVR->hBits = GlobalAlloc(GPTR, lpVR->dwSize);
        if (lpVR->hBits == NULL) return(FALSE);
        lpVR->hpBits = (HPBYTE)GlobalLock(lpVR->hBits);
        bm.bmBits = (LPVOID)lpVR->hpBits;
        if (bm.bmBits == NULL) return(FALSE);
        lpVR->hBitmap = CreateBitmapIndirect(&bm);
        if (lpVR->hBitmap == NULL) return(FALSE);

    lpVR->world = ReadWorldFile(".\\test.wld", &GamePalette);
        lpVR->renderer = wt_CreateRenderer(bm.bmBits, bm.bmWidth, bm.bmHeight);
    lpVR->view = wt_CreateView(WT_FLOAT_TO_FIXED(3.14159265 / 2.0), WT_FLOAT_TO_FIXED(1.0));
    wt_SetViewpoint(lpVR->view,
                                          WT_FLOAT_TO_FIXED(5.0), WT_FLOAT_TO_FIXED(5.0),
WT_FLOAT_TO_FIXED(5.0),
                    WT_FLOAT_TO_FIXED(0.0));
    lpVR->lpPal = GamePalette.palette;
    if (GamePalette.palette_entries > 236)
        GamePalette.palette_entries = 236;
```

```
    lpVR->uPalEntries = GamePalette.palette_entries;
        lpVR->uPalStart = 0;
    lpVR->uMode |= MF_PALETTE;

    if (lpVR->world && lpVR->renderer && lpVR->view)
        return TRUE;
    else
        return FALSE;
}

// ...vrUpdate...is the function called by the Windows software to cause the virtual world
// to be changed. Return TRUE if there is a change in the virtual display, else return
// FALSE...

BOOL    WINAPI    vrUpdate(
        HWND      hWnd,            // handle to window instance
        LPVR      lpVR)           // far pointer to VR structure
{
    wt_SetViewpoint(lpVR->view,
                                        WT_FLOAT_TO_FIXED(5.0), WT_FLOAT_TO_FIXED(5.0),
WT_FLOAT_TO_FIXED(5.0),
                    WT_FLOAT_TO_FIXED((double) lpVR->nDirection++ / 180.0 * 3.14159265));
    wt_Render(lpVR->renderer, lpVR->world, lpVR->view);

        SetBitmapBits(lpVR->hBitmap, lpVR->dwSize, lpVR->hpBits);
        return(TRUE);
}

// ...vrEnd...this is the function called when the application is exiting and we're
// shutting down. Give the VR system a chance to dump everything...

void    WINAPI    vrEnd(
        HWND      hWnd,            // handle to window instance
        LPVR      lpVR)           // far pointer to VR structure
{
        if (lpVR->hBits != NULL)
        {
          GlobalUnlock(lpVR->hBits);
          GlobalFree(lpVR->hBits);
          if (lpVR->hBitmap != NULL) DeleteObject(lpVR->hBitmap);
        }
}
```

winmain.c

winmain.c is the module that contains the **WinMain()** function. As shown in the flowchart in Figure 4.1. test to see if there is another copy of the application. Exit if so.

Is this the Only Copy of the Application?

When a memory model is used which contains multiple, writeable data segments, only one copy may be executing. In addition, normally, you don't want more than one copy at one time anyway. Determine that here by examining the previous instance handle passed by Windows. Exit if not.

Figure 4.1—WinMain() flowchart

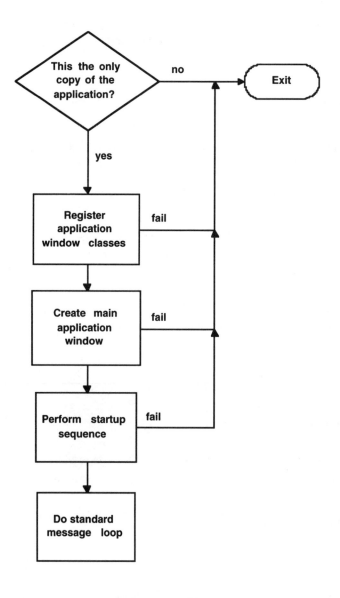

Register Application Window Classes

Now is when the window classes to be used in the application should be registered; we're going to need them soon. Exit on error.

Create Main Application Window

Actually, combine creation of the main application window with creation of the other application windows. Exit on error.

Perform Startup Sequence

I wanted a way to show a number of different techniques, this works nicely and we have some fun at the same time.

Do Standard Message Loop

The ubiquitous message loop. Note, however, that this message loop is somewhat different. There is a new function: **TranslateAccelerator()**. This translates any keystrokes found in the ACCELERATORS resource table to WM_COMMAND messages.

```
// ---------------------------------------------------------------------------
        //
// "Plunging Into Virtual Reality", WINMAIN.C
        //
// Copyright 1994, 1995 Russell J. Berube Jr. ALL RIGHTS RESERVED.            //
// This software is published, but is NOT public domain. It remains the exclusive    //
// property of Russell J. Berube Jr. and Brookside Systems, Inc. This software may not
        //
// be reproduced or integrated with other software without the prior written permission
        //
// of Russell J. Berube Jr. and Brookside Systems, Inc. It is provided herein for     //
// instructional purposes only.
        //
// ---------------------------------------------------------------------------
        //

#include "includes.h"          // include the world
```

```
#include "startup.h"           // include startup definitions...
#include "funcs.h"             // include miscellaneous functions definitions...

// There are a number of compile time definitions that affect the generated code. Define,
// or not, the specified options to include/exclude the specified options as follows:
//
// DEFINE         RESULT
// no defines     Bitmaps are loaded as DIBs (device-independent bitmaps) then converted to
//                DDBs (device-dependent bitmaps) with palettes. All processing done as DDBs.
//                Opening scene bitmaps are 8-bit color images.
//
// _LESSON1       Bitmaps are loaded as DIBs (device-independent bitmaps) with palettes. All
//                processing done as DIBs. Opening scene bitmaps are 8-bit color images.
//
// _LESSON2       Bitmaps are loaded as DDBs (device-dependent bitmaps) without palettes. All
//                processing done as DDBs. PIVR image 24-bit true color image.
//
// _LESSON3       All images made with identical rainbow palette. Can be used with or without
//                _LESSON1.
//
// _LESSON4       Include to remove automatic generation of rainbow palette for true color
//                images on a palettized device.
//
// _LESSON5       Include to remove keyboard accelerators.


// Global data...


HINSTANCE       ghInstance;        // handle to application instance

// ...WinMain...is the standard Windows application start function. This is identical to the
// "main()" function in a non-Windows program...
//
// On entry we're passed:
//
// hInst A handle which uniquely identifies this occurance (instance) of the
//                application.
//
// hPrevInst      A handle which uniquely identifies the previous instance of this application
//                which is currently executing. This is NULL if there are no other instances.
//
// lpszCmd        A far pointer to the command line entered when the application was started.
//
// nShow Initial "ShowWindow()" value. One of SW_xxx as found in      windows.h.
//
// This function registers the window class and creates the application window. When complete,
// we go into the standard message loop...

// Any comment line ending with [nnn] indicates further and more detailed discussion can be
// found in the appropriate section, item <nnn>...

int     PASCAL  WinMain( // Windows entry function
        HINSTANCE hInst, // handle to application instance
        HINSTANCE hPrevInst,      // handle to previous instance
        LPSTR   lpszCmd,          // pointer to command parameter string
        int     nShow)            // initial show value
{
#ifndef _LESSON5
HACCEL  hAccel;          // handle to accelerators table instance
#endif
HWND    hWnd;                     // handle to main window instance
```

```
MSG      Message;          // message structure

// First things first, if we're not the only instance executing, exit. Only want to run once.
// I prefer the construct "(xxx != NULL)" rather than simply "(xxx)". It's slightly more
// readable: it shows specifically what we're testing for. Besides, I like to use "(xxx)" and
// "(!xxx)" for booleans...

        if (hPrevInst != NULL) return(0);

// Save handle to our application instance. We'll need it occasionally...

        ghInstance = hInst;

// Register window classes. Exit if fail. Note that this function, along the startup functions
// are located in a separate module. Since we only need these functions on startup, pack'm away
// in a discardable segment, probably never be of any use, but Windows can use all the help it
// can get...

        if (!RegisterWindowClasses()) return(0);

// Create application window. Again, exit if fail...

        if (!(hWnd = CreateMainWindow())) return(0);

// Show application main window (the frame, etc). Then update (paint) it...

        ShowWindow(hWnd, nShow);
        UpdateWindow(hWnd);

#ifndef _LESSON5
// Load keyboard accelerators from resource file...

        hAccel = LoadAccelerators(hInst, "ACCEL");
#endif

// Show startup sequence, do all one time initializations. Exit if we fail. However, if we
// succeed, update the VR window with our first glimpse of that terrifying landscape. I
// suppose the vrUpdate() call could go in DoStartUp(), but it feels? more...correct here,
// somehow...

        if (!DoStartup(hWnd, lpszCmd)) return(0);
        UpdateView(hWnd);

// Now begin standard message loop. Stay in this loop forever as long as GetMessage() returns
// TRUE. Which it will do until it processes a WM_QUIT message...

#ifdef _LESSON5
        while (GetMessage(&Message, NULL, 0, 0))
        {
            TranslateMessage(&Message);
            DispatchMessage(&Message);
        }
#else
        while (GetMessage(&Message, NULL, 0, 0))
          if (!TranslateAccelerator(hWnd, hAccel, &Message))
          {
            TranslateMessage(&Message);
            DispatchMessage(&Message);
          };
```

```
#endif

// Time to leave...

        return(Message.wParam);
}
```

wndproc.c

wndproc.c is the module that contains the **WndProc()** function, as shown in the flowchart in Figure 4.2.

Messages are optionally processed or given to Windows for default processing. One thing you should never do, is intercept a message, then ignore it, or return a value other than what Windows expects.

A comment about the structure of this code. It's tempting, and I've done it myself time and time again, to simply include the actual code for the messages directly inline, within the **switch** statement. I don't recommend it. Is there anything wrong with it? Well, wrong isn't the right word, but you're about to expose your code to some poor practices, you can easily get lost within the cases, and you lose the ability to see the flow of the code. It's certainly more work to put the actual message code in separate functions, and it's microscopically slower as well, but the benefits far outweigh the bad points.

Put all the message handling code for an application of even moderate complexity inline, within a switch statement, then forget one, just one, case statement **break**, and have fun trying to debug that.

Note also that, unlike most **switch** statements used for generic WndProc functions, I don't use the **default** case for **DefWndProc()**. This gives us a more flexible structure. Now, if a message code is **case**-d, we can either examine and process it and then **return()**, which causes Windows not to process it, or we can **break** and Windows will handle it. If we ignore the message entirely, it's the same as if we used the **default** clause.

One more comment about comments. You should have noticed by now that virtually every code line is commented. One of the most common and worst tendencies to develop is not commenting "quick fixes," thinking something on the order of "Well, it's only one line." Without having experienced the frustration of encountering a mysterious, uncommented, orphan code line, many simply don't believe how troublesome they can be. Even for those of us who have ground their teeth and threatened the unknown programmer with a horrible death for not commenting the wayward line, there is *still* the temptation to skip the comment. It is only one line, after all, isn't it?

Figure 4.2—WndProc() flowchart

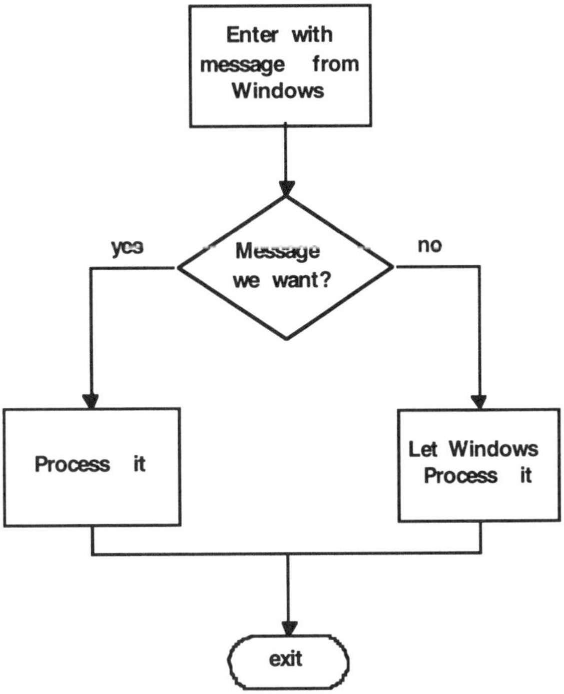

```
                    ┌─────────────────┐
                    │   Enter with    │
                    │ message  from   │
                    │    Windows      │
                    └─────────────────┘
                             │
                             ▼
         yes         ◇ Message    ◇        no
      ┌──────────────   we want?   ──────────────┐
      │                                           │
      ▼                                           ▼
┌──────────────┐                         ┌──────────────┐
│              │                         │ Let Windows  │
│ Process   it │                         │ Process   it │
│              │                         │              │
└──────────────┘                         └──────────────┘
      │                                           │
      └───────────────────┬───────────────────────┘
                          ▼
                      ( exit )
```

Well, I stuck one in the WM_CLOSE code section. See what you think. If it leaves you contemplative and thinking, "Gosh!" then my life and this book have been worth all the pain and suffering (just kidding). In any event, you'll find the answer in the *Don't Peek!* appendix.

Note that Windows has different return values for different messages. Pay attention. This leads me to one of my final thoughts, which I've repeated throughout this book.

Take your time. If you haven't discovered it yet, attention to detail is profoundly important when programming. Take your time!

```
// ---------------------------------------------------------------------------------
//          //
// "Plunging Into Virtual Reality", WNDPROC.C
//          //
// Copyright 1994, 1995 Russell J. Berube Jr. ALL RIGHTS RESERVED.                //
// This software is published, but is NOT public domain. It remains the exclusive  //
// property of Russell J. Berube Jr. and Brookside Systems, Inc. This software may not
//          //
// be reproduced or integrated with other software without the prior written permission
//          //
// of Russell J. Berube Jr. and Brookside Systems, Inc. It is provided herein for    //
// instructional purposes only.
//          //
// ---------------------------------------------------------------------------------
//          //


#include "includes.h"           // include the world...
#include "message.h"            // include message functions prototypes...

// External data...

extern   HBRUSH   ghbrBkgnd;        // handle to background brush
extern   HFONT    ghfView; // handle to view angle font
extern   HINSTANCE      ghInstance;       // handle to application instance
extern   int      gnPaintMode;      // current painting mode
extern   int      gnScrollInc;      // scroll increment for monologue
extern   RECT     grMono;           // monologue rectangle

// Global data...

int      gnHeight;              // client area height
int      gnRepeat;              // key repeat time
int      gnWidth;           // client area width

// ...WndProc...is the exported callback function used to process the messages sent to us by
// Windows...
//
// On entry we're passed:
//
// hWnd         A handle to our window instance.
//
// wMsg         A WORD containing the Windows message code we're being passed.
//
// wParam       A WORD containing a parameter specific to this message.
//
// lParam       A LONG containing a parameter specific to this message.

LRESULT CALLBACK WndProc(
          HWND    hWnd,           // handle to window instance
          WORD    wMsg,           // windows message code
          WPARAM  wParam,         // word parameter
          LPARAM  lParam)         // long parameter
{
HDC      hDC;                   // handle to display device context
PAINTSTRUCT      ps;            // PAINTSTRUCT used by WM_PAINT

// This function must process the messages passed to it by Windows. The simplest way to
// handle them is with a switch (case) statement. However, there are more than 200 messages
// which can be sent by Windows that makes for a huge, unwieldy source file it we put all
// that code inline. Instead we'll try to make the source as readable as possible. One thing
```

```
// I've learned, which never fails to amaze me: I can live with a program and the source code
// for months, know it intimately, see the stuff in my sleep no less, then leave it for a few
// months/ and when I come back, I'm convinced I never wrote it in the first place.
Especially,
// especially, if it's not commented up to its eyeballs. Virtually every line. You wont
believe
// how easy it is to completely forget this stuff as soon as you leave it.

// It can't possibly be wrong (one of my favorite sayings) to heavily comment your code. DO
IT!!

// Note that the messages are case'd in alphabetical order. Simply one of my quirks, I'm fussy
// that way, consistency is important. When I come back and look at this stuff again, it helps
// get me realigned. All my code is the same way. Always structured the same, same sort of
// comments, parameter notation, module layout, etc. I suppose it's like traveling and finding
// a McDonalds off in outer space, it's reassuring. Also, it proves to me I wrote this and not
// my doppelganger...

        switch (wMsg)
        {

// ...WM_CLOSE...this message is received when Windows wants to close the application.
// Use this time to decide whether or not the application can be closed or do any
// required cleanup. If OK to close the app, execute DestroyWindow() and return 0 or
// don't process it. Either way Windows will close the application. Return 0 without
// executing DestroyWindow() and nothing happens...

            case    WM_CLOSE:
                if (gnPaintMode != eNORMAL) return(0);
                DestroyWindow(hWnd);
                return(0);

// ...WM_COMMAND...this message is received when a menu item has been selected or a child
// button is activated (like MODE and UPDATE). The only menu we've got is the floating popup,
// but that'll work anyway...

            case    WM_COMMAND:
                MsgCommand(hWnd, wParam, lParam);
                return(0);

// ...WM_CREATE...this message is received when Windows is about to create the application
// window. It is generated as a direct result of the Create() function. Use this time to do
// any global initialization required. Return 0, if OK, else return 1...

            case    WM_CREATE:
                MsgCreate(hWnd);
                return(0);

// ...WM_DESTROY...this message is received when Windows is about to destroy the application
// window. It is generated as a direct result of the DestroyWindow() function. Use this time
// to do any final application cleanup. Here, we delete the class name for our application
// window with the UnregisterClass() function. Send ourselves the WM_QUIT message with the
// PostQuitMessage() function. That'll finally end us (see the WinMain module). Return 0, if
// OK, else return 1...

            case    WM_DESTROY:
                MsgDestroy(hWnd);
                return(0);

// ...WM_DRAWITEM...this message is received when Windows is about to draw a control. Since
```

```
// we have owner-draw controls, the processing is done here. If the OwnerDrawControls()
// function returns TRUE, it handled the drawing, so return TRUE, else leave it for the
// default WndProc...

        case   WM_DRAWITEM:
            if (MsgDrawItem(hWnd, (int)wParam, (LPDRAWITEMSTRUCT)lParam)) return(TRUE);
            break;

// ...WM_KEYDOWN...this message is received when Windows detects a key has been pressed on the
// keyboard. But not a system key (ALT+anything), that generates a WM_SYSKEYDOWN...

        case   WM_KEYDOWN:
            if (MsgKeyDown(hWnd, wParam)) return(0);
            break;

// ...WM_INITMENUPOPUP...this message is received just prior to Windows displaying a popup
// menu. Since, by a strange coincidence we have one, we're going to process this message.
// We'll modify the menu items to check whichever item is currently selected...

        case   WM_INITMENUPOPUP:
            MsgInitMenuPopup(hWnd, (HMENU)wParam);
            return(0);

// ...WM_LBUTTONDOWN...this message is received when the user clicks the left mouse button in
// the client area. Windows passes us the point where the mouse was clicked, relative to the
// CLIENT AREA...

        case   WM_LBUTTONDOWN:
            MsgLeftButtonDown(hWnd, MAKEPOINT(lParam));
            return(0);

// ...WM_LBUTTONUP...this message is received when the user releases the left mouse button,
// provided in the client area or anywhere if we've captured the mouse. Windows passes us the
// point where the mouse was clicked, relative to the CLIENT AREA...

        case   WM_LBUTTONUP:
            MsgLeftButtonUp(hWnd, MAKEPOINT(lParam));
            return(0);

// ...WM_PAINT...this message is received when Windows has determined that all or part of the
// client area has changed or if we (the application) tell Windows to force a WM_PAINT with
// the InvalidateRect() or InvalidateRgn(). UpdateWindow() does NOT generate a new WM_PAINT,
// it only forces any WM_PAINT in the queue to be acted on immediately...

        case   WM_PAINT:
            hDC = BeginPaint(hWnd, &ps);
            MsgPaint(hWnd, hDC, &ps);
            EndPaint(hWnd, &ps);
            return(0);

// ...WM_RBUTTONDOWN...this message is received when the user clicks the right mouse button in
// the client area. Windows passes us the point where the mouse was clicked, relative to the
// CLIENT AREA...

        case   WM_RBUTTONDOWN:
            MsgRightButtonDown(hWnd, MAKEPOINT(lParam));
            return(0);

// ...WM_SIZE...this message is received whenever the window size changes. Including window
// creation. Windows passes us the new size...
```

```
          case   WM_SIZE:
            gnWidth = LOWORD(lParam);
            gnHeight = HIWORD(lParam);
            return(0);

// ...WM_TIMER...this message is received whenever a timer goes off...

          case   WM_TIMER:
            MsgTimer(hWnd, wParam);
            return(0);
       }

// Any message we don't process, pass through to the Windows default message handler. Return
// whatever result it returns...

          return (DefWindowProc(hWnd, wMsg, wParam, lParam));
}
```

bitmap.h

```
// ---------------------------------------------------------------------------------
          //
// "Plunging Into Virtual Reality", BITMAP.H
          //
// Copyright 1994, 1995 Russell J. Berube Jr. ALL RIGHTS RESERVED.                    //
// This software is published, but is NOT public domain. It remains the exclusive     //
// property of Russell J. Berube Jr. and Brookside Systems, Inc. This software may not
          //
// be reproduced or integrated with other software without the prior written permission
          //
// of Russell J. Berube Jr. and Brookside Systems, Inc. It is provided herein for      //
// instructional purposes only.
          //
// ---------------------------------------------------------------------------------
          //

void     WINAPI   Blit(HWND, HBITMAP, int, int, HPALETTE);
void     WINAPI   BlitDC(HDC, HBITMAP, int, int, HPALETTE);
HPALETTE WINAPI   MakeRainbowPalette(HWND);
void     WINAPI   DrawDIB(HWND, LPDIB);
void     WINAPI   DeleteDIB(LPDIB);
BOOL     WINAPI   LoadDIB(HWND, int, LPDIB);
BOOL     WINAPI   LoadDDB(HWND, int, LPDDB);
void     WINAPI   DrawDDB(HWND, HBITMAP, HPALETTE);
```

funcs.h

```
// ---------------------------------------------------------------------------------
          //
```

```
// "Plunging Into Virtual Reality", FUNCS.H
//          //
// Copyright 1994, 1995 Russell J. Berube Jr. ALL RIGHTS RESERVED.              //
// This software is published, but is NOT public domain. It remains the exclusive   //
// property of Russell J. Berube Jr. and Brookside Systems, Inc. This software may not
//          //
// be reproduced or integrated with other software without the prior written permission
//          //
// of Russell J. Berube Jr. and Brookside Systems, Inc. It is provided herein for    //
// instructional purposes only.
//          //
// ------------------------------------------------------------------------------
//          //

void     WINAPI   Draw3DBorder(HWND, HDC);
int      WINAPI   MBox(HWND, int, int, UINT);
void     WINAPI   UpdateAzimuth(HWND, int);
void     WINAPI   UpdateControlMode(HWND, int);
void     WINAPI   UpdateDirection(HWND, int);
void     WINAPI   UpdateElevation(HWND, int, BOOL);
void     WINAPI   UpdatePalette();
void     WINAPI   UpdateSpeed(HWND, int);
void     WINAPI   UpdateView(HWND);
void     WINAPI   WaitFor(enum PAINTMODE);
POINT    WINAPI   WaitForLeftButtonDown();
POINT    WINAPI   WaitForLeftButtonUp();
void     WINAPI   WaitForManual();
```

includes.h

```
// ------------------------------------------------------------------------------
//          //
// "Plunging Into Virtual Reality", INCLUDES.H
//          //
// Copyright 1994, 1995 Russell J. Berube Jr. ALL RIGHTS RESERVED.              //
// This software is published, but is NOT public domain. It remains the exclusive   //
// property of Russell J. Berube Jr. and Brookside Systems, Inc. This software may not
//          //
// be reproduced or integrated with other software without the prior written permission
//          //
// of Russell J. Berube Jr. and Brookside Systems, Inc. It is provided herein for    //
// instructional purposes only.
//          //
// ------------------------------------------------------------------------------
//          //

#include <windows.h>          // include standard windows definitions
#include <math.h>             // include abs definition...
#include <memory.h>           // include _fmemcpy definition...
#include <stdlib.h>           // include itoa definition...
#include <string.h>           // include string functions definition...

// Application-wide type definitions...

#ifndef HPBYTE
```

```
typedef BYTE      huge*    HPBYTE;
#endif

typedef struct   _BM                     // structure for 16 color DDB
{
        HBITMAP hBM;             // handle to bitmap
        RECT    rect;            // bitmap rectangle
} BM,   FAR*      LPBM;

typedef struct   _BAR
{
        LPBM    lpBM;            // far pointer to bar BM structure
        int     nInc;            // increment/position
        LPINT   lpInc;           // far pointer to increment value
} BAR,  FAR*      LPBAR;

typedef struct   _BUTTON
{
        HWND    hWnd;            // handle to child window
        HBITMAP hbmUp;           // handle to UP bitmap
        HBITMAP hbmDown; // handle to DOWN bitmap
} BUTTON,         FAR*    LPBUTTON;

typedef struct   _DDB                     // structure for 256 color DDB
{
        HBITMAP hBM;             // handle to bitmap
        HPALETTE hPal;   // handle to palette
} DDB,  FAR*      LPDDB;

typedef struct   _DIB
{
        HGLOBAL hBI;             // handle to internal image
        HGLOBAL hPI;             // handle to palette index area
        HPALETTE hPal;   // handle to PALETTE structure
        DWORD   dwTable; // size of color table
} DIB,  FAR*      LPDIB;

// System definitions...

// Note all numeric values are defined within parentheses. That isn't just for the heck of it.
// Consider the following:

// #define      EXPR    1+2
//
//      EXPR*3
//
// this returns a value of 7 (1+2*3) whereas what you wanted was 9, ((1+2)*3). Big difference.

#define tAppName "ClassPinballApp" // application window name
#define tBarName "ClassPinballBar" // slider bar window name
#define tDirName "ClassPinballDir" // ball direction window name
#define tSpdName "ClassPinballSpd" // ball speed window name
#define tViewName        "ClassPinballView"       // view window name
#define KEYREPEAT        (250)    // key repeat time
#define KEYACCEL (20)    // acceleration rate
#define KEYFAST          (50)    // max acceleration
#define STUCKTIME        (30000) // time to wait for "stuck?"
#define PALSIZE          (256)   // max number of colors in palette image
#define VWHEIGHT (240)   // view window height
#define VWWIDTH          (480)   // view window width
```

```
#define  UPDATEx1 (1000)    // x1 autopilot update rate

// Paint modes...

enum      PAINTMODE          {eUNKNOWN, eMONO, eBRP1, eBRP2, ePIVR, eNORMAL};

// Control modes...

enum      CONTROLMODE        {eVIEWER, eBALL};

//· Colors...

#define  COLOR_BLACK         (RGB(0, 0, 0))
#define  COLOR_BLUE          (RGB(0, 0, 255))
#define  COLOR_GREEN         (RGB(0, 255, 0))
#define  COLOR_RED           (RGB(255, 0, 0))
#define  COLOR_YELLOW        (RGB(255, 255, 0))
#define  COLOR_DKGRAY        (RGB(128, 128, 128))
#define  COLOR_WHITE         (RGB(255, 255, 255))
#define  COLOR_FRAME         (RGB(192, 192, 192))
```

message.h

```
// --------------------------------------------------------------------------------
        //
// "Plunging Into Virtual Reality", MESSAGE.H
        //
// Copyright 1994, 1995 Russell J. Berube Jr. ALL RIGHTS RESERVED.              //
// This software is published, but is NOT public domain. It remains the exclusive  //
// property of Russell J. Berube Jr. and Brookside Systems, Inc. This software may not
        //
// be reproduced or integrated with other software without the prior written permission
        //
// of Russell J. Berube Jr. and Brookside Systems, Inc. It is provided herein for    //
// instructional purposes only.
        //
// --------------------------------------------------------------------------------
        //

void      WINAPI   MsgCommand(HWND, WPARAM, LPARAM);
void      WINAPI   MsgCreate(HWND);
void      WINAPI   MsgDestroy(HWND);
BOOL      WINAPI   MsgDrawItem(HWND, int, LPDRAWITEMSTRUCT);
void      WINAPI   MsgInitMenuPopup(HWND, HMENU);
BOOL      WINAPI   MsgKeyDown(HWND, UINT);
void      WINAPI   MsgLeftButtonDown(HWND, POINT);
void      WINAPI   MsgLeftButtonUp(HWND, POINT);
void      WINAPI   MsgPaint(HWND, HDC, LPPAINTSTRUCT);
void      WINAPI   MsgRightButtonDown(HWND, POINT);
void      WINAPI   MsgTimer(HWND, UINT);
void      WINAPI   MsgVScroll(HWND, UINT, int, HWND);
```

resource.h

```
// ------------------------------------------------------------------------------
//        //
// "Plunging Into Virtual Reality", RESOURCE.H
//        //
// Copyright 1994, 1995 Russell J. Berube Jr. ALL RIGHTS RESERVED.              //
// This software is published, but is NOT public domain. It remains the exclusive   //
// property of Russell J. Berube Jr. and Brookside Systems, Inc. This software may not
//        //
// be reproduced or integrated with other software without the prior written permission
//        //
// of Russell J. Berube Jr. and Brookside Systems, Inc. It is provided herein for    //
// instructional purposes only.
//        //
// ------------------------------------------------------------------------------
//        //

#define IDI_ICON1                        101
#define IDB_BITMAP1                      102
#define IDB_BITMAP2                      103
#define IDB_BITMAP3                      104
#define IDB_LAU                           105
#define IDB_LAD                           106
#define IDB_RAU                           107
#define IDB_RAD                           108
#define IDB_GAUGE1                        109
#define IDB_GAUGE2                        110
#define IDB_AUTOON                        111
#define IDB_AUTOOFF                       112
#define IDB_SLIDE                         113
#define IDB_KNOB                 114
#define IDS_MONO1                        201
#define IDS_MONO2                        202
#define IDS_MONO3                        203
#define IDS_MONO4                        204
#define IDS_MONO5                        205
#define IDS_ERROR                        301
#define IDS_ERRNOGM                      302
#define IDS_ERRNOLM                      303
#define IDS_ERRDDB1                      304
#define IDS_ERRDDB2                      305
#define IDS_ERRDDB3                      306
#define IDS_ERRDIB1                      307
#define IDS_ERRDIB2                      308
#define IDS_ERRDIB3                      309
#define IDS_ERRLGM                       310
#define IDS_ERRLLM                       311
#define IDS_ERRPCF                       312
#define IDS_ERRLR                        313
#define IDS_NOT256                       314
#define IDS_STUCK                        315
#define IDS_QUERY                        316
#define IDC_VIEW                 401
#define IDC_MODE                 402
#define IDC_DIRECTION                    403
#define IDC_SPEED                        404
#define IDC_UPDATE                       405
#define IDC_X1                           406
```

```
#define  IDC_X2                             407
#define  IDC_X5                             408
#define  IDC_X10                            409
#define  IDC_FAST                410
#define  IDC_AUTO                411
#define  IDC_3D                              412
#define  IDC_FRAME                           413
#define  IDC_EXIT                414
```

startup.h

```
// -----------------------------------------------------------------------
//
// "Plunging Into Virtual Reality", STARTUP.H
//
// Copyright 1994, 1995 Russell J. Berube Jr. ALL RIGHTS RESERVED.          //
// This software is published, but is NOT public domain. It remains the exclusive   //
// property of Russell J. Berube Jr. and Brookside Systems, Inc. This software may not
//
// be reproduced or integrated with other software without the prior written permission
//
// of Russell J. Berube Jr. and Brookside Systems, Inc. It is provided herein for    //
// instructional purposes only.
//
// -----------------------------------------------------------------------
//

HWND     WINAPI  CreateMainWindow();
LRESULT  WINAPI  GlobalInit(HWND);
BOOL     WINAPI  RegisterWindowClasses();
BOOL     WINAPI  DoStartup(HWND, LPCSTR);
```

vr.h

```
// -----------------------------------------------------------------------
//
// "Plunging Into Virtual Reality", VR.H                                     //
// Copyright 1994, 1995 Russell J. Berube Jr. ALL RIGHTS RESERVED.          //
// This software is published, but is NOT public domain. It remains the exclusive   //
// property of Russell J. Berube Jr. and Brookside Systems, Inc. This software may not
//
// be reproduced or integrated with other software without the prior written permission
//
// of Russell J. Berube Jr. and Brookside Systems, Inc. It is provided herein for    //
// instructional purposes only.
//
// -----------------------------------------------------------------------
//

#include "wt.h"
```

```
// Constant definitions. Two things to notice, the parentheses and the use of #define.
// One advantange C++ has over C is its support of constants using the syntax:

// const int AZINC = 1;

// Much better than a define. The parentheses are there to ensure disasters such as:

// #define        foo        1+2
//                fee = foo*3;

// don't happen...

#define  AZINC           (1)        // azimuth increment
#define  DIRINCMAX       (90)       // max direction increment
#define  HGTINC          (1)        // height increment
#define  SPDINCMAX       (50)       // max speed increment
#define  MAXELEVATION    (9)        // max viewer height
#define  MAXSPEED (100)    // max ball speed value (+/-)

// the VALUE typedef is used in case we want to switch to another data type: int, float,
// etc. You can't be assured of going through the source and changing each instance of a
// data type reliably. Do it this way instead. You should use this method for virtually
// all data types. There's nothing wrong with defining a data type called MILESperGALLON
// for example...

typedef  LONG     VALUE;           // numeric values
typedef  VALUE    TDA[3];          // 3D array

// This is the structure used to communicate between the 3D rendering software and the
// Windows code. All communications take place in the module VR.C...

typedef  struct   _VR
{
        int     nAzimuth;          // viewer azimuth (0-360)
        int     nElevation;        // viewer elevation (0-MAXELEVATION)
        int     nSpeed;            // ball speed
        int     nDirection;        // ball direction
        int     nSpdInc; // ball speed increment
        int     nDirInc; // ball direction increment
        UINT    uMode;             // mode flags
        TDA     Position;          // current position
        HBITMAP hBitmap; // handle to bitmap
        int     nWidth;            // bitmap width
        int     nScan;             // bitmap scan line width
        int     nHeight; // bitmap height
        DWORD   dwSize;            // image size
        HGLOBAL hBits;             // handle to global image area
        HPBYTE  hpBits;            // huge pointer to bitmap bits
        LPPALETTEENTRY   lpPal;    // far pointer to array of PALETTEENTRY structures
        UINT    uPalEntries;       // number of palette entries
        UINT    uPalStart;         // beginning palette entry
        wtWorld world;             // world structure for the wt renderer
        wtRenderer renderer;       // info used internally by the renderer
        wtView view;               // camera location, angle, etc. for renderer
} VR,    FAR*    LPVR;

// VR mode flags...

#define  MF_AUTO         0x0001    // auto mode
```

```
#define  MF_STOP        0x0002  // stop motion
#define  MF_UPDATE      0x0004  // update in manual mode
#define  MF_3D          0x0008  // 3D image
#define  MF_PALETTE     0x0010  // update palette flag (from vrXXX)

// Function prototypes...

BOOL     WINAPI  vrBegin(HWND, LPVR, LPCSTR, int, int);
BOOL     WINAPI  vrUpdate(HWND, LPVR);
void     WINAPI  vrEnd(HWND, LPVR);
```

pivr.def

The .DEF file contains the linker control statements. If this were a .DLL, the EXETYPE line would be **LIBRARY** instead of **WINDOWS**. Note the single quotes on the DESCRIPTION line and no quotes on the NAME line. Make a mistake here and the linker accepts it, but you get an application which doesn't function.

Remember we're using the large memory model, so multiple data segments are specified. This also precludes multiple concurrent instances of the application: The Windows loader can't handle it. Also, regardless of what you specify, both CODE and DATA segments are loaded as MOVEABLE.

Finally, note that no stack size has been specified using the STACKSIZE statement. That's because the Windows C++ Workbench system I used adds it to the linker command line. You can add it here.

```
NAME        PIVR
DESCRIPTION     'Plunging Into Virtual Reality'
EXETYPE   WINDOWS
CODE      PRELOAD MOVEABLE DISCARDABLE
DATA      PRELOAD MOVEABLE MULTIPLE
HEAPSIZE  1024
IMPORTS
        GetTimerResolution        = User.GetTimerResolution ;Q112386
```

The IMPORTS: GetTimerResolution... line has been added because of an error in Windows. The function was not included in the Windows import library LIBW.LIB and must be specifically included. Refer to Microsoft Knowledge Base article number Q112386 for more information.

pivr.rc

The .RC module contains all resource definitions used in the application. Note the inclusion of **resource.h** for the *numeric* ID definitions. Resource names can also be text strings. When they are referenced as numeric values, you must use the **MAKEINTRESOURCE** macro, which converts the numeric value to a text string.

The bitmap file name endings are:

x8   8 bit/pixel

x8r   8 bit/pixel, rainbow palette

x24   24-bit/pixel

The remaining bitmaps (**IDB_LAU-IDB_BAR**) are all "normal" 16-color (4 bit/pixel) images which fit into the basic system palette.

A comment on string tables resources vs. in-line text strings. Use them! In-line text strings will come back to bite you. That application you're contemplating may just become the next international bestseller and you won't like having to go through each source module searching for text strings every time you want to send out a version in a different language.

One final comment on text strings. Have a little class. Use a dictionary. There's nothing (to me at least) as embarrassing as seeing a dialog box pop up:

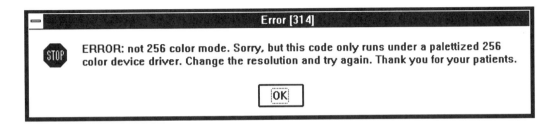

with a spelling error.

***Don't tell the entire world you think they're not worth the time it takes to
use a dictionary.***

```
// -------------------------------------------------------------------------------
        //
// "Plunging Into Virtual Reality", PINBALL.RC
        //
// Copyright 1994, 1995 Russell J. Berube Jr. ALL RIGHTS RESERVED.              //
// This software is published, but is NOT public domain. It remains the exclusive    //
// property of Russell J. Berube Jr. and Brookside Systems, Inc. This software may not
        //
// be reproduced or integrated with other software without the prior written permission
        //
// of Russell J. Berube Jr. and Brookside Systems, Inc. It is provided herein for    //
// instructional purposes only.
        //
// -------------------------------------------------------------------------------
        //

#include "resource.h"

// ICONS...

IDI_ICON1          ICON     DISCARDABLE              "res\\ICON1.ICO"

// BITMAPS...

#ifdef  _LESSON2
IDB_BITMAP1        BITMAP   DISCARDABLE              "res\\brp1x8.bmp"
IDB_BITMAP2        BITMAP   DISCARDABLE              "res\\brp2x8.bmp"
IDB_BITMAP3        BITMAP   DISCARDABLE              "res\\pivrx24.bmp"
#else
#ifdef  _LESSON3
IDB_BITMAP1        BITMAP   DISCARDABLE              "res\\brp1x8r.bmp"
IDB_BITMAP2        BITMAP   DISCARDABLE              "res\\brp2x8r.bmp"
IDB_BITMAP3        BITMAP   DISCARDABLE              "res\\pivrx8r.bmp"
#else
IDB_BITMAP1        BITMAP   DISCARDABLE              "res\\brp1x8.bmp"
IDB_BITMAP2        BITMAP   DISCARDABLE              "res\\brp2x8.bmp"
IDB_BITMAP3        BITMAP   DISCARDABLE              "res\\pivrx8.bmp"
#endif
#endif
IDB_LAU            BITMAP   DISCARDABLE              "res\\lau.bmp"
IDB_LAD            BITMAP   DISCARDABLE              "res\\lad.bmp"
IDB_RAU            BITMAP   DISCARDABLE              "res\\rau.bmp"
IDB_RAD            BITMAP   DISCARDABLE              "res\\rad.bmp"
IDB_GAUGE1         BITMAP   DISCARDABLE              "res\\gauge.bmp"
IDB_GAUGE2         BITMAP   DISCARDABLE              "res\\gauge.bmp"
IDB_AUTOON         BITMAP   DISCARDABLE              "res\\autoon.bmp"
IDB_AUTOOFF        BITMAP   DISCARDABLE              "res\\autooff.bmp"
IDB_SLIDE          BITMAP   DISCARDABLE              "res\\slide.bmp"
IDB_KNOB BITMAP    DISCARDABLE               "res\\knob.bmp"

// STRINGTABLE...

STRINGTABLE        DISCARDABLE
BEGIN
IDS_ERROR          "Error"
IDS_QUERY          "I have a question for you"
```

```
IDS_MONO1        "I was exhausted.\n\nI'd been up most of the night working on a virtual
reality application, trying to decide how to explain the concepts. +"
IDS_MONO2        "I fell asleep immediately and dreamt I was dreaming that I woke from a
dream, and there, floating in front of me was a big red pushbutton. +"
IDS_MONO3        "Somehow, even in the dream I knew that pushing that button would give me the
answer I was seeking. +"
IDS_MONO4        "I knew it would be scary, but I took a deep breath, pushed the button and
was...\n\n\n+"
IDS_MONO5        "Plunged into Virtual Reality!"
#ifdef _LESSON1
IDS_ERRDIB1      "ERROR: failed to load the device-independent bitmap resource IDB_BITMAP1."
IDS_ERRDIB2      "ERROR: failed to load the device-independent bitmap resource IDB_BITMAP2."
IDS_ERRDIB3      "ERROR: failed to load the device-independent bitmap resource IDB_BITMAP3."
IDS_ERRPCF       "ERROR: palette creation failed."
IDS_ERRLR        "ERROR: load resource failed."
#else
IDS_ERRDDB1      "ERROR: Windows failed to load the device-dependent bitmap resource
IDB_BITMAP1."
IDS_ERRDDB2      "ERROR: Windows failed to load the device-dependent bitmap resource
IDB_BITMAP2."
IDS_ERRDDB3      "ERROR: Windows failed to load the device-dependent bitmap resource
IDB_BITMAP3."
#endif
IDS_ERRLGM       "ERROR: failed to lock a global memory handle."
IDS_ERRLLM       "ERROR: failed to lock a local memory handle."
IDS_ERRNOGM      "ERROR: insufficient global memory."
IDS_ERRNOLM      "ERROR: insufficient local memory."
IDS_NOT256       "ERROR: not 256 color mode. Sorry, but this code only runs under a palettized
256 color device driver. Change the resolution and try again. Thank you for your patience."
IDS_STUCK        "Stuck? Try the F1 key."
IDC_X1           "Autopilot x1\tCtrl+1"
IDC_X2           "Autopilot x2\tCtrl+2"
IDC_X5           "Autopilot x5\tCtrl+3"
IDC_X10          "Autopilot x10\tCtrl+4"
IDC_FAST "Autopilot Real Fast\tCtrl+5"
IDC_AUTO "Auto update in Manual\tCtrl+A"
IDC_3D           "Anaglyph Images\tCtrl+I"
IDC_FRAME        "Show frame rate"
IDC_EXIT "Exit\tAlt+F4"
END

#ifndef _LESSON5
// ACCELERATORS...

ACCEL    ACCELERATORS
BEGIN
        "1",     IDC_X1,          VIRTKEY, CONTROL
        "2",     IDC_X2,          VIRTKEY, CONTROL
        "3",     IDC_X5,          VIRTKEY, CONTROL
        "4",     IDC_X10, VIRTKEY, CONTROL
        "5",     IDC_FAST,        VIRTKEY, CONTROL
        "A",     IDC_AUTO,        VIRTKEY, CONTROL
        "I",     IDC_3D,          VIRTKEY, CONTROL
END
#endif
```

Good hunting.

PART II

VIRTUAL ENVIRONMENTS PAST, PRESENT, AND FUTURE

CHAPTER 5

WELCOME TO VIRTUAL ENVIRONMENTS

Virtually Speaking ...

First let's clarify a few terms. According to Webster's:

> display—a device (as a cathode-ray tube) that gives information in visual form in communications.

If we simplify this definition:

> display—a device that gives information in communications.

We now have a term which may be used in reference to a visual stimulus—a computer screen; an auditory stimulus—a stereo sound source; and a motion stimulus—motion, tactile, or force-feedback equipment.

haptic—relating to or based on the sense of touch.

The term haptic includes all displays which present stimuli to the broad human sense of touch including texture, force, motion, temperature, and pressure.

virtual—being in effect but not in actual fact.

artificial—humanly contrived, often on a natural model.

environment—the conditions, circumstances, and influences surrounding and affecting an organism.

reality—of or relating to practical or everyday concerns or activities.

The term virtual reality was first coined by Jaron Lanier, founder of VPL Research. That term, and indeed Lanier himself in many ways, has garnered the lion's share of media usage. Artificial reality was coined by Myron Kruegar and is generally applied to his work. The terms virtual environments and virtual worlds are used by many of the premier researchers in the field, including Frederick Brooks of the University of North Carolina in Chapel Hill; Scott Fisher, formerly of NASA Ames, now of Telepresence Research; and Thomas Furness of the HIT Lab. This book will use these terms indiscriminately.

Virtual environment display types are one of the major ways to categorize different types of virtual environments. Haptic displays vary dramatically and thus are usually explicitly described. However, visual display type is undoubtedly the defining characteristic of most virtual environments. The most important distinction is between immersive and non-immersive environments, and here is where a great deal of debate about what constitutes a virtual environment rages. This is certainly due in part to the modern origins of virtual worlds research, when Ivan Sutherland presented "The Ultimate Display" to the Triennial Conference of the International Processing Societies. Therein Sutherland described "a program of research in computer graphics which has challenged and guided the field ever since."[1] Sutherland said that one must look at a computer display screen as a window through which one beholds a virtual world.

The challenge to computer graphics is to make the window look real, sound real, and the objects act real. Indeed, in the ultimate display, one

Figure 5.1—HMD, data glove, and elevator

will not look at that world through a window, but will be immersed in it, will change viewpoint by natural motions of head and body, and will interact directly and naturally with the object in the world, hearing and feeling them, as well as seeing them.[2]

Many researchers and advocates discount any environment that does not immerse the participant's vision in a three-dimensional world. It should be pointed out that few systems can immerse all of the senses, so this distinction seems somewhat arbitrary. This book will consider any environment that presents a display of another world to some participant, be it artificial world or not.

It is important to note that the field of virtual reality is in its infancy. A certain amount of skepticism and objectivity is important as we look at the accomplishments and the possibilities of this field. Of course, these are exciting times. Let's get started.

If we perceive our role aright, we then see more clearly the proper criterion for success: a toolmaker succeeds as, and only as, the users of his tool succeed with his aid. However shining the blade, however jeweled the hilt, however perfect the heft, a sword is tested only by cutting. That swordsmith is successful whose clients die of old age.

—F. Brooks, "Grasping Reality Through Illusion: Interactive Graphics Serving Science"

CHAPTER 6

THE HISTORY OF VIRTUAL ENVIRONMENTS

With Respect to ...

As we gaze toward horizons yet unconquered, feeling the zeal of recent discoveries and new technologies, it is appropriate to cast a glance and a "thank you" towards those whose enabled us to get here. Throughout history, visionaries, artists, scientists, and engineers have crafted the infrastructure we now use. The modern roots of the virtual environments field are generally traced to Ivan Sutherland's visionary work in 1965. Things aren't quite that simple, however. Sutherland credits Edwin Link's work in flight simulation, which dates to the 1930s.

A great debate raged starting at the turn of the century about who founded broadcast radio. This war lasted formally until 1943, when the Supreme Court overturned Marconi's patents in favor of Tesla's prior art and patents. Although Tesla is often still overlooked by Marconi, he wasn't overlooked by the Supreme

Court because of his vision. Nikola Tesla foresaw, well ahead of his peers, how radio could affect the way people think.

> World Telegraphy constitutes, I believe, in its principle of operation, means employed and capacities of application, a radical and fruitful departure from what has been done heretofore. I have no doubt that it will prove very efficient in enlightening the masses, particularly in still uncivilized countries and less accessible regions, and that it will add materially to general safety, comfort, and convenience, and maintenance of peaceful relations. . . . A cheap and simple device, which might be carried in one's pocket may then be set up anywhere on sea or land, and it will record the world's news or such special messages as may be intended for it. Thus the entire earth will be converted into a huge brain, capable of response in every one of its parts. . . . [I]t must needs immensely facilitate and cheapen the transmission of intelligence.[3]

The Contributions of Science Fiction

> science fiction—fiction dealing principally with the impact of actual or imagined science upon society or individuals.[4]

The field of literature known as science fiction has often presented ideas long before they were achieved in the real world. The classic age of science fiction introduced the tactile feedback glove in the 1940 Robert Heinlein story "Waldo." A waldo consisted of a pair of gloves, the master worn by a human operator and a slave which performed some task remotely, duplicating the movements of the master. These waldoes were used for remote and hazardous work, including at microscopic levels. Aldous Huxley described the virtual environments version of the movies called "feelies"—the "All-Super-Singing, Synthetic Talking, Colored, Stereoscopic Feely." Arthur C. Clarke described "personalized television safaris" which allowed couch potatoes to explore remote and hazardous places from the safety of their home. Ray Bradbury's story "The Veldt" described a sentient simulation, set in an African Veldt, which evolved from a psychological experiment into a form of entertainment for children which read minds. "The Happiness Machine," also by Ray Bradbury, described a technology which allowed people to live their fantasies. However, the people became depressed when they had to return to live in their dull, drab, everyday unaugmented existence.

A more modern form of science fiction called cyberpunk was spawned in the mid-1980s. The defining points of cyberpunk came from the 1982 movie *Blade Runner* and William Gibson's 1984 book entitled *Neuromancer*. The inhabitants of these grim and gritty worlds were people of the street, immersed in technology that was simply taken for granted, as Gibson put it, "the street has its own uses for technology." Gibson's book also coined the terms "cyberspace" and the "matrix."

Bruce Sterling—Texan, writer, publisher, and friend of William Gibson— adopted the term cyberpunk as the focal point for his issues. Soon media from the *Wall Street Journal* to MTV were applying the label to everything from youngsters committing computer crimes to people who wear black, read *Mondo 2000*, and listen to techno-pop. Cyberpunk fiction soon evolved beyond its original definitions, but its impact on the literature of science fiction, among other places, is still being felt.

Flight Simulation

Virtual reality derives its heritage (roots) from flight simulation. Edwin Link and company founded one of the best known flight simulation companies in the world. Link's original technology was based on the same pneumatic control systems found throughout his family's mechanical musical instruments company. This technology, based on mechanical linkages and pressurized air, dominated the flight simulation industry through the end of World War II.

Link's first flight simulators were closer to imitators than simulators. They featured a simple cockpit with no instrumentation which rolled, pitched, and yawed in response to simple controls provided by the pilot. Link spent a great deal of time empirically tuning the responses of his simulator so they acted appropriately. Consequently, the Link simulators were the most popular of their time.

In an effort to build a flight simulator based on the real-time dynamical solution of equations, Jay W. Forrester of the Massachusetts Institute of Technology (MIT) Servomechanisms Lab embarked in 1944 on a military-funded project called "Whirlwind." The project was to employ the Electronic Numerical

Integrator and Computer (ENIAC). Although the Whirlwind project never succeeded in creating a generalized flight trainer, it did reveal some entirely unexpected things. Late 1948 and early 1949 brought the discovery that certain computer instructions would cause certain patterns on the oscilloscope test equipment. The researchers even created a game including a dot called the "ball," which could be made to fall through a "hole" in the "floor" by adjusting some input variables. The dynamics of the ball could be predicted using pure math. Thus was born the first interactive computer graphics game. Another interesting development by the Whirlwind team was the "light gun." System

Figure 6.1—IVEX Corporation flight simulator showing cockpit and view

state information of the computer was displayed on an oscilloscope as a series of dots. The team developed a light-sensitive detector that they could point at the oscilloscope to determine what device was represented on the scope. Thus was born the light gun, the first interactive graphics tool.

Near the end of World War II, under an Air Force contract, Fred Waller developed a multiple-projector, multiple-screen flight simulator. The system had two projectors on top and three on the bottom which provided a much wider field of view than ordinary film. After WWII, Waller decided to try to sell a three-projector version to Hollywood. Waller teamed up with producer Mike

Todd to create *This Is Cinerama*. Although Cinerama was never in more than one hundred theaters even at its peak, it was credited with bringing people back to the movies. Further, it inspired a man by the name of Morton Heilig.

Morton Heilig and the Experience Theater

Morton Heilig nearly created the field of virtual environments more than 30 years ago from the field of cinematography sponsored by Hollywood. As a young man, Heilig was interested in cinematography and had dreams of multisensory experiences. He was drafted near the end of World War II and served in postwar Europe. After his time was served, Heilig took his G.I. Bill money and two Fulbright fellowships to study film-making in Rome. He began work as a self-employed documentary maker. He learned about Cinerama in the early 1950s. After he exhausted his research on the subject in Italy, he decided to go to Broadway to see it all for himself.

Heilig was excited by the possibilities he saw for Cinerama. He began to envision the next step, totally immersing the participant in the experience. He wrote a manifesto calling for Hollywood studios or the government to mount a broad-based research and development effort on sound, peripheral vision, vibration, smell, and wind. Unfortunately Heilig was an unknown, and his calls went unheeded.

Heilig set off to Mexico to film documentaries. While there, he met the great Mexican muralist Siqueiros, who invited him to lecture on his multisensory ideas to a group of intellectuals, engineers, and artists who regularly met at Siqueiros' house. Heilig published his manifesto in 1955 in a bilingual Mexican journal named *Espacios*. His discussion included sketches and schematics of his vision of an Experience Theater.

> Celluloid film is a very crude and primitive means of recording light and is already being replaced by a combination television camera and magnetic tape recorder. Similarly, sound recording on film or plastic records is being replaced by tape recording . . . a reel of the cinema of the future being a roll of magnetic tape with a separate track for each sense material. With these problems solved it is easy to imagine the cinema of the future. Open your eyes, listen, smell, and feel—sense the world in all its magnificent colors, depths, sounds, odors and textures—this is the cinema of the future!

The screen will not fill only 5% of your visual field as the local movie screen does, or the mere 7.5% of Wide Screen, or 18% of the "miracle mirror" screen of Cinemascope, or the 25% of Cinerama—but 100%. The screen will curve past the spectator's ears on both sides and beyond his sphere of vision above and below. In all the praise about the marvels of "peripheral vision," no one has paused to state that the human eye has a vertical span of 150 degrees as well as a horizontal one of 180 degrees. The vertical field is difficult, but by no means impossible to provide. ... This 180 degree by 150 degree oval will be filled with true and not illusory depth. Why? Because as demonstrated above this is another essential element of man's consciousness. Glasses, however, will not be necessary. Electronic and optical means will be devised to create illusory depth without them.

Heilig's article received enough notice that the Minister of Education of Mexico decided to support his project. With Mexican support, the project built a "huge semispherical screen." They designed and built one of the first bug-eye lenses. They proceeded to take and display test pictures on the screen. Unfortunately Heilig's sponsor died in a plane crash and support for the project crumbled. Heilig decided to return to New York.

Without a prototype, he was unable to interest any financial backers. He resolved to build an arcade-sized one-person version to make it obvious to anyone that this was the direction in which to go. Heilig took a job teaching film appreciation and set out to build his system. He found a partner and they started a company named Sensorama. They built the first working prototype, but still no one would back them. They had tried to sell the prototype as a showroom display to Ford and International Harvester. They tried to sell to educators. They also tried to sell to industry. Finally, an arcade owner allowed them to put the machine in an arcade at 52nd and Broadway in New York, but it broke within hours. Even with many months of work, the system was simply too complex for harsh arcade treatment. Eventually, Heilig's partner lost interest.

One night, Heilig received a call from a man who had seen the Sensorama on Broadway—he was interested in discussing it further. The backer turned out to be interested in mass-producing Sensoramas. The man's $50,000, a vending machining company, and an engineer built the second prototype Sensorama.

This Sensorama prototype consisted of a wooden booth which partially surrounded the participant, who was seated on a motorcycle-like contraption. A nickelodeon-like viewer provided stereographics. Right below the faceplate, a small grill provided smells. Two speakers were strategically placed near the participant's ears. The seat lurched and wind blew by the face of the rider, acting as a passenger, rode a motorcycle through Brooklyn or rode through California on a bicycle. This prototype failed to win any further financing, and Heilig's backer lost interest.

Heilig did have some successes. He built a "Stereoscopic Television Apparatus for Individual Use" in 1960. He was granted another patent in 1962 for a "Sensorama Simulator." Heilig's head-mounted display (HMD) predates Ivan Sutherland's, which is generally credited as the ancestor of modern HMDs.

J.C.R. Licklider and Interactive Computing

Shortly before the launch of Sputnik, a professor at the Massachusetts Institute of Technology (MIT) named J.C.R. Licklider was developing mathematical models to understand how humans hear, a field called psychoacoustics. One day while surrounded by stacks of paper, he began to wonder how other research scientists spent most of their time. A thorough, if brief, search revealed that no relevant studies were in existence. Licklider proceeded to record his own activities. To his utter dismay, he learned than 85 percent of his "thinking" time was spent "getting into a position to think, to make a decision, to learn something I needed to know." He wondered if specially designed computers could assume some of the mechanical acts of shuffling paper.

Computers of those days were very large, very expensive, and kept in special rooms in which the temperature and humidity were carefully controlled. Programmers wrote Fortran and COBOL programs which were then encoded on stacks of punch cards; a program often consisted of several boxes of these punch cards. The results of the program would be printed out on paper and returned to the programmer. This was the system called "batch processing." Batches of punch cards would be fed into the computer by its specially trained servants. Days or weeks later the resulting printout would be returned. Expensive computer cycles were not wasted on catering to the vagaries of humans. All of the translation between human and computer was done on the human side. A sort of priesthood of highly skilled people who were able to understand the computer grew into power around these systems. They became as restrictive of their secrets as they were of their computer cycles. Computers were simply not accessible by most researchers, many of whom could greatly benefit from their use. Among the computer cognoscenti, it was tacitly understood that each new generation of computers would be bigger, more powerful, and always under the control of the priesthood.

About this same time, a radical new concept in the use of computers was being developed by aircraft designers. Lists of numbers were being turned into graphic models of air flow over the surfaces of wings. This process, which became known as modeling, is the ancestor of scientific visualization. Digital Equipment Corporation (DEC) released the PDP-1, an unprecedented event. The PDP-1 was the first "minicomputer," a machine that was less powerful than a

Figure 6.2—Stereo VR glasses at work

"mainframe," merely the size of a refrigerator instead of a room and costing merely hundreds of thousands of dollars instead of millions of dollars. This machine used high-speed paper tape for programming, allowing programmers to do in hours what had once taken days. For the first time, hard-core programmers had a taste of interactive computing. The minicomputer allowed many more people to have access to computers than ever before.

Licklider had attained tenure, so he began consulting with Bolt, Beranek, and Newman (BB&N), a company in the possession of a PDP-1. Licklider found that it was indeed possible to use a computer to build models from experimental data. Indeed, the computer was an excellent device to help make sense out of the complicated interrelationships of data. In 1960, Licklider wrote "Man–Computer Symbiosis," in which he predicted that "in not too many years, human brains and computing machines will be coupled together very tightly, and that resulting partnership will think as no human being has ever thought and process data in a way not approached by the information-handling machines we know today."

The was created as a direct response to the Soviet's launching of Sputnik on October 4, 1957. ARPA's mandate was to directly fund unconventional ideas in hopes of leapfrogging the Soviets in computer technology. MIT's was employed to build the computerized Semi-Automatic Ground Environment (SAGE) to help protect the United States from nuclear attack. Licklider, while working on the SAGE project, became acquainted with Jack Ruina, the director of ARPA. Licklider's "interactive computing" views were just the kind of ideas for which ARPA was looking to lead to an important breakthrough.

Licklider became the director of the ARPA's Information Processing Techniques Office (IPTO) in October 1962. Licklider's new job was to raise the state of the art in information processing. He recruited all over the country for eager young minds. One of those he found was Bob Taylor, a NASA administrator. Taylor had been funding another young man with new and unusual ideas, Douglas Engelbart.

Douglas Engelbart and Intelligence Augmentation

Douglas Engelbart was driving to work one morning in 1950 musing about to what he should devote the remainder of his life and talents. After serving as a naval radar technician during World War II, he had earned an electrical engineering degree. He had a wife and a challenging profession. In short, at the age of 35 he had already accomplished everything he had set out to achieve. His musings led him to a vision of computers and humans collaborating closely to solve problems.

Engelbart realized—based on his radar experience—that computers should be capable of displaying graphical, symbolic information, which could be manipulated by an operator with knobs and levers to present the information space in different manners. He even imagined a theater-like environment where researchers could work together, with and through the computer.

Engelbart quit his job and went to the University of California, home to one of the two computers in California. He was unsuccessful in convincing anybody to waste precious computer time learning how to help people solve problems. Eventually he took a job as an orthodox computer researcher at the Stanford Research Institute. He wrote a conceptual framework for his vision in his spare time during the 1950s and early 1960s. This framework reads much like a blueprint for our work in the 1990s and beyond. In 1963, more than a decade before word processors, Engelbart published "A Conceptual Framework for Augmenting Man's Intellect." He thought it would be possible to use a computer and a video display screen to enhance the entire process of writing.

Though nobody was listening at the time, Sputnik's launch would eventually change all that. When an ARPA team visited Engelbart in 1964, he had his conceptual framework and the complete design for a laboratory to build it. The ARPA team promised him the equipment and the funding to build his dreams.

Engelbart chose to name his new lab the Augmentation Research Center (ARC)—augmentation implies using computers to enhance human labor, in contrast to automation, a popular concept of the time, which implies replacing human labor with computers. Some of the inventions which the ARC created that we take for granted today include the mouse (invented in the 1960s, although not commercially feasible until the 1980s); a rudimentary form of hypertext which enabled users to jump from one word or phrase in one part of a document to another related word or phrase elsewhere; the use of multiple windows to display text on a screen; and the presentation of text and graphics in the same document.

At the Fall Joint Computer Conference in 1968, Engelbart gave an amazing demonstration. On stage, he had a keyboard, a video display screen, a crude mouse, and an earphone-microphone headset. From an iconic display, he selected a document from which to read. He collapsed the full text document to a single-line descriptive outline format. He used the mouse to cut and paste text from one part of a document to another. Engelbart had built and was demonstrating the computer of the future at a time when those few people who dealt with computers did so through punch cards and printouts. Douglas Engelbart demonstrated the first personal computer many years before its time.

Flight Simulation Revisited

The 1960s also saw the commercial development of digital computer-based flight simulation with the release of the LinkMark I. The system responded to the pilot's manipulation of the controls according to the laws of aerodynamics, which were solved in real time. This simulator included landscape displayed through the cockpit windows, wind, and engine noise. The pilot's controls included force-feedback.

Ivan Sutherland and Sketchpad

In 1962 a graduate student named Ivan Sutherland was invited to attend a meeting of the top researchers in computer graphics, though he was not asked to give a paper. A number of reasons led to this invitation, including that he was a Ph.D. student of Claude Shannon (father of information theory and known for sponsoring extraordinary graduate students) and ARPA was looking for just this type of prodigy to create a major breakthrough. Toward the end of the meeting, Sutherland asked a question which indicated that this unknown young man might have something important to say. He was invited to speak the next day. Sutherland presented his dissertation, entitled Sketchpad, which proved to be far more innovative than any of the other work presented; he had leapfrogged their research.

Ted Nelson saw the implications of Sketchpad. In the 1977 book *The Home Computer Revolution,* Nelson entitled a chapter "The Most Important Program Ever Written." His description recounts the wonder of Sutherland's creation. The computer operator could draw a picture on the screen using a lightpen. This picture could be saved and later combined with other pictures. The computer would only display the detail necessary, but would allow you to zoom in to see more detail.

> There had been lightpens and graphical computer screens before, used in the military, but Sketchpad was historic in its simplicity—a simplicity, it must be added, that had been deliberately crafted by cunning intellect— and its lack of involvement with any particular field. Indeed, it lacked any complications normally tangled with what people actually do. It was, in short, an innocent program, showing how easy human work could be if a computer were set up to be really helpful.

. . . [T]his would do so much for blueprints, or electronic diagrams, or all the other areas where large and precise drafting is needed.

It was suddenly very clear to all who watched that computers could be used for far more than data processing. Much of what is said about this program may seem familiar to any of the readers who have watched skilled computer-aided design (CAD) operators or people using the sophisticated desktop drawing programs now available. In fact, the entire field of CAD is the direct descendant of this single program.

In 1964, J.C.R. Licklider recommended Ivan Sutherland, now aged 26, for the post of IPTO director. Sutherland held the post until the following year when he passed the job to Bob Taylor, another young man in his twenties. Ivan Sutherland was off to MIT to build head-mounted displays.

Ivan Sutherland and the Ultimate Display

In 1965, Sutherland published an article called "The Ultimate Display" which challenged the rest of the computer world. This paper is generally credited with

Figure 6.3—In another world (Virtual Research HMDs)

the beginning of the field of virtual reality and led us directly to where we are now.

> We live in a physical world whose properties we have come to know well through long familiarity. We sense an involvement with this physical world which gives us the ability to predict its properties well. For example, we can predict where objects will fall, how well-known shapes look from other angles, and how much force is required to push objects against friction. We lack corresponding familiarity with the forces on charged particles, forces in non-uniform fields, the effects of nonprojective geometric transformations, and high-inertia, low friction motion. A display connected to a digital computer gives us a chance to gain familiarity with concepts not realizable in the physical world. It is a looking glass into a mathematical wonderland.

> The ultimate display would . . . be a room within which the computer can control the existence of matter. A chair displayed in such a room would be good enough to sit in. Handcuffs displayed in such a room would be confining, and a bullet displayed in such a room would be fatal. With appropriate programming such a display could literally be the Wonderland in which Alice walked.[5]

Having just vacated the ARPA post of IPTO director, Sutherland had little trouble finding sponsors for his next project. The ARPA and the Office of Naval Research cosponsored the development of the first head-mounted display (HMD) at MIT's Lincoln Labs. Sutherland moved to the University of Utah in 1970, where he continued his research. Sutherland was building the tools necessary to fulfill his prophecy in "The Ultimate Display."

The first HMDs were test models and partial systems designed to solve problems and test theories. These HMDs became known as the "Sword of Damocles" because the operator's head was wrapped in heavy machinery suspended from the ceiling. The machine was suspended because it was heavy and employed a mechanical gaze-tracker. The display was provided by 6-inch-long, 13/16-inch-diameter CRTs mounted near the temples and viewed, through lenses and mirrors, as a virtual image 14 inches in front of the operator's face. Six interconnected computers, most of which were custom-built, created the images composed of 3000 lines at 30 frames per second (quite respectable even by today's standards). The user was free to move, turn around, tilt his or her head up or down up to 40 degrees. In all, the user had an area 6 feet in diameter and 3 feet in height in which to move around.

The first virtual object was a cube of light, two inches on a side, which floated before the wearer of the HMD. Daniel Vickers, a University of Utah student who was responsible for the integration of the different systems, was the first to view this object on January 1, 1970. Another early object was a molecular model of cyclohexane.

Later experiments used a PDP-10 to create a square virtual room with boundaries painted in light and walls marked N (North), S (South), E (East), W (West), C (Ceiling), and F (Floor). Eventually, a pistol-grip—shaped wand with four buttons, a slide switch, and a small dial was used to create and interact with the virtual objects in the virtual world. By pointing at a wall chart and pushing a button, the wand could cause objects to appear, disappear, shrink, stretch, rotate, fuse together, or fall apart. The incantations of a participant wearing the HMD and using the wand's user to interact with a world only he or she could see led the wand to be called the "Sorcerer's Apprentice."

Evans and Sutherland

While working on head-mounted displays, Sutherland realized that computers, instead of cameras, could generate the images for flight simulators. Sutherland and David Evans teamed up in 1968 to form Evans and Sutherland and to develop electronic scene generators.

The old system of constructing scale models for the scenes used paint, foam, and glue. Any three-dimensional object can be recreated on a computer with points and lines, at which point the object is said to be digitized. The view of the object may be transformed with a series of calculations. It has long been known that the closer to reality the simulation is, the more use it is. The problem with this is that "realism" involves a great number of calculations. These calculations have to be done quickly enough that the scene can be rendered before it is out of date. Every computer has a limit on what complexity can be achieved in what time frame. If the rendering is too slow, no amount of detail will make the system appear real. In fact, it can cause the operator to experience "simulator sickness," a feeling very much akin to motion sickness, which is described later.

Xerox PARC

Xerox had been exploiting a technology called photocopying, abandoned by IBM in the 1950s. Peter McColough became the new leader of Xerox in 1970s amidst worries about the "paperless office." Xerox decided to redefine itself as an information company and, to that end, set up an interdisciplinary research laboratory called the Palo Alto Research Center (PARC) near the Stanford University campus. They were given the funds and the mandate to create "the architecture of information for the future," as the president of Xerox called it.

The Mansfield Amendment, drafted during the height of the Vietnam War, effectively prevented ARPA from funding non--weapons-related research. Bob Taylor, the director of the IPTO, was hired by Xerox to assemble a team. Taylor recruited a number of former ARPA researchers including Alan Kay, who became chief scientist.

Kay came from the University of Utah, had studied Ivan Sutherland's Sketchpad, and watched Evans and Sutherland leading the way in computer graphics. Kay had been working on Sutherland's project to find way to display information on an ever-changing interactive computer display.

Kay derived his inspiration from Marshall McLuhan, Seymour Papert, and Ivan Sutherland. McLuhan led him to think of the computer as a medium rather than a tool. The ideas of Papert showed him that computer languages could be thinking tools, that graphical communication can be a powerful means of human--computer interaction, and that children can and should be able to use computers. Ivan Sutherland's Sketchpad showed him that computers could be used as interactive tools. Kay led the way away from the command line interface that all interactive computers used to a new type of computer and computer interface.

The new machine created by Kay and his crew used a direct manipulation interface, first described by Engelbart and shown by Sutherland. This computer's name was the Altos. The Altos used a new technology called "bit-mapped graphics," where every element of the graphic display system (pixel) is exactly described by a piece of computer memory. It displayed all of the computer's resources graphically on the screen, depicted by small pictures called icons, and using the concept of metaphors. The computer operator had a desk on which could be found a filing cabinet complete with folders and files and a trashcan in which to dispose of these things. ARC researchers brought the mouse with them, which enabled the operator to move and interact in the virtual computer world.

The first microcomputer revolution was in full force. In 1979, Xerox decided to invest in the leading microcomputer company of the day, and so bought 100,000 shares in Apple Computer. In exchange, Apple was allowed access to the PARC's research. Peter McColough left Xerox. Competition from the Japanese gave Xerox too much to worry about, so the Alto was shelved. Steve Jobs, cofounder and representative of Apple, found the Alto while touring the PARC facility. And thus was the course of computer history changed.

1982 saw the introduction of the Apple Lisa. Although this computer was not itself very successful, it was a breakthrough and the prototype of the very popular and successful Macintosh. It also heralded the introduction of the graphical user interface (GUI), today's computer interface of choice. Other common modern GUIs include Microsoft Windows and MIT's X-Windows. Xerox itself is developing a new generation of GUI which features a three-dimensional look featuring rooms, doors, and pockets in which to carry your tools as you wander the halls of your computer.

Myron Krueger's Artificial Reality

In April 1969 at the Memorial Union Gallery of the University of Wisconsin at Madison, GLOWFLOW opened to the public. GLOWFLOW combined networks of tubes filled with phosphorescent colored fluids, hidden minicomputers, and sound synthesizers to produce a new type of art form. Hidden lights would illuminate phosphorescent particles in the glass tubes to created different light effects in the otherwise dark room. Pressure-sensitive plates embedded in the floor enabled the audience to control the performance, although they were unaware of exactly how.

In 1983, Myron Krueger wrote about GLOWFLOW:

People had rather amazing reactions to the environment. Communities would form among strangers. Games, clapping, and chanting would arise spontaneously. The room seemed to have moods, sometimes being deathly silent, sometimes raucous and boisterous. Individuals would invent roles for themselves. One woman stood by the entrance and kissed each man coming in while he was still disoriented by the darkness. Others would act as guides explaining what phosphors were and what the computer was doing. In many ways the people in the room seemed primitive, exploring an environment they did not understand, trying to fit into what they knew and expected. Since the GLOWFLOW publicity mentioned this responsiveness, many people were prepared to experience it and would leave convinced that the room had responded to them in ways that it simply had not. The birth of such superstitions was continually observed in a sophisticated university public.

Krueger had been part of the team of artists who created GLOWFLOW. The artists who had recruited him wanted to maintain a contemplative quality to the place, but Krueger wanted to experiment with the strong human emotions created by the "responsive environment."

Kruegar has created a number of exhibits since GLOWFLOW including METAPLAY, PSYCHIC SPACE, and VIDEOPLACE, which was the basis of Kruegar's 1974 doctoral dissertation, "Computer Controlled Responsive Environments," later published as *Artificial Reality* (Addison-Wesley, 1983), in which he also coined the term artificial reality. The concept for VIDEOPLACE is a world in which full physical participation is possible.

VIDEOPLACE is a dark room with a real-time silhouette image of the participant displayed on a large video projection screen in the room. The computer analyzes the participant's motion and responds accordingly. More than 30 interactions are possible within VIDEOPLACE. The participant can draw on the screen without operator intervention by holding up one finger. Closing the hand ceases the drawing. An open hand can erase the drawing. Participants can interact with other participants and a small graphical creature called CRITTER which can chase you, climb on you, and even dance on you.

Krueger believes that at the center of every VR system is a human experience, including the experience of being in an unnatural or remote world. Attention is the instrument wielded by the artist, and "response is the medium," for virtual reality art. VR art must be fundamentally interactive.

In a time when many are considering donning gloves, suits, and helmets to enter another world, Krueger is creating a responsive world, an artificial reality, that leaves the participant unencumbered and able to move in more natural ways. Krueger believes that "human interface research will branch in two directions. One fork will have the objective of completing an artificial reality technology that includes force and tactile feedback, using whatever intrusive and encumbering means that are necessary. The other fork will pursue an interface that merges seamlessly with the rest of our environment."[6]

MIT's Arch-Mac and the Media Lab

In 1970 Nicholas Negroponte outlined his vision for combining the presentation capabilities of cinema and the information handling capabilities of computers. He believed that the fusion of digital computers, audio, video, broadcast, and networks would evolve into an integrated "media technology" (Alan Kay called this a "metamedium"). Negroponte and co-researcher Richard Bolt endeavored to lead MIT's Architecture Machine Group down this new trail with strong backing from ARPA.

The Arch-Mac Group always had their sights firmly fixed on the next great breakthrough, the newest technologies, and future possibilities. They made ample use of voice commands, eye trackers, and holographic film. The group consisted of a liberal mix of researchers from the cognitive and computer sciences. Their research featured ideas brought from the theater and cinema as well as the latest telecommunications technologies. This group was never enamored of all the gear associated with VR; they prefer the "sexier" unencumbered view of people interacting with computers.

Bolt stressed that gaze direction is very important in human communications which meant that many of the Arch-Mac and Media Lab systems made use of

Figure 6.4—Three-dimensional scanner image

this technology. Related areas of research included three-dimensional displays and techniques for transmitting facial expressions and gaze directions in telecommunications.

In 1976 Negroponte and Bolt began work on the spatial data management system (SDMS). The concept involved turning a computer into an office. The display became the metaphorical desktop including a diary, telephone, and in box. The exploration of ways in which to place the individual within the office led to the creation of the Media Room—a "room-sized personal computer where the whole body [is] the cursor-director and your voice the keyboard."[7] The computer operator sat in a chair at the center of a room whose walls were covered with computer displays. The operator could point to an object on one of the screens and say, "Put that . . .", then point to the desired location and say "there." Motion sensors and gaze trackers would decide on which object was to be moved where and execute the procedure.

The Media Room was used to explore other important concepts including different methods of the exploration of "data space." A prototype named "Dataland" allowed the Media Room operator to fly through the two-dimensional representation of three-dimensional data. This was part of the SDMS system for visually navigating databases.

The World of Windows system still continues to influence VR research. Large windows of information could be opened on wall-sized screens under the direction of eye-trackers and motion sensors. The screens could show text, photographs, and full-motion video, including live data feeds from satellites, news wires, and videodisk databases.

One of the most intriguing projects created at the Arch-Mac was the Aspen Movie Map created by Andrew Lippman, Scott Fisher, and others of the Arch-Mac crew. The idea was to create a movie of the town of Aspen, Colorado—a movie which the viewer could direct by pointing at the screen to determine what direction (literally) the movie would take. This project introduced the idea of a personal simulator: a place where an operator felt totally immersed in an alternate reality over which he or she had some control.

A special camera system mounted on a car filmed every street, corner, and building of Aspen. These pictures were combined with images from cranes, airplanes, and helicopters. This system allowed the viewer to be totally surrounded with images of Aspen without wearing any headgear. Interesting buildings would yield descriptive text for the participant, many could even be entered. The wealth of information stored on videodisks would even allow time travel through various seasons.

The mid-1980s saw a transition from the Arch-Mac to the Media Lab, newly founded by Negroponte. "Our charter is to invent and creatively exploit new media for human well-being and individual satisfaction." [8] Their focus is on what media technology might become in the future. To further that end, they build prototypes for demonstration. Indeed, their in-house slogan is "Demo or Die." Today the Media Lab is still working on some VR-related research. They have created autonomous computer characters that inhabit virtual worlds and devices the can transmit human tactile and kinesthetic senses.

> [Negroponte's] view of the future of desktop computing . . . is one where the bezel becomes a proscenium and agents are embodied to any degree of literalness you may desire. In the longer term, as holography prevails, little people will walk across your desk (if you have one) dispatched to do what they know how.
>
> The picture is simple. The stage is set with characters of your own choice or creation whose scripts are drawn from the play of your life. Their expressiveness, character, and propensity to speak out are driven by an event (external) and a style (yours). If you want your agents to wear bow ties, they will. If you prefer talking to parallelpipeds, fine. [9]

Atari Research

Nolan Brushnell was an engineer for Ampex, a recording equipment and tape manufacturer. He had an idea to build a coin-operated computer game. Although his first attempt was unsuccessful, his second—Pong—was a smash hit. Brushnell left Ampex and started his own company, Atari. In 1976 Atari was acquired by Warner Communications.

For a brief period of time during the early 1980s, while video games were generating huge profits and personal computers were new on the scene, Atari Research blossomed. Alan Kay was hired to assemble a team of researchers to dream up the entertainment and education media of the future, and they gave him the budget to make it happen. Kay's crew included former Xerox PARC and researchers including such names as Scott Fisher, Michael Naimak, Kristina

Hooper, and Eric Hulteen. Thomas Zimmerman, Brenda Laurel, Susan Brennan, Warren Robinett, and Jaron Lanier also joined the team.

The Atari Research crew was intent on building the system of the future, so they began by developing an extensive conceptual framework on which to hang their research. Their goal was to create a computer-generated responsive environment into which people could walk, and of which people could become a part. They followed Sutherland's vision with the unencumbering, Media Lab twist. While the video game boom didn't last, the conceptual framework and its creators moved on to such places as Apple Computers and NASA Ames.

Thomas Furness and the U.S. Air Force

The U.S. Air Force began to experiment with head-mounted displays (HMDs) in 1979 with the idea of reducing expenses and the system size by projecting the whole cockpit display directly into the pilot's eyes. One of the first of these systems, called VITAL, was produced by McDonnell Douglas. It made use of an electromechanical head tracker to determine head orientation and gaze. It had two monochromatic cathode ray tubes (CRTs) mounted next to the pilot's ears and projected using beam splitters. VITAL allowed the pilot to view and manipulate the mechanical controls in the cockpit while simultaneously viewing the world painted by computers. Problems with the bulky helmet and the unnaturalness of looking through beam splitters limited VITAL's usefulness.

The initial problem was encountered for the first time in the 1970s when the capabilities of advanced fighter aircraft began to exceed the capabilities of the humans that flew them. The F-15 has nine different buttons on the control stick, seven more on the throttle, and a bewildering array of gauges, switches, and dials. Using this system in the midst of the stress and confusion of battle, perhaps even when performing maneuvers at high-Gs on the verge of blackout, the pilot must always choose the correct combination of manipulations.

Thomas Furness III, chief of the Human Engineering Division of the Armstrong Aerospace Medical Research Laboratory (AAMRL) at Wright-Patterson Air Force Base, Ohio held a Ph.D. in engineering and applied science from the University of Southhampton, England and possessed a background in the creation of visual displays for the military back to 1966. Furness had some ideas on how to manage this deluge of information provided to pilots. He secured funding for a prototype system called Visually Coupled Airborne Systems Simulator (VCASS), first demonstrated in 1982.

VCASS test pilots wore Darth Vader—style helmets and sat in a cockpit mockup. The helmet featured a Polhemus tracking sensor to determine position, orientation, and gaze direction in six degrees of freedom. It used one-inch-diameter CRTs which displayed images at two thousand scan lines (about four times that of a television). VCASS totally immersed the pilot in a symbolic world, a world which was created to streamline the presentation of relevant information to the pilot. The world was created of symbols for much the same reason we use maps instead of photographs to find our way—it's easier.

The U.S. Air Force saw promise in VCASS and funded its second phase, called Super Cockpit. Thompson, in an *Air & Space* article, described what a Super Cockpit pilot might see:

> When he climbed into his F-16SC, the young fighter jock of 1998 simply plugged in his helmet and flipped down his visor to activate his Super Cockpit system. The virtual world he saw exactly mimicked the world outside. Salient terrain features were outlined and rendered in three dimensions by two tiny cathode ray tubes focused at his personal viewing distance. Using voice commands, the pilot told the associate to start the engine and run through the checklist . . .
>
> Once he was airborne, solid clouds obscured everything outside the canopy. But inside the helmet, the pilot "saw" the horizon and terrain clearly, as if it were a clear day. His compass heading was displayed as a large band of numbers on the horizon line, his projected flight path a shimmering highway leading out toward infinity.
>
> A faint whine above and behind him told the pilot even before the associate announced that his "enemy" . . . was closing in . . . .

Furness found a new way to combat the informat overload facing pilots of advanced fighter aircraft. His symbolic virtual worlds intelligently presented the important information from the aircraft's instruments and sensors while filtering out the irrelevant. He incorporated voice and sound cues to simplify the pilot's tasks and allowed the radar and sensor to become the pilot's eyes and ears.

NASA Ames Research Human Factors Division

Michael McGreevey, a Ph.D. student of Stephen Ellis at the University of California at Berkeley, was greatly interested in the psychological and technological aspects of three-dimensional and immersive displays. In 1981 McGreevey began a research program at NASA. McGreevey had been following Ivan Sutherland's pioneering work and knew of Thomas Furness and the system of the U.S. Air Force. In 1984 Scott Fisher was invited to speak at NASA about stereoscopic head-mounted displays. Ellis and McGreevey thought that this was a natural technology for the visual perception experiments they wished to explore. McGreevey created a proposal to build a prototype head-mounted display, for which he was granted $10,000.

McGreevey's first thought was to contact Furness. Unfortunately, a price tag of $1 million for the helmet alone was clearly outside of McGreevey's budget. A hardware contractor named James Humphries at Sterling General showed McGreevey a new technology called liquid crystal displays (LCDs), which were being used for small televisions and which could replace the most expensive part of the VCASS helmet, the CRTs. While the LCDs could only display 10,000 picture elements as opposed to the millions available on the VCASS system, the price was right. A motorcycle helmet with a special visor attachment and some additional optics to focus and expand the images completed the Virtual Visual Environment Display (VIVED), for a mere $2000.

McGreevey and Amy Wu, his support programmer, proceeded to create a computer system capable of driving their new display. They added a Polhemus head-tracking sensor to provide position and orientation information about the operator's head. The heart of the system was a PDP-11/40. The first virtual environment consisted of data from one of McGreevey's earlier projects involving air traffic control issues. The operator appeared to be standing on a computer-generated grid with three-dimensional wire-frame aircraft suspended in the surrounding air. McGreevey had a steady stream of visitors from academia, industry, and the U.S. military.

In 1985 NASA hired Scott Fisher, at which time Michael McGreevey went to Washington, D.C., for a two-year training assignment. Fisher brought the conceptual framework along with him from Atari Research. Fisher began to extend VIVED into a general-purpose test bed for visualization tools, surgical simulators, telerobotics, virtual workstations, among other research interests. While Fisher built, McGreevey ensured that the money continued to flow.

The VIVED HMD totally obscured the outside world, so keyboards and buttons were useless. Fisher added an off-the-shelf voice recognition system and later a voice synthesis package to echo your commands back to you. Fisher began searching for a contractor who could build a three-dimensional audio system. His search ended with Dr. Elizabeth Wenzel, Dr. Frederick Wightman of the University of Wisconsin, and Scott Foster of Crystal River Engineering. Their device, called the Convolvotron, mathematically modeled the human signal processing functions. This audio system allowed an operator to accurately pick out four different conversations and their directions—a natural capability of

Figure 6.5—View over Georgia Tech campus and downtown Atlanta from the north

human hearing known as the cocktail party effect, but not a capability of a conventional stereophonic system.

Fisher wished to experiment with tactile feedback (output) devices to enable an operator to easily manipulate objects in the virtual world. Fisher began negotiations with VPL Research. Thomas Zimmerman and Jaron Lanier created and patented a glove-based input device. Additional benefits came from adding the glove to the system: It greatly enhanced the virtual experience, and even a stick hand provides a perceptual anchor to the virtual world.

Warren Robinett joined the NASA team in 1986 and began to write the application code to tie the system together. He managed to create dramatic demonstrations even though he was constrained by the inexpensive equipment. His wireframe creations included architectural structures, hemoglobin molecules, the space shuttle, turbulence flow patterns, and stick figures. Douglas Kerr also joined the team and assumed the system software responsibilities.

In 1988 McGreevey returned from the East Coast and resumed control of the VIVED project, now called VIEW (Virtual Interfaces Environment Workstation). Kerr succeeded Robinett when he left, and began to port the software to a Hewlett Packard 9000 workstation which would provide enough power to draw shaded surfaces instead of wireframes. Scott Fisher left in 1990 to form Telepresence Research with Brenda Laurel.

NASA's low-cost virtual reality system was the first of its kind and proved that such a system could be built. They established a commercial contractor syndicate that could supply virtual environment components off-the-shelf. The NASA system also combined a head-mounted display with a glove in one system for the first time. The infancy of the commercial virtual reality market was at hand.

Jaron Lanier and VPL Research

Jaron has become a figure of virtual myth and legend. He is "a large, shaggy bear of a man, with his brown hair falling naturally around his bearded face like Jamaican-style dreadlocks." [10] Marvin Minsky believes "he is one of the few computer scientists who looks at a larger picture."

Lanier learned the art of programming at the height of the video game boom. He created his own games for Atari, including Moondust, which made enough money for him that he quit his job to pursue his other interests.

Thomas had an undergraduate degree from MIT and he loved to build things. He believed that the most significant part of the human body for gestural input to a music synthesizer had to be the hand; he really wanted to play air guitar. Zimmerman created a simple mechanism using bendable plastic tubes, an old glove, and some miscellaneous electric parts. The tubes were used to conduct light in much the same way as fiber optics. This system was not terribly accurate, but it worked and earned Zimmerman U.S. Patent No. 4,542,291.

Zimmerman worked at Atari Research while awaiting his patent, where he met Scott Fisher and Jaron Lanier, among others. In 1983 Lanier and Zimmerman attended a meeting of computerized musicians (people who used personal computers with their electronic synthesizers), at which Lanier spoke. Lanier discovered Zimmerman's glove-based interface to a computer. Lanier was in search of just such a device for his programming language, which used images and sounds instead of cryptic text.

Zimmerman and Lanier combined to form VPL Research. Jean-Jacques Grimaud joined VPL as president, while Lanier remained CEO. Grimaud brought a conservative business approach and a management background to VPL which served as counterpoint to Lanier's eclectic style. All of this is very important when you are trying to sell a $250,000 system to a conservative company.

Marvin and Margaret Minsky were VPL's first investors after Lanier's Moondust money ran out. Indeed, Margaret Minsky was responsible for telling Lanier to contact Scott Fisher, now of NASA. Thompson Avionics also became a major financial backer of VPL.

Zimmerman went to work on the next version of the glove. At Lanier's behest, the new glove included a Polhemus sensor to allow glove position and orientation to be determined. The new glove also incorporated fiber optics, Young Harvill's idea. Along with Charles Blanchard and Steve Bryson, Harvill also helped write the software to make the glove useful to a computer.

VPL Research delivered the glove to NASA for the VIVED system in 1986. Since all of NASA's work is in the public domain, VPL was well positioned to use the technology commercially. In 1988 VPL created the field of complete virtual reality systems, including an improved head-mounted display, based on the NASA design and dubbed EyePhones, and Scott Foster's Convolvotron for three-dimensional sound.

VPL went on the create a virtual world that could be shared by two people, called Reality Built for 2 (RB2), which used two Silicon Graphics workstations and an Apple Macintosh. They also introduced the DataSuit, which was essentially a DataGlove for the whole body including the orientation of the knees, neck, ankles, and wrists.

In 1987, VPL combined with Abrams-Gentile Entertainment and Mattel to create the ill-fated Mattel PowerGlove. The PowerGlove was an input device to the popular Nintendo video game. While the PowerGlove didn't have the accuracy of a DataGlove, it did sell for under $100. Unfortunately, the PowerGlove is no longer commercially available.

In mid-1992, Lanier removed himself from the day-to-day operations of VPL. In December 1992, Thompson CSF, VPL's largest creditor, seized the company's patents, which were being held as collateral for $1 million in loans. When VPL had failed to repay the loans and had run out of cash, management, backed by Thompson, fired the entire staff including Jaron Lanier. "Despite demand for its systems, VPL suffered from poor management, the failure to satisfy orders on time and disorganized research," claimed Jean-Jacques Grimaud, CEO of VPL. "Attempts to find fresh financial backing have also been unsuccessful."[11]

Frederick Brooks at the UNC Chapel Hill

The Department of Computer Science at the University of North Carolina at Chapel Hill has been quietly working on virtual environments–related research since the 1960s. Frederick Brooks Jr., directs the efforts at the facility, supported by many capable researchers including Henry Fuchs, Stephen Pizer, and until recently Warren Robinett. Unlike many other institutions, UNC has used tactile feedback since the beginning.

Brooks is already a legend in the computing field. He directed the team that developed the IBM 360 series operating system, undoubtedly the greatest programming feat of its time. Brooks authored *The Mythical Man-Month*, a very important book of computer culture. This book attempted to discredit the still-prevalent notion that the measurement of labor called the man-month can be applied to software programming. He demonstrated that doubling the number of programmers will in effect guarantee that the project will become at least six months farther behind schedule—an idea with which most programmers will agree.

Brooks espouses a concept called intelligence amplification, a concept similar to Engelbart's intelligence augmentation. Brooks sees three areas in which human minds are more powerful than any computer yet designed. "The first of these is pattern recognition, whether visual or aural. Computer Scientists don't even have good ways of approximating the pattern recognition power a one-week-old baby uses to recognize its mother's face from an angle and with lighting it has never seen before." The second area he calls evaluations. "Every time you go to the supermarket, you're performing the kind of evaluations that the computer algorithms we have today can only roughly approximate." The third area is in "the overall sense of context that enables us to recall, at the appropriate moment, something that was read in an obscure journal twenty years previously, in reference to a completely different subject, that we suddenly see to be meaningful."

Brooks also sees three areas in which computers are more capable than humans. These are the "evaluations of computations, storing massive amounts of data, and remembering things without forgetting." Brooks wishes to combine human and computer strengths in one system. The most difficult part of building such a system is creating the interface. Brooks points to Sutherland's 1965 paper "The Ultimate Display" as the reference for designing such an interface.

Brooks believes in using a "driving problem" philosophy to make technological advances. The best such advances are made when real applications are created while attempting to solve a carefully selected problem. Good collaborators are essential to keep everybody honest. Brooks has selected several driving problems that both push computer science and solve real problems of value.

In 1965 Brooks attended a conference where Ivan Sutherland spoke about "The Ultimate Display." Brooks became excited about the possibilities and committed himself to research that allows people, in Sutherland's words, "to gain familiarity with concepts not realizable in the physical world." In 1969, Brooks acquired a special graphics computer from IBM. Brooks also had a very capable graduate student named William Wright. Brooks went to the UNC provost to find out, "Who on this faculty most deserves to have his intelligence amplified?" He wanted a collaborator whose problem had a high geometric content—might as well deal in three-space as an abstract space. The problem should be too hard for a machine algorithm alone and too hard for a human to solve by insight alone. The problem must require a great deal of calculation. Eventually Brooks began working with Jan Hermans, a protein chemist; the first driving problem became the structure of life molecules in nucleic acids. Brooks wrote, "If watching imaginary objects move and alter as one manipulates them endows them with a kind of real existence, and if this process yields more power for understanding and designing imaginary objects, can we build yet more powerful tools by using more sense?"

The GRIP-71 system was designed by Wright and Hermans in 1971. The GROPE-I system was also finished in 1971 by James Batter, another graduate

Figure 6.6—One time step in a molecular dynamics simulation. A NaCl cluster smashing into a Ne surface.

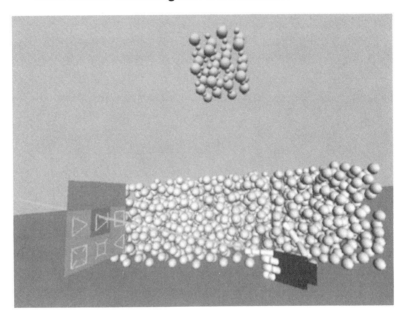

student of Brooks. In 1972 Brooks and his students began combining force-reflection feedback with interactive computer graphics. By serendipity the team ended up with a pair of orphaned Argonne Remote Manipulators (ARMs) from Argonne National Laboratories, with thanks to Raymond Goertz, the original ARM designer. The ARM was a master–slave system that enabled humans behind a lead shield to manipulate radioactive substances by using machines that mimicked what they did with their own hands. The team substituted the computer for the slave part of the ARM. The GROPE-II system allowed seven virtual children's blocks to be manipulated by tongs on a table in a wireframe world. Anything beyond this task was simply beyond the capability of computers at this time, so the project was mothballed.

In 1986 Ming Ouh-Young undertook to produce the GROPE-III system using a Vax computer. This system allowed a chemist to manipulate virtual molecules with the ARMs, twisting and turning molecules until they "fit" together and made a proper bond. This system worked twice as well as the next-best system for determining new chemical combinations. Currently a consolidation of the many different molecular studies tools developed is under way as a new project called Trailblazer. Trailblazer is to bring "a unified support base that will radically reduce the effort at building new prototype visualization tools, for each tool will have data structures and many classes of graphics, interaction, molecular computation, and geometric functions already built, tested, and available."

In 1985 Brooks and his team selected another driving problem, termed architectural walkthrough. Brooks says, "It has the tremendous advantage that sooner or later the building gets built and you can compare the real and the virtual worlds and see how far away you are from realism." The heart of the problem is that while architects and engineers claim to be able to visualize three-dimensional structures from working drawings, few of their clients can make this claim. This leads to costly revisions when things don't work right. One way of dealing with this is to immerse someone in a three-dimensional world of that structure built from its design specifications. This allows people to wander around in the building and suggest changes long before expensive working drawings have been constructed.

Medical imaging is the latest driving problem adopted by Brooks. These projects include Radiation Treatment Planning in the field of radiation oncology. Computer graphics and virtual environments are allowing more precise use of radiation, maximizing effectiveness while minimizing exposure. See-Through Ultrasound allows a physician to "look into" a pregnant mother and "see" the developing baby. This would be useful for such things as watching an amniocentesis probe in relation to the baby. The X-Ray Vision project is superimposing a computer-generated world on the real world allowing ultrasound, computed tomography (CT), magnetic resonance imaging (MRI), or other imaging techniques to be overlaid on a patient. In this manner, a surgeon planning reconstructive surgery can see the real soft tissue and underneath it the three-dimensional bone at the same time.

Brooks and the UNC Chapel Hill staff are quietly pushing the envelope of virtual environments research. They utilize a driving problem philosophy to push the limits of computer science while solving real problems of value.

Thomas Furness and the HIT Lab

Thomas Furness III founded and became the director of the Human Interface Technology Laboratory (HIT Lab) in 1989. Furness was previously chief of the Visual Display System Branch, Human Engineering Division of the Armstrong

Aerospace Medical Research Laboratory (AAMRL) at Wright-Patterson Air Force Base, Ohio, and brought 23 years of virtual worlds experience to the HIT Lab. Furness is also a professor of industrial engineering at the University of Washington, conducting classes in human factors and the design of virtual world technology.

The HIT Lab is part of the Washington Technology Center (WTC), located on the University of Washington campus in Seattle, Washington. The HIT Lab was established "to transform virtual environment concepts and early research into practical, market-driven products, and processes." The Lab is strongly backed by ARPA and the Virtual Worlds Consortium—a commercial team who financially back, help chart research directions for, and make use of HIT Lab technology.

The GreenSpace project will demonstrate an immersive trans-Pacific communications medium. The U.S. participants will appear to be seated in a Japanese-style meeting room with Mt. Fuji in the background, while the Japanese participants will be immersed in an American-style meeting room with Mt. Rainier in the background. The participants will see photorealistic facial texture maps of their counterparts which are animated with a speech vowel recognition system. This teleconferencing system will initially feature a teamwork-making game. The HIT Lab hopes to connect more than 100 participants over broadband networks such as SONET/ATM.

One of the most exciting projects at the HIT Lab is the Virtual Retinal Display (VRD). The VRD is a display that draws an image directly on the retina. The system uses a custom-developed mechanical resonant scanner which provides both vertical and horizontal scanning, with large scan angles. This full-color, stereo display will eventually be provided in a package about the size of a pair of glasses, priced to compete with conventional displays.

The sci.virtual-worlds Usenet newsgroup was originally established through the efforts of Howard Rheingold, with help from Furness. Rheingold passed the moderating responsibilities on to the HIT Lab staff, currently led by Toni Emerson, "Cybrarian Extraordinaire." Emerson is also responsible for creating and maintaining the extensive virtual environments research facilities and repositories, including an excellent web server. The sci.virtual-worlds newsgroup acts as a clearing house for discussion, ideas, and technology transfer in the virtual environments field.

Other initiatives include Chemistry World, Telemedicine, and Architecture VR. All of the HIT Lab projects emphasize the pragmatic basis of this organization.

Conclusion

The history of virtual environments is somewhat longer and more complex than such a seemingly young and vital field would dictate. No doubt exists that Sutherland should be credited with the modern beginnings of this field. However, honorable mentions must be made of Heilig for his early efforts and of Link for his work in flight simulation.

Now that you've got some understanding of the past of virtual environments, let's take a look at the current applications and research directions of the field.

CHAPTER *7*

A TOUR OF APPLICATIONS

Introduction

You should now have some perspective on the past of virtual worlds research. Now it's time to explore present and near-future applications for virtual environments. Although many of these systems are prototypes or under development, they represent common themes about problems that may be solved using virtual environments technology. So here begins a tour of virtual environment applications.

Architectural Walkthroughs and Computer-Aided Design

Computer-aided design and architectural walkthroughs are among the most intuitive applications for virtual environments. Both types of applications are essentially representations of three-space designs: objects meant to be built or manufactured. This category enables virtual environments designers to test concepts, constructions, and realism—which is why many of the major research institutions, such as UNC Chapel Hill, Georgia Tech, and the HIT Lab, are undertaking advanced concept programs in this area.

Frederick Brooks and the University of North Carolina in Chapel Hill are pioneers in the field of architectural walkthrough—one of Brooks' driving problems. They create virtual environments from architectural drawings and renderings—environments through which clients may walk and view a building long before the costly working drawings are created. The UNC researchers use

Figure 7.1—Aerial view of the GVU Center lab

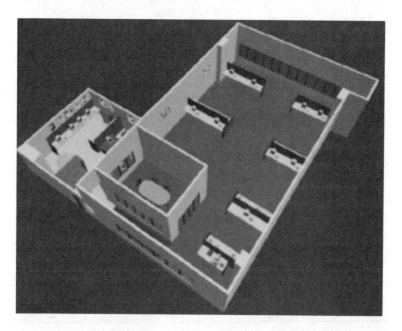

head-mounted displays or large-screen monitors to provide video; joysticks; a custom three-dimensional mouse; a steerable treadmill; and even a room-sized area with a ceiling-based head-tracker.[12]

The Human Interface Technology Lab (HIT Lab) and the Cascadia Community and Environment Institute at the College of Architecture and Urban Planning (CAUP) at the University of Washington is developing the Community and Environmental Design and Simulation (CEDeS) Lab. This lab will feature design and simulation facilities capable of supporting three-dimensional architectural design and modeling with virtual environments technology. The

CEDeS Lab will become integrated into the CAUP cirriculum and used to study methods of design, planning and community development. Perhaps most importantly, it will make virtual environments more accessible to the design community.[13]

The city of Berlin, now no longer divided, contracted with the German company Art+Com and VPL Research to model the city of Berlin in VPL's Virtual Reality environment. The model will help in planning the reconstruction of the city and many of its buildings. Several buildings are completely modeled, including the national gallery.[14]

A department store's kitchen sales area in Tokyo, Japan has a VPL system. "The salesman takes down the measurements of the kitchen at your house. Then you put on goggles and glove and suddenly you're in a room the size of your kitchen." You can design your kitchen by moving things around the virtual environment until everything is the way you want it. The cabinet doors open and the water faucet works. If you're happy with the design, you sign a form, and the store delivers and installs your new kitchen. Matsushita Electric Works intends to extend this vision to include a complete house, allowing the owner to design and try out the house in cyberspace. [15]

Lockheed Corporation's Optical Design Group under the auspices of NASA created a virtual prototype of the Hubble Space Telescope primary mirror aberration repair equipment. This virtual environment allowed engineers to find several problems before the physical prototype was built, as well as determine the best positions for cameras to properly test the space hardware and ensure all the parts would fit. This virtual prototype saved time and money by finding errors that would have slipped the construction schedule.[16]

NASA's Marshall Space Flight Center in Huntsville, Alabama has constructed a "low fidelity space station to help pathfind and check out the system." They have also created a virtual mockup of the shuttle payload bay which is used by astronauts to familiarize themselves with equipment storage layouts for their missions.[17]

Communications and Interfaces

Enabling communications in manners never thought of before, including as interfaces to computers and machinery, is perhaps the area with the largest potential for virtual environments applications. Communicating with other people in ways that more resemble fact-to-face communications has long been a goal of virtual environments creators. Telepresence and teleoperation are terms gaining rapidly in popularity that essentially provide humans better ways to communicate, explore, analyze, and diagnose remote and potentially hazardous areas from the safety and convenience of home.

Paul Marshall of Maxus Systems International has created a desktop, three-dimensional virtual landscape of multicolored squares that have varying heights. The rows of data represent financial markets such as Hong Kong or Tokyo, while columns represent different stocks. Textures are used to identify columns and rows. The whole system is supplied with data from a Reuters news feed. The financial analyst can "fly" over the landscape, scoping for information about the changing relationships of the world's stock markets. [18]

The Boeing Company, the Human Interface Technology Lab, and the University of Washington are exploring ways of augmenting factory floor workers. These applications superimpose information such as overlays or templates directly on the work. This allows information to be updated and customized easily without the need to manufacture expensive precision templates. Other augmented realities include virtual manuals, oscilloscope readouts, schematics, or drill-hole locations which can be positioned anywhere within easy reach or sight.[19]

Ronald Pickett of the University of Massachusetts at Lowell has developed a virtual world that looks like grass. The blades of grass may change length, curve, and arc to represent data such as income level, age, and sex. According to Pickett, the selection of grass goes back to our genetic makeup and the reflexes our forebears needed for survival. Our highly optimized information-gathering systems can be put directly to use with the selection of a proper metaphor (such as grass).[20]

The Virtual Environment Vehicle Interface (VEVI) created by NASA Ames has been successfully interfaced to a Russian Mars rover. VEVI provides a three-dimensional view to the operator. The system can manipulate a remote vehicle even with a time delay of up to 40 minutes (which is how long it takes to send a command to Mars and get an image back). VEVI has also been used to pilot an unstaffed submarine to explore the waters of McMurdo Sound in the Antarctic. Researchers learned about operating vehicles remotely under harsh conditions, while exobiologists learned about the life evolving under the permanently frozen lakes.[21]

Figure 7.2—Interaction with a three-dimensional visualization of molecular data

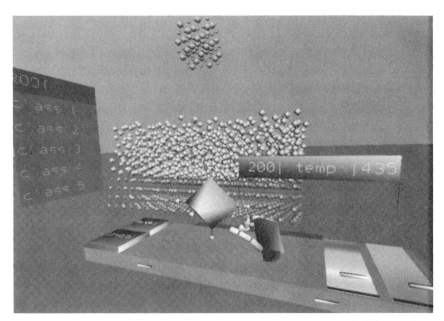

The Monterey Bay Aquarium Research Institute in Monterey, California, has been "using a remotely operated vehicle to compile a detailed record of the cavernous underwater Monterey Cavern." The system includes a three-dimensional stereoscopic view, which provides distinct advantages over two-dimensional views, especially when the robot arm is being used to pick up a delicate object off the ocean floor. [22]

Scientific Research

Virtual environments are giving researchers in basic science and the applied sciences a whole new set of tools with which to visualize and analyze theories and gather data. It is interesting to note that many of the first virtual environments involved the creation of molecules. Scientific visualization is one of the big buzz words these days. Virtual environments provide an excellent way to study micro-sized worlds and the collision of galaxies. Virtual environments also provide a more intuitive way of studying abstract spaces by providing more dimensions with which to work.

Frederick Brooks and the University of North Carolina in Chapel Hill's Computer Science Department chose the study of the structure of life molecules in nucleic acids as their first driving problem in virtual worlds research. The GROPE and SCULPT systems combine a large-screen monitor and goggles to provide a three-dimensional real-time display of the environment. An Argonne Remote Manipulator (ARM) provides force feedback during interactions with the virtual world. The system allows chemists to interactively manipulate molecular models which obey physical laws—in this manner chemists can determine potential new compounds of interest. These researchers have also created a virtual e nvironment interface, called a nanomanipulator, for a scanning--tunneling microscope. This allows the scientist to "approximate presence at the atomic scale" and modify the environment interactively. In effect, the scientist could build a custom silicon chip, one atom at a time. [23]

The Electronic Visualization Laboratory at the University of Illinois in Chicago has created a fully immersive virtual environment called the Cave (Cave Automatic Virtual Environment). The Cave uses projectors to display a three-dimensional image on three walls and the floor; participants don special glasses to see this image in three dimensions. Three-dimensional sound cues are also provided. One of the Cave's strengths is that several participants may work together in the shared environment. [24]

The Virtual Reality Applications Research Team of the Department of Manufacturing Engineering and Operations Management at the University of Nottingham is comparing quicker virtual reality systems using collision detection and "traditional labor-intensive mathematical modeling procedures to see whether the VR system can provide comparable accuracy in describing particle behavior" in a simulation of "discrete element flow both through static walled hoppers and rotating elliptical hoppers." [25]

NASA has a virtual wind tunnel where, using a boom-mounted display and a glove, a scientist can "explore the aerodynamic intricacies of air streaming past an airplane in a virtual wind tunnel." [26]

Training

Flight simulation provides some of the original history for virtual environments research as well as some of the high-end research. The original reason for the creation of flight simulators was to train pilots safely. Training is a natural field in which virtual environments are flourishing—practicing hazardous maneuvers in the safety of a warm computer.

The Advanced Research Projects Agency (ARPA) has created SIMNET, a worldwide network of (relatively) inexpensive simulators that allow soldiers in vehicle simulators to fight mock battles without regard to cost, safety, environmental impact, geographic boundaries, or the constraints of time. Simulators ranging from the M1 Abrams main battle tank to the A-10 close combat support fighter to the AH-64 Apache attack helicopter all fight together

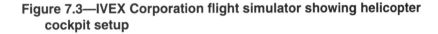

Figure 7.3—IVEX Corporation flight simulator showing helicopter cockpit setup

in the same battles. While these simulators are not full-blown training simulators, all of the viewports show the battle going on around the vehicle while battle sounds thunder around the operators. These battles provide a great deal of real operational training both for the unit operators and for their commanders—some tanks get lost, some run out of fuel, all briefings and debriefings are handled in the same manner as for a real battle.

NEC Corporation has developed a virtual ski training system. The trainee dons a three-dimensional, wide-field-of-view, head-mounted display, stands on two movable steel plates, and grasps the ski poles. The computer monitors foot

Figure 7.4—"A virtual party" (Virtual Research HMD and a Cyberglove data glove)

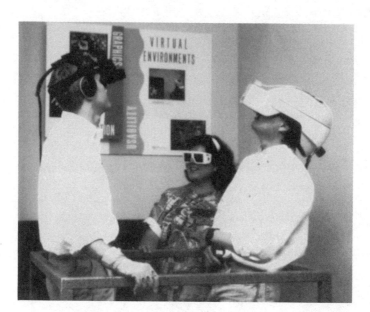

position, stance, and blood flow through a finger (to estimate stress). The system decides an appropriate difficulty and speed of the simulation. [27]

SRI International of Menlo Park, California, has built a virtual environment to train the ground crew that direct aircraft to park. The combination of a head-mounted display and gloves allows a trainee to direct aircraft, even into virtual buildings which cost (virtually) nothing to repair. [28]

Entertainment

In many ways entertainment may become the driving force for virtual environments. A great deal of money is available for research and creation and a great deal of money exists to be made. Certainly the entertainment industry will drive down the cost of low-end virtual environment equipment.

Carnegie Mellon University has a team of researchers creating a Networked Virtual Art Museum. The multicultural contributors will be invited to create galleries or individual works for the distributed museum. "Guest curators will have the opportunity to organize special exhibitions, explore advanced concepts, and formulate the basis for critical theory pertaining to virtual reality and cultural expression."[29]

W Industries of the United Kingdom has created several "Virtuality" games including Dactyl Nightmare, Capture the Flag, and Legend Quest. Each unit consists of a single-person-sized stand, a head-mounted display with built-in sound and position sensors, and a joystick that controls walking and a virtual weapon. The virtual worlds are three-dimensional, if cartoon-like, and the illusion suffers from lag. However, consumers are presented with an inexpensive and enjoyable trip into a virtual environment and are often so engrossed in the action that the quality is of less importance. [30]

Chicago may be the home of the largest installed base of virtual reality units, BattleTech. Thirty-two people can sit in separate BattleMech—robo-tank— cockpits, each surrounded by controls, a large forward-view screen, and a small satellite-view screen. All of the units may play against each other or in teams. [31]

Medicine and Virtual Environments

The field of medicine may be fundamentally changed by the application of virtual environments techniques. Here is presented an overview of many of the types of applications being researched and tested to give you an idea how many different facets of one field of technology can be affected. For instance, minimally invasive surgical techniques were introduced in 1987; by 1992 these techniques accounted for 85% of all gallstone operations performed in the U.S.[32] Minimally invasive surgery consists of inserting a catheter into the patient. This catheter must wind its way through the human body to the point of the intended operation or diagnosis. Small cameras and miniature instruments allow the surgeon to guide and perform surgery. While these techniques have been wonderfully successful for reducing postoperative problems, the interfaces are totally foreign to the conventional skills possessed by most surgeons. For instance, typically displays are two-dimensional, while the operating space is three-dimensional. No force-feedback exists that can replace a surgeon's ability to poke and prod tissue.

Figure 7.5—Ocular surgery simulator—fusable stereo pair

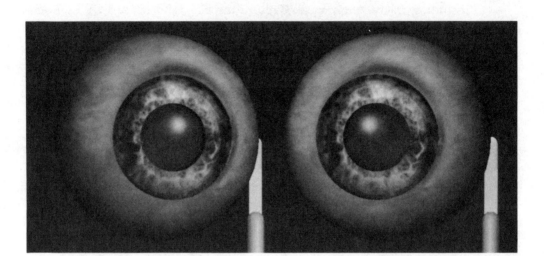

Visualization Tools

Philip Green at SRI International has developed a Telepresence Surgery System which provides a more natural human interface to minimally invasive procedures. Surgeons can operate at a workstation with all the "motor, visual and sensory responses that they would experience having their heads and hands right inside the patient." A system designed especially for laparoscopic surgery is under development. [33]

The Department of Neurosurgery at the Mayo Clinic in Rochester, Minnesota, has developed the COMPASS system. COMPASS is a three-dimensional stereotactic system that interactively utilizes robotic technology and a carbon dioxide laser to perform volumetric tumor resection and digital angiography. [34]

Brigham and Women's Hospital is working with General Electric's Research and Development Center to combine two-dimensional magnetic resonance imaging (MRI) pictures to form three-dimensional pictures of the brain. With special goggles, the brain may be viewed in three dimensions from any angle, even from inside. A few keyboard clicks allow the gray matter to be peeled away to show the white matter. [35]

Henry Fuchs at the University of North Carolina in Chapel Hill is heading a large effort to employ computer graphics and virtual environments techniques in medicine. James Chung is developing a CAD tools to help radiotherapists in radiation treatment planning. The See-Through Ultrasound project is combining two-dimensional ultrasound images to provide real-time video which can be overlaid on stationary objects. For example, a physician can "see" the baby inside a pregnant woman while guiding an amniocentesis probe. The X-Ray Vision project is using x-ray, computed tomography (CT) , magnetic resonance imaging (MRI), ultrasound, or other image sources in a similar fashion.[36]

Communications

The Virtual Reality Applications Research Team of the Department of Manufacturing Engineering and Operations Management at the University of Nottingham, working with a local Nottingham school, has developed a system to help teach intellectually handicapped children the Makaton communications scheme. The system provides three-dimensional virtual images, the symbol, the word, and the sign language representation if applicable. Video sequences are planned to allow the children to interact with the system.[37]

A number of organizations have combined gloves with voice synthesizers to allow the translation of either a sign language or custom gestures to speech or as an input to a computer or telephone. Some of these organizations include: Stanford University; Greenleaf Medical; Artificial Realities Systems with the Department of Computer Science at the Universita' degli Studi di Milano and the Ente Nazionale Sordomuti; the University of Tasmania Computer Science Department, in Hobart, Tasmania, Australia; the University of Toronto, Canada; and Loma Linda University's Advanced Technology Center.[38]

Figure 7.6—Virtual view from a balcony overlooking a lobby

Treatment

The Phobia Project, at the Georgia Institute of Technology's Graphics, Visualization, and Usability Center under the direction of James Foley and Larry Hodges, is studying the use of virtual reality graded exposure in the treatment of acrophobia—the fear of high places. As part of the treatment, patients are exposed to a 50-story virtual glass elevator.[39]

The Loma Linda University Advanced Technology Center is developing a Neuro-Rehabilitation Workstation (NRW). The system incorporates pressure sensors, biofeedback, EEG, electromyogram, TekScan sensors, an eye-tracking system, a glove, and a Convolvotron in an advanced visualization workstation. The NRW is being used as a diagnostic and therapeutic device for such problems as "Parkinson's disease, Huntington's chorea, Alzheimer's disease, and physical disorders resulting from severe accidents and birth defects" in a manner that interjects play with rehabilitation to improve motivation.[40]

Training and Simulation

Michael Sinclair and the Georgia Institute of Technology's Multimedia Lab, in collaboration with the Medical College of Georgia, has developed a prototype ocular surgery simulator. This system combines photorealistic three-dimensional stereo images of the anterior ocular structures with surgical instrumentation which provides elementary tactile feedback. The tool–tissue interaction algorithms are very realistic and provide reasonable tactile feedback.[41]

Dartmouth Hitchcock Medical Center, in conjunction with MIT's Media Lab Computer Graphics and Animation Group, is developing a finite-element—based surgical simulator which models the nonlinear characteristics of skeletal muscles. The simulator utilizes a whole-hand input glove and a head-mounted display. Eventually the system could be used to "perform microsurgery on nerves or blood vessels, controlled through Virtual Reality techniques at a 'human scale' more comfortable for people."[42]

Dr. Richard Satava of the U.S. Army Medical Center at Fort Ord is developing a surgical simulator for the inner abdomen. It includes several instruments to support virtual surgery, but will also support flying through the system to help learn anatomy. [43]

For the past 10 years the University of Washington's Department of Biological Structures has been developing a digital model of the human body for the Digital Anatomist program. Two-dimensional tissue sections are hand-digitized by anatomists, then combined by computer to form three-dimensional computer images. The Human Interface Technology Lab has been collaborating with the UW to create a virtual interface browser to the Digital Anatomist database. The browser may be overlaid on a simulation of opthalmic surgery using a see-through head-mounted display. The simulator handles video display and the collision detection of instruments with virtual objects. [44]

Conclusion

In many ways the virtual environments field is in its infancy, and while many problems exist which must be addressed, the field seems to have achieved some sort of critical mass. Governments, academia, and industry from all around the world are investing large sums of money in research and development. Most virtual environments projects are prototypes and proof-of-concept models. However, applications are beginning to become available, and the hardware prices are dropping. Before too long, it appears that virtual environments will graduate from a trendy topic to a ubiquitous and unnoticed one.

CHAPTER 8

HUMAN PERCEPTION

Introduction

Human beings are tremendously versatile and adaptable creatures. This may be our greatest strength as a species. We live in nearly every climate all over the world, from the frigid wastelands of the north to the steamy jungles of the equator and pretty much everywhere in between. Much of our adaptability is based on our brain's ability to perceive patterns of information from relatively little data. This strength comes at a price—we are extremely susceptible to illusion. Yet illusion is not all bad by any means. Without illusion we could never match colors, or be fooled into believing we were immersed within a three-dimensional, virtual environment.

Okay, this is all fine and dandy, but what does this have to do with creating virtual environments? If you want to create useful, believable virtual environments where people will live and play, you must possess some understanding of how the human body functions, in addition to understanding

199

all the mathematics of creating worlds from pixels on a screen. So let's take a brief tour of the human senses to learn how they work and how they can be fooled.

The Human Eye

> The eye, whilst it makes us see and perceive all other things, takes no notice of itself.
>
> —John Locke, *Essay Concerning Human Understanding*

The human eye may be the most flexible and advanced viewing system on the planet. Other animal eyes can beat the human eye in a particular category—the hawk at distance, the harbor seal for dark sensitivity—but only the human eye can zoom from watching a fly washing its nasty little head to picking out the Andromeda Galaxy two million light years away. It can display 10 million colors, yet register a single photon. Animals can be nearly as cleanly separated from the plant kingdom by the presence of eyes as by motility. Indeed, the very origin of eyes is thought to lie in the demands of motility: Early swimming life forms developed visual pads to enable them to swim towards the light and away from shadows (or hovering predators blocking the light). This theory also neatly explains the crossover of the visual fields in the brain: To swim toward the light, you wiggle your fin on the opposite side of your body.

The human eye sits in a bony socket on a cushion of fat. Six muscles hold the eyeball in a sling, allowing it to rotate freely. Light entering the eye initially encounters a transparent tissue called the cornea. Beneath the cornea is the colored part of the eye known as the iris, at the center of which is a dark hole called the pupil. Radial and circular muscles in the iris allow the pupil to expand and contract. Bright lights and close focusing cause the iris to contract, while dim lights and far focusing cause it to expand, allowing more light to enter the eye. Emotions also affect the pupil; an unpleasant sight can make the pupil contract (to shut out the pain?). Danger, and the opposite sex, cause the pupil to expand (some sort of relationship, maybe?).

Residing just beneath the pupil is the lens. Between them is a nutrient-rich fluid called aqueous humor. The pupil deforms to focus an image of light on the

Figure 8.1—The human eye

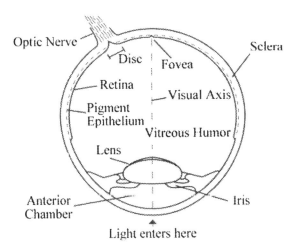

retina, all the way at the back of the eye. While the lens of a camera changes focus by moving back and forth, the lens of the eye changes focus by thickening and rounding to focus near images and flattening to focus far images. Age causes the geometry of the eye to change: The lens thickens, requiring many of us to need reading glasses.

The interior of the eye is filled with a fluid called vitreous humor. At the back of the eye, the retina, converts light images into nerve impulses. This conversion process requires light to be absorbed by light-sensitive chemicals such as rhodopsin. Carrots and other vegetables help replenish our body's supply of these chemicals, helping us to see.

Our eye contains two types of light-sensitive cells, named for their shapes: rods and cones. The 125 million rod cells are responsible for dim, gray-scale—night—vision; they may be found all over the retina, but are more concentrated at the periphery. Rod cells also respond to light more slowly than cone cells, which explains why it takes longer for your eyes to adapt to a dark theater than to the bright street afterwards. However, once adapted, the rods are quicker to detect fleeting movement out of the "corner" of your eye.

The 7 million cone cells are predominately located at the center of the retina, an area called the macula lutea. For hundreds of years scientist have felt that three types of color receptors must account for our color vision, but until recently—through the microspectrophotometry of excised retinas and reflection densitometry of living eyes—no objective evidence of this had been presented.[45] These three receptors are often referred to as red, green, and blue. However, they don't all peak at these colors, and their responses overlap, especially the red and green. This overlap is important in that it allows us to distinguish related colors, because the brain measures the ratios of excitations. While this is a powerful strategy for identifying colors, side effects result. Certain look-alike colors, called metamers, may be built from different spectral components; the eye cannot distinguish these differences although a spectrophotometer can. This turns out to be a good thing: Without metamers, color printing, photography, and color television would not exist as we know them. Worse, Barney purple on dolls would not match the Barney purple of rugs (gasp! horror!). As it turns out, the three-primary video system is an efficient way of driving the color vision of humans. Red, green, and blue (say, 650, 520, and 436 nm) are chosen as the primary colors because they encompass most colors.

The center of the macula lutea, at the center of the retina, is a pinhole-sized region called the fovea which contains roughly 4000 cones but no rods. Almost every cone in the fovea has its own nerve fiber, which provides this region the highest bandwidth available anywhere directly to the brain. The rest of the cells on the retina must share time on a nerve fiber, which reduces the sharpness of the image. The fovea is directed anywhere requiring sharpness, because this is such a small area it is kept moving constantly, flicking from letter to letter on a page.

You might think that what with the fovea moving constantly, the lens focusing, the pupil contracting and expanding, and the eye rotating rapidly that the image held by the brain would be bouncing constantly like an amateur camcorder video. The eye is wholly unlike any video or still camera; the eye has no shutter and no scanning raster (at least, not like any camera). The bundles of ever-changing streaks on our retina are translated by an incredibly efficient image processing system, the brain. In short, those creatures whose visual processing systems failed to stabilize the scenery died in short order. The human visual system is also not hampered by any adherence to Euclidean geometry; parallel lines can and do converge on the retina. Interestingly, the light-sensitive cells on the retina of vertebrates are *beneath* the blood supply system. The signal processing of the brain "hides" these from our image. This same trick is used to hide our blind spot.

The blind spot has neither rods nor cones. This is the part of the retina where the one million nerve fibers combine to form the optic nerve, the pathway to the brain. The optic nerves travel from the retinas to a meeting place in front of the pituitary gland, the optic chasm. Here, those optic nerve strands carrying signals from the right side of each eye split to send their signals to the left hemisphere, while those from the left side of each eye head for the right hemisphere of the brain for further processing.

The optic nerve dumps out at the lateral geniculate body, deep inside the brain. Oddly, the information stream is next sent all the way to the rear of the brain, the area farthest from the eyes, called the striate cortex. The striate cortex passes the data along to the inferior temporal cortex and the posterior parietal cortex for advanced processing. In these areas objects are broken up into different attributes; edges are analyzed independently of overall shape, spots of color are handled separately from areas of widespread color—this constitutes the object pathway. Position, with respect to visual landmarks, is assessed separately in its own spatial pathway. The brain works massively in parallel, with individual neurons flagging certain object properties only and no others. The tremendous efficiency of the brain allows us to recognize a pattern from almost no information; the flip side to this strange attribute processing is that we are vulnerable to a wide variety of optical illusions. [46]

Despite the fact that Aristotle described the "waterfall" illusion in the fourth century[47] (where after a few minutes of watching a waterfall, the scenery around you appears to move up), people still generally have the attitude that "seeing is believing" and can be quite reluctant to admit that their eyesight can play tricks on them.[48] Illusions that fool most of us may not even be perceived by other people. For instance, geometrical illusions are not normally perceived by people who live in "non-orthogonal" worlds. The Zulus live in round huts which have round doors; they plow their fields in curves and they don't even have a word for "square" in their language.[49] The Jalé tribe of New Guinea describe things only in terms of lightness and darkness—they have no specific words for color.[50] Cultural background and previous visual experience can greatly affect the perception of illusions that are the basis of computer graphics today; this must be considered as part of virtual environments design.

Three-dimensional computer graphics uses optical illusions to fool our eyes into believing that some object on a computer monitor is closer or farther than the actual monitor. Illusions of this nature work because humans have two eyes whose visual fields overlap significantly. As a result, we have developed binocular vision, the ability to locate objects in three dimensions (out to about 100 feet). Although it is apparent to us today that these separate visual channels can be fed different perspectives artificially to mimic the sensation of seeing in three dimensions, this experiment apparently was not attempted until 1832, when Sir Charles Wheatstone invented the stereoscope. Holograms, head-mounted displays, and wicked fast computers have revived an interest in three-dimensional displays, although most of us still stare at flat, two-dimensional displays.

An interesting fact for all virtual environments designers to bear in mind is that stress impairs our binocular vision. A case in point is the naval battle of Jutland, in 1916. The British rangefinders used to aim the big battleship guns were mechanical contraptions that matched two images with the turn of a crank. In contrast, the Germans had state-of-the-art Zeiss rangefinders which were based on an optical enhancement of the gunners' stereo vision. When the big shells began to fall, they lost their stereo perception and were helpless. The British were just as terrified, but their horribly antiquated coincidence rangefinders scored hit after hit.

Sound and the Human Ear

Those born blind dream of touch, sound, smell.[51]

The sounds of falling bomb shells, the wind blowing in trees, little feet pattering, and dogs barking all conjure up vivid ideas of our dynamically changing environment. Sound provides most humans with a natural complement to sight and, along with gestures, forms the basis of most human languages. Our two ears provide most of us with binaural hearing; we hear in stereo. This provides us with the ability to determine from what direction most sounds originate. An even more interesting ability is known as the cocktail party effect, where a listener in a crowded and noisy room full of people can "tune into" and follow several different conversations without them becoming entangled. Present us with even the highest fidelity monaural (mono) recording of that same party, and we would be helpless to repeat this process. Well-made binaural recordings, delivered to our ears by headphones or surround sound systems, enable us to

Figure 8.2—The human ear

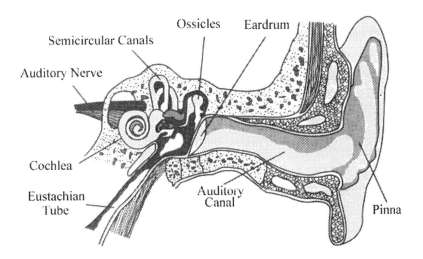

recover much of this ability. One of the most recent developments is three-dimensional sound reproduction, which can fully duplicate this effect.

A sound, such as a corn chip bag rustling, is actually composed of lots of air molecules bumping around. When the bag moves, it forces some of the air molecules away from it—this group of molecules is called a shell of compression. As this shell moves, it bumps into other molecules, setting them into motion. Behind the shell is an area with fewer than average molecules, called rarefied air, which encourages the surrounding air with more molecules to expand into its space. The moving bag creates three-dimensional "waves" of sound. The peaks contain more molecules than the troughs, moving at 1100 feet per second through air and even faster through liquids and solids. Eventually, the sound encounters a human ear. . . .

The human ear is primarily concerned with two physical attributes of sound, frequency and amplitude. Frequency (pitch) describes the number of compression shells (vibrations) observed at a given point per unit time. The standard unit of measure for frequency is hertz (Hz). Human hearing typically ranges from 20 Hz, lower than a string bass, to 20,000 Hz, higher than a flute. Amplitude is related to volume. The standard unit is decibels (dB), which is a logarithmic scale. Zero dB is the quietest sound a human can hear. A ticking watch is about 20 dB. Whispering in a quiet library is about 30 dB (10 times louder than the watch). The hum of a refrigerator runs about 50 dB (one thousand times louder than the watch). Jet engines and metal bands tip the scale at 140 dB, well past the point where pain and permanent hearing damage occur. Another aspect of sound, often called sound quality or timbre, is also important: the manner in which different sounds intermingle. As sounds of different frequency and their harmonics combine, the sound appears to change. A piano, violin, and flute may all produce the same note, but each instrument contributes different overtones to add a different quality to the music. This is how we recognize different instruments.

Eventually the sound encounters a human ear. The outer ear is skin-covered cartilage which primarily acts as a sound funnel, although the folds do contribute to signal processing. The ear flap, called the auricle, opens onto a curving tube, the auditory canal. The canal is roughly an inch long and ends at the eardrum. The outer ear is where the middle frequencies resonate. It buffers the middle and inner ear from the environment, which is where ear hair and earwax figure into the equation. Wax is secreted by glands inside the ear to help keep foreign particles out.

Between the outer ear and the middle ear is the eardrum, which measures a third of an inch in diameter and 1/50th of an inch thick (paper-thin). The eardrum is a membrane covered with skin on the outer ear side and a mucous lining on the middle ear side. The eardrum displaces air as sounds pound on it from the outside. The eardrum transfers energy to the three smallest bones in the human body, each named for its shape: the malleus (hammer), the incus (anvil), and the stapes (stirrup). These bones transform and transmit sound energy across the air-filled middle ear to the inner ear, matching the impedance of the outside world to that of our specialized, liquid organ, bringing the sounds of the dry land to the sea where we evolved. The middle ear lowers the sound's amplitude while increasing its intensity and maintaining its frequency.

The stapes attaches to the oval window of the inner ear, one of two small openings between the middle and inner ear. The other is round (called the round window) and compensates for the vibrations of the oval window. In order for the eardrum to vibrate properly, air pressure on both sides of the eardrum must be the same. The one-and-a-half-inch long eustachian tube connects the middle ear and the pharynx to balance the air pressure; this accounts for the "popping" we often hear when we yawn or swallow and the e-tube does its job.

The inner ear is an irregularly shaped bone cavity in the skull, behind the eye socket. This cavity is a labyrinth of bone-encased membrane channels, each filled with fluid. Sound is represented as pressure waves moving through this liquid. Inside the oval window is an area called the vestibule, home to the pea-sized, snail-shell spiral called the cochlea. The cochlea contains a duct which winds from the oval window to the round window. Along the spiral is tissue containing the basilar membrane, home to the 25,000 auditory receptor hair cells that are known as the organ of Corti. The sound pressure waves gently bend these hairs, causing small electrical signals to be sent along the auditory nerve.

Very loud noises and some diseases can cause these hairs to break. Once broken, these hairs are dead forever. Traffic or restaurant noise (70 dB) is generally considered safe, while a loud lawn mower or chainsaw (90—100 dB) will cause some hearing loss. Walkman headphones can reach 100 dB and rock concerts over 120 dB, both causing permanent hearing loss. The deterioration of hearing is not necessarily due to age; the Mabaan, a people who live in the Sudan, often have sensitive hearing even when they are old—of course, their world is a quiet one.

Our two ears provide most humans with stereo hearing, much as we have stereo vision. We can resolve sounds such as clicks to within 4 degrees azimuth under ideal conditions.[52] This system is limited to locating sounds in the horizontal plane (we can't distinguish up from down). However, since we don't fly much, this isn't a particularly important ability. We also have trouble locating the direction of pure tones.

Humans use a variety of techniques to localize sound, most of which are dependent on the sound's duration and spectrum. The simplest technique is based on which ear hears a sound loudest. A more subtle trick is based on the relative arrival time of the sound. Another subtle technique can detect as little as one hundred-thousandth of a second difference based on the phase difference of the sound between the ears. Interestingly, the ear cannot hear phase relationships that extend over more than several milliseconds.[53] This limitation makes sense, since remembering phase relationships over more than a dozen cycles wouldn't be terribly useful.

Modern virtual environment designers must consider the effect of sounds on their illusion because humans value sound to a great degree. Sound is often taken for granted, until it is missing or somehow wrong—then it becomes of paramount concern. Now that we've explored sight and sound, we'll explore the most complex and least understood of the human senses, the haptics system.

Figure 8.3—Georgia Tech's 1996 Atlanta torch carrier used in city demonstration

The Human Haptic System

> Haptic perception—the touch senses, tactile, proprioception (informs us about the position of our limbs relative to us and the space around us), internal sensors at joints and in muscles which sense changes in pressure and position, the effectors for transmitting commands from the sensing and sense-making systems to muscles.[54]

The senses of touch, pressure, temperature (heat and cold), and pain are often referred to as the cutaneous senses (from cutin, the Latin word for skin). As humans, one of our primary interfaces with the world is our skin—our largest organ at two meters and massing 2.8 kilos. Embedded in the surface of our skin are millions of information receptors, some of which are highly specialized, such as those responsible for taste sensitivity and those hair cells which can feel a slight breeze. We have other types of receptors, such as the free nerve endings, which are less sensitive and react slowly to pressure and touch. Our dynamically adapting proprioceptive system can accommodate changes in our environment which remain constant over time; this is why a cat can sit on your lap and not be continuously exciting your pressure detection system.

Humans spend most of their lives walking upright on two legs. Having evolved in a gravity well, we prefer to orient ourselves with respect to that well—feet down, head up. Our balance system expects a gravity field, and when astronauts are plying the starways, the lack of gravity can cause "space sickness," a form of motion sickness caused by the lack of an orienting gravity field. Interestingly, gymnasts and others who make more precise use of gravity than most of us are more susceptible to space sickness. Our balancing abilities do not depend on sound, although the heart of the system lies within the inner ear. Part of the cochlear duct are three fluid-filled bony loops called the semicircular canals. At the bulbous end of each canal, the ampula, are hair cells. The fluid bends the hairs, sending signals to the brain. The three canals are perpendicular, and each is most sensitive in its own plane—head side-to-side, up and down, or twisting left and right. Usually a tiny lag exists between the change in a motion and the brain's registration of this event. If you're twirling quickly and stop, the fluids in your head are still spinning, telling your brain that you are still spinning, which is why you feel dizzy.

Two other organs of balance may also be found in the inner ear. These are sacs known as the saccule and utricle, both of which are fluid-filled and use hair cells, although these hairs are enclosed in a gelatinous material. On this membrane can be found small calcium carbonate crystals called the otoliths, or ear stones. These little stones are like gravity magnets; they can detect the direction and strength of a gravity field. Where the semicircular canals provide the brain with angular acceleration data, the otoliths and their neighbor hair cells provide linear acceleration data—bending over or standing up, and which direction is "up."

Other sensors in our body are responsible for measuring such things as joint angles, position in space, and muscle tension. Some of these receptors help us balance at rest, others when we are in motion. Our ability to know where all our limbs are positioned in space without conscious thought is called the kinesthetic sense. Many aspects of our senses—touch, force, texture, pressure, temperature, pain, motion, and balance—overlap; collectively they are known as the haptic system.

Holistically Speaking

The human senses cannot truly be considered in isolation. The overlaps and redundancy provided by our sensing systems are important ingredients in the understanding of our environment. The constantly changing database of our surrounding environment is fed with information from all of our senses, and the brain decides which bits to use in what manner and which bits to ignore. The senses of smell and taste, for instance, interact in subtle ways (e.g., by holding your nose, you can alter the taste of many foods).

Research into the human senses has led some to believe that humans may be able to orient themselves in a magnetic field much as birds do. The sense of smell may help us to determine our mate. Different senses also have different "priorities." If you view a straight rod through a curvy lens, you will think the rod is curvy—even if you handle the rod! Rapidly spinning ballerinas and ice skaters defeat their balance system by spinning their heads faster than their body, then locking their eyes on certain "still" objects. The seeming "still" eye image, with some training, can carry more weight with the brain's processing system than your inner ear. Visual stimuli generally outweigh other information—this is important information for virtual environments designers.

A problem occurs when all of this overlapping sensory information fails to agree, leading to a condition generally termed simulator sickness. Flight simulators have a long history with this problem, and virtual environments are even more susceptible. Simulator operators and passengers have been known to experience motion sickness—like symptoms—sometimes lasting or reoccurring several hours after the exposure. Severe cases of simulator sickness cause operator performance problems and can even lead to safety hazards. Common symptoms include eye strain, headaches, fatigue, nausea, vertigo, and general discomfort; after-effects include sudden disorientation and flashbacks.

The trivial case of simulator sickness is not a simulator flaw at all, but rather a result of creating a simulation that is all too realistic. Consider as an example an aircraft making a 10-G turn, causing you to black out—the event seems real enough to make you sick. Although the causes of simulator sickness appear to be varied, sensory conflict appears to play a major role. Transport delays and uncoordinated simulator displays (especially visual and haptic) are often cited. In fact, visual delay by itself is enough to cause sickness, which affects simulators with no motion platform.

The causes and cures for simulator sickness are still being researched and debated. One result of all this is that most participants are forced to limit their exposure to such systems. Faster and higher-quality hardware and software will undoubtedly help matters, but so does better design. Even though problems persist, flight simulators and virtual environments can and should be used. Indeed, they have already proved their usefulness.[55]

Conclusion

The human ability to understand its surrounding environment may be unmatched on this planet. We possess high-quality sensors capable of filtering data and presenting an information display of unparalleled accuracy and detail which is based on seemingly small, even insignificant, amounts of data. To build virtual environments capable of fooling this system requires an understanding of the capabilities and limitations of the human beings who will work and play in these worlds. Failure to fully consider the creature at the heart of these systems will surely lead to eventual disaster.

PART III

A LOOK AT THE VIRTUAL REALITY GRAPHICS RAY-CASTING TEXTURING ENGINE

CHAPTER 9

GETTING STARTED

The Windows-Based Games on the Diskette

In the previous sections of this book, you learned about programming Windows applications, and about the history and applications of virtual reality technologies. The remainder of this book is primarily a *reference guide* dedicated to tying those two fields together through the development of a graphics engine similar to that found in Wolfenstein 3-D and DOOM. This graphics ray-casting texturing engine is used to generate the three-dimensional worlds with which you will interact. Issues of database, image generation, fixed-point arithmetic for speed, creation of worlds, collision detection, textures, sprite figure animation, and palette manipulation are covered. We will start with a look at the games that we will develop.

Virtual Pinball

Here in Virtual Pinball the viewer is the pinball, and he gets launched into the pinball machine with a keyboard or mouse press. There are two modes of view. The first is where the viewer is locked onto the direction of the pinball, so when he bounces off of the wall, he follows the direction of travel. Note that we simulate ideal bounces (incident angle = reflected angle). And the final is where the viewer can look around, as he, the pinball, bounces around the "machine" (i.e., view not locked onto the direction of travel). Various obstacles are placed in the pinball-machine playing area for the viewer/pinball to hit. When he hits an object of some geometric shape, it changes color, jitters, and there is some sort of sound. Different bumpers are given different values, and some pseudo-score kept. Two flappers are used to keep the ball in the playing area. Gravity will always tend to pull the ball down into and past the flappers. If the ball passes the flappers, the game is over. Otherwise, some pseudo-physics is used to calculate the new ball direction (incident angle = reflection angle, for the orientation of the flapper at the time of contact). Two keys or mouse buttons are used for flapper controls. Sprite creatures may also appear every so often to try and push the pinball (i.e., the viewer) down past the flappers faster than gravity. A three-dimensional rendering mode for *3-D anaglyph glasses* is included so that you can see your three-dimensional world in 3-D. Another option for this virtual pinball game is to use the keyboard or mouse to "drive" the pinball around the playing area. This leads us to the next game, Virtual Dungeon. . . .

Virtual Dungeon

In Virtual Dungeon, the viewer can move around (much as in the DOS wt program with the addition of collision detection, and also much like an architectural walk-through). Sprite creatures run about the couple of rooms in which you move. The graphics are more like those found in Wolfenstein 3-D and DOOM, in order to lure DOOM-engine game programmers to purchase this book. 3-D anaglyph glasses once again, so that you can see your world in 3-D.

Notes on Database Structure and Fixed-Point Mathematics

Lists

wt makes extensive use of singly linked lists internally. The lists are used within the wtWorld structure to keep track of the vertices, walls, and objects used in the world. All list related functions are defined in list.c; their declarations, the definition of the list type, and a few useful macros are in list.h There's nothing new or unusual in the way these are handled, so we'll just give a brief overview of the module.

Here is how the generic list type is defined:

```
typedef struct List_s {
        void *node;
        struct List_s *next;
} List;
```

Declaring node a pointer to void is the only way in C to make the list type somewhat generic; unfortunately, such loose typing makes use of lists quite dangerous. In order to prevent list-related bugs from cropping up into the code, we've tried to use just the functions and macros declared in list.h for list handling.

Here are the basic list functions:

```
List *new_list(void);
Boolean add_node(List *l, void *node);
void delete_node(List *l);
void remove_node(List *l);
void delete_list(List *l);
```

new_list() returns a pointer to a new, empty list structure. This call can fail if there is not enough memory to allocate a new list; in this event, the function returns NULL.

add_node() creates a new list entry for node. It returns True if the node could be added, or False if there was an error. add_node() does not make a copy of node; thus, if node is freed before its list entry is deleted, the list will contain an invalid pointer.

delete_node() and *remove_node()* both delete the list entry l; the difference between the two functions is that remove_node() frees the memory used by l->node, while delete_node() does not.

delete_list() calls *delete_node()* repeatedly on the list l until it reaches the end.

Our list module also has some support for scanning and searching lists:

```
typedef Boolean Scan_list_function(List *l, void *data);
extern List *scan_list(List *l, void *data, Scan_list_function *func);
extern Boolean find_node(List *l, void *data);
```

scan_list applies the function func to successive elements of the list l until either the end of the list is reached or until func returns True. If it reached the end of the list, scan_list returns NULL; otherwise, it returns a pointer to the list element for which func returned True. find_node is a *Scan_list_function* for searching lists. It returns True when the list's node points to the same place as data.

There are places in wt where we opted to not call scan_list for the sake of speed; scan list requires a function call for every element of the list scanned. For these situations, we've written a FOREACH macro, and some supporting macros.

```
#define LIST_NODE(l, type) ((type) (l)->next->node)
#define LIST_END(l) ((l)->next == NULL)
#define LIST_NEXT(l) ((l) = (l)->next)
#define FOREACH(l, start)  for ((l) = (start); \\
         !LIST_END(l); \\
         LIST_NEXT(l))
```

The FOREACH macro is used when scanning every element of a list sequentially. l is initially set to the first element of the list, and is advanced through the list with each iteration. If the nodes of the list are integers, the following bit of code could be used to print out all the list entries:

```
List *list_of_numbers;
List *l;

FOREACH(l, list_of_numbers)
{
        printf("%d\n", *LIST_NODE(l, int *));
}
```

Certainly a more extensive library of list functions could be implemented, but the current set seems to suffice for wt.

Fixed-Point Arithmetic

We have used fixed-point arithmetic extensively in wt for speed. It is especially important to use fixed-point arithmetic for fast graphics on machines without an FPU, but they provide a great speed benefit even on 486s and Pentiums with fast, on-chip FPUs. Three different fixed-point formats are used in wt, depending on how much fractional precision is needed for a particular task. The general-purpose fixed-point type used in wt has 16 integer bits and 16 fractional bits—this variety is by far the most often used. A few functions in render.c use a format with 8 integer bits and 24 fractional bits or a format with 2 integer bits and 30 fractional bits. Most of the macros in fixed.h apply to the 16.16 fixed-point numbers only; macros for the other types are defined privately in render.c, as that is the only place where they are used.

The fixed type is really a long:

typedef long fixed;

There are four basic fixed-point conversion macros:

```
// fixed point conversions
#define INT_TO_FIXED(i) ((i) << 16)
#define FIXED_TO_INT(f) ((f) >> 16)
#define FIXED_TO_FLOAT(f) (((double) (f)) * 1.52587890625e-5)
#define FLOAT_TO_FIXED(f) ((fixed) ((f) * 65536.0))
```

These should be self-explanatory; nevertheless, a few points should be made. First of all, the FIXED_TO_INT macro does a right shift of a signed number. The C Standard says that the behavior of this operation is undefined, although every compiler which we have ever used gives the reasonable and expected result: there's certainly not going to be a problem on an x86 system. We just think it's a good idea to be aware of subtleties in your code that make it nonportable. The FIXED_TO_INT macro does not round to the nearest integer; instead, it truncates to the nearest integer less than or equal to the argument. The FIXED_TO_FLOAT macro multiples by 1/65,536 rather than dividing by 65,536 because multiplication is usually a faster operation than division.

```
#define FIXED_ABS(f) ((f) < 0 ? -(f) : (f))
#define FIXED_TRUNC(f) ((f) & 0xffff0000)
#define FIXED_SIGN(f) ((unsigned int) (f) >> 31)
#define FIXED_PRODUCT_SIGN(f, g) ((unsigned int) ((f) ^ (g)) >> 31)
#define FIXED_HALF(f) ((f) >> 1)
#define FIXED_DOUBLE(f) ((f) << 1)
#define FIXED_SCALE(f, i) ((f) * (i))
```

FIXED_ABS gives the absolute value of a fixed point number.

FIXED_TRUNC gives a fixed point representation of the nearest integer less than or equal to its argument.

FIXED_SIGN evaluates to 1 if its argument is negative and to 0 otherwise.

FIXED_PRODUCT_SIGN gives the sign of the product of two fixed-point numbers without actually doing any multiplication. This macro is used in render.c for optimizing wall visibility calculations; it is perhaps more proper to move it from here to render.c since it is such a special-purpose macro.

FIXED_HALF and FIXED_DOUBLE perform obvious operations.

FIXED_SCALE scales a fixed-point number by an integer. This is implemented by just doing an integer multiply. It may seem silly to macro-ize this, but it helps reinforce the fact that integers and fixed-point numbers must be treated differently even though they have the same reputation. Unfortunately, C makes it necessary for us to maintain this distinction.

Here are some useful fixed point constants from fixed.h:

```
#define FIXED_ZERO     (INT_TO_FIXED(0))
#define FIXED_ONE      (INT_TO_FIXED(1))
#define FIXED_ONE_HALF (FIXED_HALF(FIXED_ONE))
#define FIXED_PI       (FLOAT_TO_FIXED(3.14159265))
#define FIXED_2PI      (FLOAT_TO_FIXED(6.28318531))
#define FIXED_HALF_PI  (FLOAT_TO_FIXED(1.57079633))
#define FIXED_MIN      LONG_MIN
#define FIXED_MAX      LONG_MAX
#define FIXED_EPSILON  ((fixed) 0x100)
```

The only constant which needs explanation is FIXED_EPSILON. This is a constant needed in order to work around an inherent limitation of fixed-point arithmetic: division overflow. In order to used fixed-point arithmetic safely, we had to impose a limit on the size of walls in wt. No wall may be more than 255 units in length or be more than 255 units high. Given this restriction, you can safely divide any fixed-point number used within the renderer by another fixed point number with an absolute value greater than FIXED_EPSILON. At least, this is the case so far . . . modifications to the renderer could invalidate this rule. The name of this constant should probably be changed to something else like FIXED_FUDGE. FIXED_EPSILON used to mean something, but no longer does.

```
#define MIN(a, b) ((a) < (b) ? (a) : (b))
#define MAX(a, b) ((a) > (b) ? (a) : (b))
```

MIN and MAX are defined in `fixed.h` merely for convenience—their use is obviously not restricted to fixed-point numbers.

We did not define macros for fixed-point addition and subtraction, since these operations are no different for fixed-point numbers than integers. Multiplication and division are another matter; extra bits are needed for an intermediate result. The multiplication of two 16.16 fixed-point numbers can be done in C, but it's much more efficient to do it in assembly language, where we can take advantage of the the 386 and 486s extended multplication and division instructions. Our multiplication function looks like this:

```
static inline fixed fixmul(fixed r1, fixed r2)
{
        fixed result;
        __asm__ ("imull %2\n\t"
        "shrd $16, %%edx, %%eax\n\t"
        :"=a" (result):"a" (r1), "d" (r2):"eax", "edx");
        return result;
}
```

This is written using AT&T assembler syntax. A TASM version looks like this:

```
imul edx
shrd eax, edx, 16
```

This code fragment assumes that the operands are in eax and edx and that the result is in eax. An extra instruction or two is needed to move the result from a 32-bit register into two 16-bit registers so that we can integrate the assembly with a Borland C program.

Here's the TASM version of division with the dividend in edx, the divisor in ecx; the quotient will be in eax:

```
mov   eax, edx
```

```
sar  edx, 16
shl  eax, 16
idiv eax, ecx
```

That covers all of fixed.h. We don't know how familiar you are with fixed-point arithmetic, so we apologize if the preceeding information is not useful to you because of its terseness.

Notes on the Graphics Library

LIBWT

The wt library is designed to be a minimal set of functions needed to build a world and render it. So there are no fancy commands in the library to move objects, or to handle the physics, or to detect collisions. All of those functions belong in another library. The wt library deals with three types of objects: worlds, views, and renderers. A world is composed of vertices, walls, regions, textures, and objects. The view describes a virtual camera within the world. The renderer points to the framebuffer, and knows the height and width of the framebuffer (that is the only aspect of the renderer visible to the library caller—a lot of internal structures are maintained within the renderer structure, but the caller does not need to know anything about them). Before we start going over the interface functions, take a look at the wtResult type. Many of the functions in the library return a result code of this type:

```
typedef enum {
        wt_Ok,
        wt_NoMemory,
        wt_BadObject,
        wt_NoSuchObject,
        wt_Error
} wtResult;
```

wt_Ok means that the function returned successfully.

wt_NoMemory is returned when there is not enough memory left to allocate.

wt_BadObject means that a bad argument was passed to the function.

wt_NoSuchObject is returned when the caller tries to remove an object from a world which was never added to the world to begin with.

wt_Error is returned for miscellaneous other cases.

The library works with either 8 bits per pixel (256-color palette) or 16 bits per pixel (hicolor) depending upon the following #define:

```
#ifdef TRUECOLOR
        typedef unsigned short wtPixel;
#else
        typedef unsigned char wtPixel;
#endif
```

The Renderer

```
typedef struct {

        /* Fields private to the wt library. */

} *wtRenderer;
```

These functions are responsible for creating and destroying renderer instances:

```
wtRenderer wt_CreateRenderer( wtPixel *framebuf, int width, int height );
void wt_DestroyRenderer( wtRenderer renderer );
```

These functions set renderer parameters:

```
wtResult wt_RendererChangeSize(wtRenderer renderer, int width, int height);
wtResult wt_RendererChangeFramebuf(wtRenderer renderer, wtPixel *framebuf);
```

And this function actually renders a frame:

```
wtResult wt_Render(wtRenderer renderer, wtWorld world, wtView view);
```

In order to get the stereo pair for viewing with 3-D (red-blue) anaglyph glasses, we will make a sequence of calls like this:

```
wt_RendererChangeFramebuf(renderer, left_fb);
wt_Render(renderer, world, left_eye);
wt_RendererChangeFramebuf(renderer, right_fb);
wt_Render(renderer, world, right_eye);
```

More on this topic under stereo viewing.

While changing the framebuffer pointer takes virtually no time, changing the framebuffer size can require a substantial amount of time. The renderer maintains structures dependent on the height and width of the framebuffer and must reallocate memory for them when the size changes. The speed penalty should only be a problem if you're changing the size every frame or something. If you need two different framebuffer sizes (say, for a large front view and a small back view inset), then you should create two different renderer structures of different sizes.

The View

```
typedef struct {

        /* fields private to the wt library */

} wtint_View, *wtView;
```

As with the renderer, there are no structure fields visible to the library caller. The structure can be manipulated only through the following group of functions

Here are the usual constructor and destructor functions:

```
wtView wt_CreateView(wtFixed field_of_view, wtFixed eye_distance)
void wt_DestroyView(wtView view)
```

And here are functions to change the horizontal field of view [the vertical field of view is fixed right now at 2 * atan(1/2)] and the distance of the eye from the view plane:

```
wtResult wt_SetFieldOfView(wtView view, wtFixed field_of_view)
wtResult wt_SetEyeDistance(wtView view, wtFixed eye_distance)
```

And finally, two functions to move the viewer position and angle:

```
wtResult wt_SetViewpoint(wtView view, wtFixed x, wtFixed y, wtFixed z, wtFixed
angle);
wtResult wt_ShiftViewpoint(wtView view, wtFixed dx, wtFixed dy, wtFixed dz, wtFixed
dangle);
```

The wtFixed used in the view functions is a 16.16 fixed-point number, defined thus:

```
typedef long wtFixed;
```

The World

```
typedef struct {

        /* fields private to the wt library */

} wtint_World, *wtWorld;
```

Constructors and destructors:

```
wtWorld wt_CreateWorld();
void wt_DestroyWorld(wtWorld world);
```

Functions to add and remove world components:

```
wtResult wt_AddVertex(wtWorld world, wtVertex vertex);
wtResult wt_RemoveVertex(wtWorld world, wtVertex vertex);
wtResult wt_AddWall(wtWorld world, wtWall wall);
wtResult wt_RemoveWall(wtWorld world, wtWall wall);
wtResult wt_AddObject(wtWorld world, wtObject object);
wtResult wt_RemoveObject(wtWorld world, wtObject object);
```

Note that there are no functions to add and remove regions and textures. The reason for this is that the renderer does not need to walk through a list of textures and regions—they are referenced only through fields in walls and objects.

Here are the declarations for the world components:

```
typedef struct {
        wtFixed x, y;
        #ifdef WT_PRIVATE
                wtFixed tx, ty, proj;                   // transformed coordinates
        #endif
} wtint_Vertex, *wtVertex;

typedef struct {
        int width, height;
        int log2height;
        wtPixel *texels;
        int opaque;
```

```
} wtint_Texture, *wtTexture;

typedef struct {
        wtFixed floor, ceiling;              // floor and ceiling heights
        wtTexture floor_tex, ceiling_tex;    // floor and ceiling textures
} wtint_Region, *wtRegion;

typedef struct {
        wtVertex vertex1, vertex2;           // wall endpoints
        wtRegion front, back;                // front and back regions
        wtTexture texture;                   // texture on this wall
        wtFixed xphase, yphase;              // texture mapping paramters
        wtFixed xfreq, yfreq;
        int opaque;
        int sky;                             // 1 to mark this wall as
                                             //   sky
                                             // This only affects how the
                                             // texture is projected onto
                                             // the wall
} wtint_Wall, *wtWall;

typedef struct {
        wtFixed x, y, z;                     // object position
        wtFixed width, height;               // object size (for tex.
                                             //   mapping)
        wtTexture image;                     // picture to use for object
} wtint_Object, *wtObject;
```

The world components are the only types defined in wt.h which have fields that can be manipulated by the library caller. Every other structure has an associated set of functions which can manipulate it. Again, the philosophy in our design of the wt library is to let some other higher-level library deal with the world components. The only functions provided for handling world components are the create/destroy functions:

```
wtVertex wt_CreateVertex(void);
void wt_DestroyVertex(wtVertex vertex);

wtRegion wt_CreateRegion(void);
void wt_DestroyRegion(wtRegion region);

wtWall wt_CreateWall(void);
void wt_DestroyWall(wtWall wall);

wtTexture wt_CreateTexture(void);
void wt_DestroyTexture(wtTexture texture);

wtObject wt_CreateObject(void);
void wt_DestroyObject(wtObject object);
```

CHAPTER 10

THE KEY TO THE VIRTUAL WORLD DATABASE

World File Syntax

What follows is a discussion of the syntax of the world files. In order to build a proper world file, you need to have some understanding of how the wt renderer works. Each world file consists of a number of "directives." A directive is simply a keyword followed by a number of data fields. The data fields can be strings, numbers, or references. A reference is an integer which refers to a texture, vertex, or region, depending upon the context. A reference to texture 0 would refer to texture defined by the first texture directive in the world file, reference 1 to the second, etc.

Here's a summary of the world file directives:

- palette <string>

Load a palette from the image file named in <string>. This directive can only appear once in the texture file, and it must appear before and texture or region directives (and, consequently, before any wall directives).

- texture <string>

Load a texture from the image file named in <string>.

- vertex <x> <y>

This directive defines a vertex. The two data fields are both numbers, and they specify the Cartesian coordinates of the vertex.

- region <floor height> <floor red> <floor green> <floor blue>

<ceiling height> <ceiling red> <ceiling green> <ceiling blue>

The region directive defines a new region. All the data fields of this directive are numbers. The first four define properties of the region floor, and the last four define the ceiling. The color of the floor and ceiling are specified with RGB triples. The value of each component should be in the range 0.0 to 1.0.

- wall <start vertex> <end vertex> <front region> <back region>

<texture> <x phase> <y phase> <x freq> <y freq>

The first five data fields are all references. The last four fields are numbers which tell how the texture will be mapped onto the wall. The frequencies tell how many times the texture will be tiled across the wall; for example, an xfreq of 2 means that the texture will be tiled twice. The degree to which the texture is stretched depends upon the frequency as well as the length of the wall.

- skywall <start vertex> <end vertex> <front region> <back region>

Like the wall directive, skywall defines a new wall. However, a different type of texture mapping is used on skywalls that makes them appear infinitely far from the viewer. This makes skywalls useful for backdrops.

- object <x> <y> <z> <texture> <height> <diameter>

This directive defines an object Height and diameter give the dimensions of the object cylinder. The coordinates tell where the center of the bottom of the cylinder should be located. The texture (usually a texture with transparent parts) determines the appearance of the object to the viewer.

Overview of World Structures

This is an overview of the structures in a wt 'world.' You are probably somewhat familiar with this already, but we thought that we had better spell out the details. The world contains five different types of structures:

vertices

textures

regions

walls

and *objects*.

Some basics:

- Vertices are points in two dimensions. Two vertices give the location of a wall in the x–z plane (in the coordinate system we use for 3-D graphics, the positive z-axis points into the screen, the y-axis is up, and the positive x-axis is to the right).

- A wall separates two regions—a front and a back.

- The floor and ceiling height of a wall's front and back region
  determine its height; the wall has no height of its own.

- A wall has one texture mapped onto it.

Here's the definition of wt's vertex type:

```
typedef struct {
        wtFixed x, y;
        wtFixed tx, ty, proj; // transformed coordinates
} *wtVertex;
```

In addition to holding the coordinate of the vertex in world space, the transformed (view space and screen space) coordinates of the vertex are contained in the vertex structure. We think that's all you need to know about vertices.

Textures are images which get mapped onto walls. Regardless of the source of the texture (BMP file, GIF, PPM, etc.) the texture data ends up in this structure:

```
typedef struct {
        int width, height;
        int log2height;
        wtPixel *texels;
        int opaque;
} *wtTexture;
```

The actual image information is contained in the area of memory pointed to by texels. A texture can have any width; however, its height must be a power of two. This restriction is enforced in order to get the best performance possible from the texture mapping loop. We use log2height (log base 2 of the texture's height in pixels) to make 'wrapping' the texture as fast as possible. When the textures height is a power of two, we can use an and-mask to make the texture wrap, rather than a much more expensive mod operation. Opaque is a flag which indicates whether there are portions of the texture which are transparent. Textures used for objects will typically have this flag set; some walls use transparent textures, though the majority will not. The image pixels pointed to by texels are not the original values from the image file. They have been mapped into a different palette. This is explained in the discussion on reading textures following this section. Now on to regions . . . the only geometry we specify for the region are the heights of the floor and ceiling. The shape of the region is defined by the walls which have the region as their back or front. Since we have not been able to get floor and ceiling texture mapping to work technically correctly *and* quickly by the publishing date of this book, walls and ceilings are just painted with a solid color. This also has the advantage of making wt code *much* easier to read.

```
typedef struct {
        wtFixed floor, ceiling;
        wtPixel floor_color, ceiling_color;
} *wtRegion;
```

Now a short description of walls, and afterward a long description of how walls and regions "interact" to define the geometry of the world.

```
typedef struct {
        wtVertex vertex1, vertex2;
        wtRegion front, back;
        wtTexture texture;
        wtFixed xphase, yphase;
        wtFixed xfreq, yfreq;
        int opaque;
        int sky;
} *wtWall;
```

vertex1 and *vertex2* are pointers to the vertices that are the endpoints of the section of wall. *front* and *back* are pointers to the regions on either side of the wall. *texture* is the picture which will be mapped onto the wall. *xphase, yphase, xfreq,* and *yfreq* are the parameters or this mapping. By tuning these parameters, we can determine how large the texture will appear on the wall, its aspect ratio, etc. *opaque* is set to 1 for opaque walls and 0 for transparent walls. Transparent walls *must* use trasparent textures in order to be rendered transparently. The transparency that I'm talking about here refers to 'holes' in the texture where the background will show through completely; 'partially transparent' (translucent) textures are not supported. Either a pixel from the texture is drawn, or a pixel from the background is left. If the sky flag is set, a different type of texture mapping is used for the wall. The "sky" mapping differs from the standard texture mapping in that the mapping is dependent *only* on the viewer's facing direction and not his position. A wall with the sky mapping is effectively at an infinite distance from the viewer—at least it looks this way. Aside from its appearance, the wall with a sky mapping will behave in all other ways like a normal wall. Infinitely distant walls are useful as backgrounds in a world.

Typically, we define a square border for the world and use a wrapping texture with sky mapping on; this makes a convincing horizon. (We hacked RayShade to render 360 degree panoramas onto a cylindrical surface—the resulting images are what we usually use for our backgrounds, and one of them we're using for the DOOM-style game. There's a definite lack of public-domain panoramic images out there.)

Ok . . . now let's look at very simple world file. This is basically the test.wld file that is on the disk.

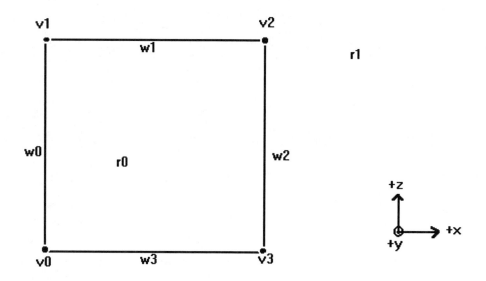

It's impossible to understand exactly what this world is supposed to look like without any perspective clues in the drawing. Rather than make our hack art any fancier, we will tell you what this is supposed to be: It's a top view of a box-shaped room. The viewer is intended to view this room from region r0. So, how should we define the vertices, walls, and regions for this world? Obviously, we want four vertices: v0, v1, v2, and v3. The walls connect the points in a straightforward way, too. The trick is in setting up the regions correctly.

This world needs two regions. Region r0 has a floor height of 0, and a positive ceiling height. (When determining the exact height of the ceiling, we need to take into account the nature of the camera; we have defined the height of the image plane to be 1 in wt, so we definitely want the difference in ceiling height and floor height to be greater than one. For `test.wld`, we chose the ceiling height to be 15.) Since we want this room to be closed off from everything else, we'll make the region r1 "solid." To do this, we just set the floor height of the region to be equal to the ceiling height.

The last thing to do is set up the front and back regions of each of the walls. Do we want the front regions of all the walls to be the same? Do we want all the back regions to be the same? Should r0 be the front or back? What we do know for certain is that if the viewer is standing surrounded by all the walls, he should be in region r0. Which region is in front or back of a wall depends upon how the vertices of the walls are ordered. In wt, if the walls in the above world are defined as a counterclockwise circuit (i.e., vertex1 of w0 is v1, vertex2 is v0 vertex1 of w3 is v0, vertex2 is v3, . . .), then r0 should be the front region and r1 should be the back region. If they are defined in a clockwise order, r1 should be the front region.

Although it makes the most sense with the above world to define the walls in a clockwise or counterclockwise circuit, we don't have to do it this way. Wall w0 could have

vertex1 == v0

and

vertex2 == v1

and w1 could point the other way with vertex1 == v2 and vertex2 == v1.

There's something more fundamental than clockwise/counterclockwise going on here, because these concepts don't make sense for single walls (although in properly contructed worlds, walls will always appear in closed polygons [as if there's any other kind :)]).

Here's the rule:

Let W be a wall with a start vertex V0, and an end vertex V1.

If P is a point in the front region of W, then

(V1 - V0) dot (P - V0) > 0.

All of the worlds in DOOM can be built from just vertexes, walls, and regions. DOOM renders the world using a different technique, but everything in DOOM (with the exception of "two-sided" walls) can be represented using wt's vertices, regions, and walls.

Last are objects. . . .

Objects exist indepently of vertices, regions, and walls. A single 3-D point represents the location of the object. The size of the objects consists just of a width and a height . . . this does not mean that objects are rectangles (though they are drawn this way). In wt, objects are considered to occupy a cylinder with a diameter width and a height.

```
typedef struct {
        wtFixed x, y, z;
        wtFixed width, height;
        wtTexture image;
} *wtObject;
```

More on Textures

The wt engine does not directly support the loading of textures from image files. Rather, a group of modules which sits on top of wt handles this. There are two relevant structs: wtTexture and Graphic_file. A wtTexture is used internally by the wt renderer. A Graphic_file is only a temporary storage place for the image as it is loaded off disk from an image file and converted into a wtTexture. The primary difference between a wtTexture and a Graphic_file is that the Graphic_file contains a palette of RGB colors and a wtTexture does not.

The implicit palette of a wtTexture is the "global palette." A single palette is used by wt for displaying rendered images—this is the palette shared by all wtTextures. The only image file types supported right now are 8-bit BMPs. If you want to add more, it is a simple matter to add another case to the switch in read_graphic_file() in `gfile.c` and then add an appropriate routine to decode whatever format it is you wish to read. The texture modules are currently set up to best handle paletted image formats such as GIFs and BMPs. The rest of this discussion assumes that we're working with a paletted image.

The main chore involved in converting from a Graphic_file to a wtTexture is palette remapping. The colors in the image file's palette may not match the ones in the global palette; in this case, for each color in the image file palette we must find the closest color in the global palette. The function quantize_texture in `texture.c` takes care of this. As a color distance metric, quantize_texture uses Euclidean distance in RGB space. Even when colors in the image file are the same as colors in the global palette, we must still remap colors. It's likely that if a particular shade of red appears in both the image file and the global palette, it will be represented by different palette entries—say, palette entry one in the image file and palette entry two in the global palette. We need all pixels in the image file with value one to have value two in the wtTexture. Otherwise, these pixels will not show up with the desired value of red in the final image. This part of color remapping is also handled in quantize_texture().

The Extras

3-D Anaglyph Stereo

The file `anaglyph.c` contains two public routines. The most important of these is called wt_AnaglyphRender. It accepts the same arguments as wt_Render, except that it requires an additional argument, which is the distance between the eyes of the viewer. The view passed to wt_AnaglyphRender is assumed to be exactly between the eyes of the viewer; the left and right views are displaced from it by one-half the eye spacing. In order to understand what happens in wt_AnaglyphRender after the left and right views are calculated, you need to know how textures are loaded differently in anaglyph stereo mode. In anaglyph mode, textures are loaded without color information. The RGB colors from the image file are converted to gray levels using the NTSC-defined conversion:

```
Y = 0.30R + 0.59G + 0.11B
```

The gray levels will be rendered as shades of blue in the right eye view and shades of red in the left eye blue. In wt_AnaglyphRender, the left eye view is rendered first. Then, the right eye view is superimposed on it using a shift and an OR for each pixel, so that the first four bits of the pixel value are the red level and the last four bits are the blue level (since we need to fit everything into a one-byte-deep framebuffer, four bits is all we can use to represent each color component). We need to set up a special palette for anaglyph mode to work correctly. The function CreateAnaglyphPalette handles this for us. What's it do? Well, we know that the last four bits of the pixel value represent the blue level and the first four are the red level. If the red level is zero, then all we have is blue; it's clear then that the first 16 palette entries should just be varying intensities of blue. When the low four bits of a pixel value are zero, there is just red, and so palette entries 16, 32, 48, . . . are pure reds. Other palette entries have mixtures of blue and red and will be various hues and shades of violet. Although we use four bits per color component, we cannot have 16 shades of gray. Windows does not let us set all 256 palette entries, and so we restrict ourselves to 14 gray levels.

CHAPTER 11

THE RENDER.C MODULE

The Include Files

In the previous chapters, we discussed some background information such as data structures and how to build a world model. Now let's take a look at the heart of the engine, the render.c module.

The module starts out with the standard system include files.

```
#include <math.h>
#include <stdlib.h>
#include <string.h>
#include <math.h>
#include "wtlib.h"
#include "slice.h"
```

Then we define MAX_ERROR; we will discuss this more later. For now, just remember that it is an important number used when we try to determine whether one wall is in front of another.

```
#define MAX_ERROR view_width
```

The Renderer Structure

Next, we look at the Renderer structure. This contains all the structures that the renderer needs to work with. It's not really supposed to be at this point in the file, as it references structs that have not been declared yet. But we can explain things more clearly and easily if we talk about this first.

```
typedef struct
{
        fixed width, height;
        wtPixel *framebuf;
        int *fb_rows;
        fixed *sin_tab, *cos_tab, *row_view;
        Wall_start *start_event_lists, *start_events, *cur_start_event;
        Wall_end  *end_event_lists, *end_events, *cur_end_event;
        Object_start *obj_start_lists, *obj_start_events, *cur_start_obj;
        Object_end  *obj_end_lists, *obj_end_events, *cur_end_obj;
        int obj_list_size, event_list_size;
} Renderer, *wtRenderer;
```

We will start with a brief explanation of each field in the structure. *height* and *width* are just the height and width of the frame buffer into which we will be rendering; *framebuf* is the actual chunk of memory used for drawing. The next few fields are used for optimization. *sin_tab* and *cos_tab* are used for drawing texture mapped floors, which unfortunately do not work as of the publication of this book. During rendering, it is often necessary to know the offset into the framebuffer of the first pixel in a row. This can be obtained by just multiplying the row number by the width of the framebuffer. But multiplication is a slow operation in 386s and 486s, and we do everything that we can to avoid it. One of the things that we do is compute ahead of time the offset of the first pixel in each row and stuff it into fb_rows; then we can replace multiplication with an array lookup later on.

Next in the renderer struct are the event lists. These are key to the working of wt—most everything in the renderer is somehow related to manipulating event lists. We will postpone the the bigger questions about event lists, and concentrate on how they are implemented. There are four types of event lists. All four types are essentially linked lists—the common structure is not as evident as it could be because we found it necessary to strip away some layers of abstraction in order to get the best performance possible. For each type of event list, there are three fields in the renderer struct. The second two are really just related to how event list entries get allocated. It would be absurd to use malloc to allocate each event list entry—there can be hundreds of events in each frame we render. Instead, prior to doing any rendering, we allocate a pool of event list entries: start_events, end_events, obj_start_events, and obj_end_events are all pointers to these pools. cur_start_event et al are pointers to the next unused element in each pool. They are reset every time we call the renderer; during rendering, the pointers are incremented as more and more event list entries are used. The *_event_lists fields are really arrays of event lists; the number of entries in each of these arrays is equal to the width of the framebuffer. This number is variable, and unfortunately C allows us no way of indicating that an array whose size cannot be determined at compile time is really an array. The elements of this array are event list entries. Before rendering each frame, all entries are initialized so that their "next" field is NULL. This indicates an empty list. The phrase "event list" probably makes you think of polygon scan conversion. The similar terminology belies the more than superficial resemblance of the wt engine to a generic scan converter. Each screen column in wt corresponds to a scanline in the scan converter; wt draw columns of texture-mapped walls into the framebuffer rather just filling spans. You should note that there are two start/end pairs of event lists—one for walls and one for objects. Here are the declarations of event list entries. We will describe the fields of the event lists later when we describe exactly how the event lists are used.

```
// typedefs for wall event lists

typedef struct Wall_start_s {
        wtWall wall;
        fixed z, dz;
        BOOL is_back_view;
        struct Wall_start_s *next;
} Wall_start;

typedef struct Wall_end_s {
        wtWall wall;
        struct Wall_end_s *next;
} Wall_end;

// typedefs for object event lists
typedef struct Object_start_s {
        wtObject o;
        fixed z;
        fixed first_slice;
        struct Object_start_s *next;
} Object_start;
```

```
typedef struct Object_end_s {
        wtObject o;
        struct Object_end_s *next;
} Object_end;
```

That's the end of the event list structs.

```
typedef struct {
        BOOL is_back_view;
        wtWall wall;
        BOOL visible;
        fixed pstart1, pend1, pstart2, pend2;
        fixed dpstart1, dpend1, dpstart2, dpend2;
        fixed z;
        fixed dz;
} Active_wall;
```

```
typedef struct {
        wtObject o;
        fixed x, dx;
        fixed z;
} Active_object;
```

The preceding two structures are active list entries. Essentially, we create event lists and then scan through them from the first entry (corresponding to the leftmost screen column) to the last (rightmost screen column). When we get a start event for a wall, we add it to the active list. Further along, we'll get an end event for that wall, signaling us to remove it from the active list. When rendering a particular screen column, we need only consider walls currently in the active list.

OOPS and Static Declarations

```
typedef struct {
        fixed screen_dy, screen_dx;
        fixed view_sin, view_cos;
        fixed sin_dx, cos_dx;
        int *fb_rows;
        fixed *sin_tab, *cos_tab, *row_view;
} View_constants;
```

Oops! This struct was really supposed to have been obsoleted by the new and improved wtRender struct. We noticed this at the last minute and didn't want to mess with the code. We will look into eliminating either this struct or the fb_rows, sin_tab, and cos_tab fields from the renderer struct. Next are all the prototypes for functions declared static within this file. We like to just declare every function in the file right at the beginning so that we never have to worry about how the functions are ordered within the file. Of course, you could argue that it forces you to update two different prototypes whenever you change how a function is defined. Whatever . . . change it if you like.

```
static void transform_vertices(wtWorld world, wtView view);
static void clip_walls(wtRenderer renderer, wtWorld world, wtView view);
static void add_wall_events(wtRenderer renderer, wtView view, wtWall wall,
fixed x1, fixed px1, fixed x2, fixed px2);
static void render_walls(wtRenderer renderer, wtWorld world, wtView view);
static int add_events(wtRenderer renderer,
Active_wall *active, int n_active, int column);
static int remove_events(wtRenderer renderer,
Active_wall *active, int n_active, int column);
static void add_objects(wtRenderer renderer, wtWorld world, wtView view);
static int add_obj_events(wtRenderer renderer,
Active_object *active, int n_active, int column);
static int remove_obj_events(wtRenderer renderer,
Active_object *active, int n_active, int column);
static fixed wall_ray_intersection(fixed Vx, fixed Vy, wtWall wall);
static BOOL wall_obscured(wtVertex common, wtVertex v1, wtVertex v2);
static void init_buffers(wtRenderer renderer);
static void clear_framebuffer(wtRenderer renderer);
static void calc_view_constants(wtRenderer renderer, wtView view);
static void do_walls(Active_wall *active, int n_active,
Active_object *active_obj, int n_active_obj,
int column, wtView view,
fixed Vx, fixed Vy);

static int view_width, view_height;
static View_constants view_constants;
static Pixel *fb;


static BOOL SafeRealloc(void **p, size_t size)
{
        void *temp;
        if (*p == NULL)
        {
                *p = malloc(size);
                if (*p == NULL)
                        return FALSE;
                else
                        return TRUE;
        }
        else
        {
                temp = realloc(*p, size);
                if (temp == NULL)
                        return FALSE;
                else
                {
                        *p = temp;
```

```
                               return TRUE;
                   }
       }
   }
```

SafeRealloc is just a wrapper for realloc that we find easier to use. In particular, it discourages us from doing evil things like this: pointer = realloc(pointer, new_size); . . . and blasting the original pointer if the call fails. Also, if *p is NULL, SafeRealloc acts just like malloc, which is what the realloc in every ANSI C library is supposed to do, too.

Changing Frame Buffer Size

```
wtResult wt_RendererChangeSize(wtRenderer renderer, int width, int height)
{
        BOOL success;
        int i;

        if (renderer == NULL || width < 1 || height < 1)
                return wt_Error;

        if (height != renderer->height)
        {
                success = SafeRealloc((void **) &renderer->fb_rows,
                sizeof(int) * height);
                if (!success)
                        return wt_NoMemory;
                for (i = 0; i < height; i++)
                        renderer->fb_rows[i] = i * width;
        }

        if (width != renderer->width)
        {
                success = SafeRealloc((void **) &renderer->start_event_lists,
                        sizeof(Wall_start) * width) &&
                        SafeRealloc((void **) &renderer->end_event_lists,
                        sizeof(Wall_end) * width) &&
                        SafeRealloc((void **) &renderer->obj_start_lists,
                        sizeof(Object_start) * width) &&
                        SafeRealloc((void **) &renderer->obj_end_lists,
                        sizeof(Object_end) * width) &&
                        SafeRealloc((void **) &renderer->sin_tab,
                        sizeof(fixed) * width) &&
                        SafeRealloc((void **) &renderer->cos_tab,
                        sizeof(fixed) * width) &&
                        SafeRealloc((void **) &renderer->row_view,
                        sizeof(fixed) * width);
                if (!success)
                                return wt_NoMemory;
        }
```

```
        renderer->height = height;
        renderer->width = width;

        return wt_Ok;
}
```

wt_RendererChangeSize should be called whenever you want to change the size of the framebuffer into which you will be rendering. Most likely, it will not be called often directly by the wt user—a framebuffer size will be specified when the renderer instance is created and left alone afterward. You'll note that there are a lot of calls to realloc going on here, indicating that it's not a good idea to call this function a lot if performance is critical. If, for example, you need to render two different image sizes in each frame, you're better off allocating two renderers rather than repeatedly changing the size of a single one.

Only the fields dependent on the size of the framebuffer are reallocated in wt_RendererChangeSize. In fact, the fields whose size depends on the width of the framebuffer will not be reallocated when just the height changes. This seems to us now like a silly detail to worry about, but the book is about due, and we are not going to mess with the code right now, as it is stable; and it is not all that important, anyway.

```
wtResult wt_RendererChangeFramebuf(wtRenderer renderer, wtPixel *framebuf)
{
        if (renderer == WT_NULL || framebuf == NULL)
                return wt_BadObject;

        renderer->framebuf = framebuf;
        return wt_Ok;
}
```

This call just changes the area of memory that image data is written to. It assumes that the size of this area has not changed. If it has, the library user had better also call wt_RendererChangeSize.

Creating and Destroying a Renderer

```
void wt_DestroyRenderer(wtRenderer renderer)
{
        FREE_SAFELY(renderer->start_events);
        FREE_SAFELY(renderer->end_events);
        FREE_SAFELY(renderer->obj_start_events);
        FREE_SAFELY(renderer->obj_end_events);
        FREE_SAFELY(renderer->fb_rows);
```

```
        FREE_SAFELY(renderer->sin_tab);
        FREE_SAFELY(renderer->cos_tab);
        FREE_SAFELY(renderer->row_view);

        free(renderer);
}
```

wt_DestroyRenderer frees all memory used by the renderer. Note that it uses the FREE_SAFELY macro, which checks to see if a pointer is null before calling free(). This makes cleanup easier after errors that occur partway through the initialization of a struct (although it forces you to initialize everything to NULL first—check out what we do in wt_CreateRenderer). Sorry if it seems like we're editorializing on programming style. Our hope is that these remarks will give you a better understanding of our code.

```
wtRenderer wt_CreateRenderer(wtPixel *framebuf, int width, int height)
{
        wtRenderer renderer;

        renderer = malloc(sizeof(Renderer));
        if (renderer == NULL)
                return WT_NULL;

        renderer->start_events    = NULL;
        renderer->end_events      = NULL;
        renderer->obj_start_events = NULL;
        renderer->obj_end_events  = NULL;
        renderer->start_event_lists = NULL;
        renderer->end_event_lists = NULL;
        renderer->obj_start_lists = NULL;
        renderer->obj_end_lists   = NULL;
        renderer->obj_list_size = 0;
        renderer->event_list_size = 0;
        renderer->fb_rows = NULL;
        renderer->sin_tab = NULL;
        renderer->cos_tab = NULL;
        renderer->row_view = NULL;
        renderer->width = 0;
        renderer->height = 0;

        if (wt_RendererChangeSize(renderer, width, height) != wt_Ok) {
                wt_DestroyRenderer(renderer);
                return WT_NULL;
        }

        if (wt_RendererChangeFramebuf(renderer, framebuf) != wt_Ok) {
                wt_DestroyRenderer(renderer);
                return WT_NULL;
        }

        return renderer;
}
```

wt_CreateRenderer allocates memory for and initializes a new renderer struct. There should be nothing very surprising in this function—it initializes all pointer fields to NULL and then calls wt_RendererChangeSize and wt_RendererChangeFramebuf to do most of the work. In order to make sure that wt_RendererChangeSize does the right thing, the width and height fields must first be set to zero (because wt_RendererChangeSize checks to make sure the old framebuffer size does not match the new framebuffer size before actually doing anything).

Let's Render

```
wtResult wt_Render(wtRenderer renderer, wtWorld world, wtView view)
{
        // Resize the object and wall event buffers if the number of vertices in
        //  the world has increased.
        if (world->n_walls > renderer->event_list_size) {
                BOOL success;

                success = SafeRealloc((void **) &renderer->start_events,
                sizeof(Wall_start) * world->n_walls) &&
                        SafeRealloc((void **) &renderer->end_events,
                        sizeof(Wall_end) * world->n_walls);
                if (!success)
                        return FALSE;
        }

        if (world->n_objects > renderer->obj_list_size) {
                BOOL success;

                success = SafeRealloc((void **) &renderer->obj_start_events,
                sizeof(Object_start) * world->n_objects) &&
                SafeRealloc((void **) &renderer->obj_end_events,
                sizeof(Object_end) * world->n_objects);
                if (!success)
                return FALSE;
        }

        init_buffers(renderer);
        calc_view_constants(renderer, view);
        transform_vertices(world, view);
        clip_walls(renderer, world, view);
        add_objects(renderer, world, view);
        clear_framebuffer(renderer);
        render_walls(renderer, world, view);

        return wt_Ok;
}
```

OK . . . now things start to get a little bit interesting. First of all, we have been very careful to see that the renderer always has enough memory. We don't want it to crash mysteriously, and we don't want to be constantly checking for adequate memory in speed critical portions of the code. Thus, you'll notice that the first thing we do in wt_Render is check to see if we need to allocate more memory for struct components dependent on the number of walls or objects in the world (which this part of the renderer allows to change dynamically; the collision detection code does not currently support the addition of walls after the world file has been loaded, though nowhere are there any restrictions on adding and removing objects from the world). Following the check to see if enough memory remains, you can see the steps in the rendering pipeline. First, the renderer struct is initialized. Next, calc_view_constants is called to calculate some values which are used over and over by the renderer and are constant for the current camera view. This values are precalculated purely for optimization. These first two stages are mostly just bookkeeping. The call to transform_vertices is the first real rendering stage. Transforming the vertices is probably the simplest rendering stage, and the part of wt most similar to a traditional 3-D renderer. Here's the function:

Transformations of Vertices

```
static void transform_vertices(wtWorld world, wtView view)
{
        List *l;
        fixed view_sin, view_cos;


        view_sin = view_constants.view_sin;
        view_cos = view_constants.view_cos;

        FOREACH(l, world->vertices) {
                wtVertex vertex = LIST_NODE(l, wtVertex);
                fixed x = vertex->x - view->x;
                fixed y = vertex->y - view->y;

                vertex->tx = fixmul(x, view_cos) - fixmul(y, view_sin);
                vertex->ty = fixmul(x, view_sin) + fixmul(y, view_cos);
                // project point onto view plane
                if (vertex->tx > view->eye_distance)
                        vertex->proj = fixdiv(vertex->ty, vertex->tx);
        }
}
```

You should see some things in this function that look pretty familiar. Every vertex in the world is translated so that the viewer's location is the origin, and then rotated so that the direction the viewer is facing is 0 degrees—the vertices are transformed from world space into view space. The last line of the loop is a division operation (done in fixed point) which is the perspective part of the vertex transformation. This is only done if the vertex lies in front of the view plane. Obviously, if the vertex is behind the view plane, we don't need to worry about projecting it onto the view plane. wt is really a two-dimensional renderer with a "faked" third dimension. The rotation and translation of points in transform_vertices are done in two dimensions. This gives a considerable savings in computation time over performing true 3-D calculations—four multiplies for the 2-D transformations vs. nine multiplies for 3-D. That wt is really a 2-D renderer can be seen again in the perspective transformation where only one coordinate in screen space is calculated. We don't have a view plane; instead, we have a view line. (We like to think of it as a bunch of flatlanders from earlier in the book sitting in front of their high-perforance 2-D workstations projecting images onto the 1-D surfaces of their high-res displays and working with these same equations.) wt could be smarter about which vertices it transforms, however. Above, you can see that it transforms every vertex in the world (using the FOREACH macro defined in `list.h`) rather than just the ones that are relevant for rendering the world from the current camera position and angle. This unfortunate reality places an upper limit on the complexity of a world.

Another thing about transforming vertices: The vertex structure contains fields for the vertex coordinates in three different coordinate systems—world, view, and screen coordinates. x and y are the world coordinates, tx and ty are the view coordinates, and *proj* gives the screen coordinate. After we transform the vertex coordinates, we're ready to clip the walls to the edges of the view line. Here again you'll see some familiar-looking algorithms which have been reduced to one dimension.

Clipping

```
static void clip_walls(wtRenderer renderer, wtWorld world, wtView view)
{
        List *l;
```

We scan through every wall in the world to see if it needs to be clipped.

```
FOREACH(l, world->walls)
{
        fixed x1, y1, px1, x2, y2, px2;
        unsigned int outcode1, outcode2;
        wtWall wall = LIST_NODE(l, wtWall);

        x1 = wall->vertex1->tx;
        x2 = wall->vertex2->tx;
        // See if the wall lies completely behind the view plane.
        if (x1 < view->eye_distance && x2 < view->eye_distance)
                continue;
```

Walls that lie completely behind the view line are skipped—we won't do anything more with them in this call to the renderer. Our choice of variable names seems confusing in retrospect. Here, x1 and x2 are the distances of the two wall endpoints from the view line. Below, y1 and y2 are coordinates along the axis parallel to the view line, and px1 and px2 are the perspective-transformed vertex coordinates.

```
y1 = wall->vertex1->ty;
px1 = wall->vertex1->proj;
y2 = wall->vertex2->ty;
px2 = wall->vertex2->proj;
```

The setup is finished—now we're going to do some real clipping.

```
/* Clipping */
/* First, clip to the view plane (or line, really, since we're
** working in only two dimensions.)
*/
if (x1 <= view->eye_distance)
{
        /* be careful for division overflow */
        if (x2 - x1 < FIXED_FUZZ)
                continue;
        y1 = y1 + fixmul(view->eye_distance - x1,
                fixdiv(y2 - y1, x2 - x1));
        px1 = y1;
        x1 = view->eye_distance;
}
else if (x2 <= view->eye_distance)
{
        if (x1 - x2 < FIXED_FUZZ)
                continue;
        y2 = y2 + fixmul(view->eye_distance - x2,
        fixdiv(y1 - y2, x1 - x2));
        px2 = y2;
        x2 = view->eye_distance;
}
```

The same process is used for each of the two wall endpoints. Which branch is taken depends on which of the wall endpoints lies behind the view line (if they both lie behind the view line, the wall has already been thrown out). If the wall crosses the view line and is also nearly parallel to it, we throw it out in order to avoid a possible fixed-point division overflow when we calculate its intersection with the view line.

Now a brief digression about the value FIXED_FUZZ. . . . We're constantly using this value in the renderer to avoid overflows. But we can only guarantee that overflows will be avoided when certains constraints in world file design are adhered to. The relevant constraint for the code given earlier is on wall length. FIXED_FUZZ is defined in fixed.h to be 1/256 (0x100 in 16.16 fixed point), and we threw out the walls where abs(x2 - x1) is less than this value. That means that we could be dividing by a value as small as 1/256, which is the same as multiplying by 256. abs(y1 - y2) is the length of the wall projected onto the view plane. In the worst case, the wall is parallel to the view plane, and its projected length is equal to its length (which really can't happen, because the wall wouldn't intersect the view plane at all. But we're fudging on the safe side). If the wall length is 256 or greater, we'll overflow a 32-bit integer when we multiply (in the worst case) by 256. Since the integer is signed, we have to be even more limiting: Wall length must be less than 128 in order to avoid blasting the sign bit. That explained, we will now get back to clipping. . . . When we clip to the view line, the wall endpoints are modified. The x coordinate is set to the view plane distance (typically we use 1 for this value); the y coordinate is set to the intersection of the wall and view line. px, the screen coordinate, is also set to y— for vertices lying right on the view line, perspective is just the identity transformation.

Now that we've clipped to the view line, we'll clip to the view polygon (instead of the truncated pyramid view volume in traditional 3-D rendering, we have a view trapezoid, though we only bother clipping to the front and sides of it).

```
// Now, clip to the sides of the view polygon.
outcode1 = FIXED_SIGN(view->view_plane_size + px1);
outcode1 |= FIXED_SIGN(view->view_plane_size - px1) << 1;
outcode2 = FIXED_SIGN(view->view_plane_size + px2);
outcode2 |= FIXED_SIGN(view->view_plane_size - px2) << 1;
```

We calculate outcodes so that we can quickly check for the trivial accept and reject cases. The outcodes are calculated useing the perspective transformed vertex coordinates. Bit zero of the outcode is set if the vertex is left of the view line segment, and bit one is set if the vertex is right of the view line segment.

```
// trivial reject
if ((outcode1 & outcode2) != 0)
        continue;
```

If the wall lies outside the view polygon, we throw it away and don't mess with it until the next time the renderer is called.

```
// check for trivial accept */
if ((outcode1 | outcode2) != 0)
{
```

If we've gotten to this point, we're going to need to clip to the sides of the view polygon.

```
// We need to clip . . .
fixed base_slope, slope, denom, y_diff;

denom = (x2 - x1);
if (FIXED_ABS(denom) < FIXED_FUZZ)
{
        if (denom < 0)
                base_slope = FIXED_MIN + view->view_plane_size;
        else
                base_slope = FIXED_MAX - view->view_plane_size;
}
else
        base_slope = fixdiv(y2 - y1, denom);
```

We've now computed base_slope, which is the slope of line from (x1, y1) to (x2, y2). The slope of a wall parallel to the view line is plus or minus infinity; the slope of a wall perpendicular to the view line is zero. We fudged around the infinity by ensuring the denominator (x2 - x1) is larger than FIXED_FUZZ. Now, we calculate the intersection of the wall with the view polygon. We perform one or two intersection calculations.

```
if (outcode1 == 1)
{
        px1 = -view->view_plane_size;
        y_diff = y1 - fixmul(x1, -view->view_plane_size);
        slope = base_slope + view->view_plane_size;
        if (FIXED_ABS(slope) > FIXED_FUZZ)
                x1 -= fixdiv(y_diff, slope);
        else
```

```
                          x1 = FIXED_MAX;
        }
        else
                if (outcode1 == 2)
                {
                        px1 = view->view_plane_size;
                        y_diff = y1 - fixmul(x1, view->view_plane_size);
                        slope = base_slope - view->view_plane_size;
                        if (FIXED_ABS(slope) > FIXED_FUZZ)
                                x1 -= fixdiv(y_diff, slope);
                        else
                                x1 = FIXED_MAX;
                }

        if (outcode2 == 1)
        {
                px2 = -view->view_plane_size;
                y_diff = y2 - fixmul(x2, -view->view_plane_size);
                slope = base_slope + view->view_plane_size;
                if (FIXED_ABS(slope) > FIXED_FUZZ)
                        x2 = fixdiv(y_diff, slope);
                else
                        x2 = FIXED_MAX;
        }
        else
                if (outcode2 == 2)
                {
                        px2 = view->view_plane_size;
                        y_diff = y2 - fixmul(x2, view->view_plane_size);
                        slope = base_slope - view->view_plane_size;
                        if (FIXED_ABS(slope) > FIXED_FUZZ)
                                x2 -= fixdiv(y_diff, slope);
                        else
                                x2 = FIXED_MAX;
                }
}
```

Regardless of whether the wall has been clipped, we call add_wall_events to put the endpoints of the wall into the wall even list. So, clip walls is really doing more than just clipping. It also sets up the wall event lists. . . . We're not really happy with overloading clip_walls like this, but the call to add_wall_events didn't seem to fit anywhere else.

```
        add_wall_events(renderer, view, wall, x1, px1, x2, px2);
    }
}
```

Wall Events

In add_wall_events, we're going to add create two events for a wall. One event will be inserted in the wall_start list and another into the wall_end list. . . .

```
static void add_wall_events(wtRenderer renderer, wtView view, wtWall wall,
        fixed x1, fixed px1, fixed x2, fixed px2)
{
        int fb1, fb2;
        fixed z1, z2;

        // convert to frame buffer coordinates
        px1 = fixdiv(px1, view_constants.screen_dx + 1);
        px2 = fixdiv(px2, view_constants.screen_dx + 1);
        fb1 = FIXED_TO_INT(px1) + (view_width >> 1);
        fb2 = FIXED_TO_INT(px2) + (view_width >> 1);
```

The first thing we do is convert the coordinates in screen space (px1 and px2) into integer coordinates in the framebuffer (fb1 and fb2.) To do this conversion, we use a value from the view_constants struct. screen_dx is the size of the view plane divided by the frame buffer width. We're sure that this sort of conversion is familiar to you. . . .

```
        /* There's no need to deal with walls that start and end in the
        **   same screen column. In a properly contructed world, we're
        **   guaranteed that throwing them away won't leave any gaps.
        */
        if (fb1 == fb2)
                return;

        /* Here we use a 2.30 fixed point format. The result of this
**   calculation
**   is always between 1 and zero, as the distance can never be less
**   than the view plane distance. The extra fractional bits are
**   critical for the inverses. Note that using 2.30 restricts the
**   size of the view plane to something less than 2.
*/
        z1 = fixdiv(TO_FIX_2_30(view->eye_distance), x1);
        z2 = fixdiv(TO_FIX_2_30(view->eye_distance), x2);
```

The z values that we are calculating here are the inverses of the distance from the view line to the points. It turns out to be much more efficient to use the inverse distance rather than the distance. In particular, we can linearly interpolate the inverse of the distance from one wall endpoint to the other. This wouldn't be a win if we had to invert the interpolated values to use them.

However, it turns out that usually we're interested in inverse distance anyhow. Consider that in perspective calculations, we're always dividing by the distance.

In the code that follows, you'll see essentially the same code replicated twice. The code which is run depends on whether the walls runs from right to left or from left to right. The code might seem redundant, but we found it easier to write a special case for both conditions rather than to use the same code for both.

You'll now get to see first-hand how the event lists are used. . . .

```
if (fb1 < fb2)
{
        /* Start off by allocating new events from the pool of free
        **  events. Allocate a start and an end event.
        */
        Wall_start *start_event = renderer->cur_start_event++;
        Wall_end *end_event = renderer->cur_end_event++;

        /* Now fill in the fields of the event. First specify which
        **  wall this start event is for.
        */
        start_event->wall = wall;
        /* Set the initial z (inverse distance) value. */
        start_event->z = z1;

        /* Compute dz, which will be used to linearly interpolate z
        **  between the left wall endpoint and the right.
        */
        start_event->dz = fixdiv(z2 - z1, INT_TO_FIXED(fb2 - fb1));

        /* The direction of the wall determines whether we're looking at
        **  it from in front or from behind. See the reference on the
        **  wt world files for more information on what it means to be
        **  in front of or behind a wall.
        */
        start_event->is_back_view = FALSE;
        /* Remember that start_event is an entry in a linked list.
        **  We're going to insert it at the beginning of the list at
        **  slot fb1, so we set next to point to the current first
        **  list element.
        */
        start_event->next = renderer->start_event_lists[fb1].next;
        /* Finally, put the start event into the event list. */
        renderer->start_event_lists[fb1].next = start_event;

        /* Now add the end event. End events are much simpler than the
        **  start events. The only field in the end event (aside from
        **  next) is a pointer to the wall which the end event is for.
        */
        end_event->wall = wall;
        end_event->next = renderer->end_event_lists[fb2].next;
        renderer->end_event_lists[fb2].next = end_event;
}
else
{
```

```
        Wall_start *start_event = renderer->cur_start_event++;
        Wall_end *end_event = renderer->cur_end_event++;

        start_event->wall = wall;
        start_event->z = z2;
        start_event->dz = fixdiv(z1 - z2, INT_TO_FIXED(fb1 - fb2));
        start_event->is_back_view = TRUE;
        start_event->next = renderer->start_event_lists[fb2].next;
        renderer->start_event_lists[fb2].next = start_event;

        end_event->wall = wall;
        end_event->next = renderer->end_event_lists[fb1].next;
        renderer->end_event_lists[fb1].next = end_event;
    }
}
```

Object Events

Now we stuff events into the object event lists. The procedure is similar in most ways to the way wall events were created.

```
static void add_objects(wtRenderer renderer, wtWorld world, wtView view)
{
        List *l;
        fixed view_sin, view_cos;

        view_sin = view_constants.view_sin;
        view_cos = view_constants.view_cos;

        FOREACH(l, world->objects)
        {
                fixed x, y, z;
                fixed tx, ty;
                wtObject o = LIST_NODE(l, Object *);

                // Skip the object if it is invisible.
                if (o->image == NULL)
                        return;
```

We begin the process by transforming the objects' coordinates into the view coordinate system. This works just as it did for vertices, minus all the complexities of clipping.

```
        x = o->x - view->x;
        y = o->y - view->y;
        z = o->z;
        // Rotate into viewer's coordinate system.
        tx = fixmul(x, view_cos) - fixmul(y, view_sin);
        ty = fixmul(x, view_sin) + fixmul(y, view_cos);
```

```
// Only worry about the object if it is in front of the view plane
        if (tx > view->eye_distance + FIXED_FUZZ)
        {
                int fb1, fb2;
                fixed pstart, pend;
                fixed z;

                // Project the object onto the view plane. The object's
                // width and it's distance from the view line determine
                // how far apart pstart
                //   and pend are.
                pstart = fixdiv(ty - FIXED_HALF(o->width), tx);
                pend  = fixdiv(ty + FIXED_HALF(o->width), tx);

                // Convert to frame buffer coordinates. This is the same
                //   conversion that was used at the beginning of
                //   add_wall_events.
                //
                pstart = fixdiv(pstart, view_constants.screen_dx + 1);
                pend  = fixdiv(pend,  view_constants.screen_dx + 1);
                fb1 = FIXED_TO_INT(pstart) + (view_width >> 1);
                fb2 = FIXED_TO_INT(pend)  + (view_width >> 1) - 1;

                // Only bother with the object if it lies somewhere in
                //   the field of view.
                if (fb2 >= 0 && fb1 < view_width)
                {
                        Object_start *start_obj = renderer->
                                  cur_start_obj++;
                        Object_end  *end_obj  = renderer->cur_end_obj++;
                        fixed first_slice = FIXED_ZERO;
                /* Calculate the inverse distance for the object,
                ** as we did for wall endpoints. You'll notice that we
                ** do not calculate a dz value. This is because objects
                ** are texture mapped onto a plane which is always
                ** parallel to the view line. This is why in DOOM
                ** and Wolfenstein 3D objects appear to rotate as you
                ** move around them. The term we have heard for this is
                ** 'billboarding'
                */
                        z = fixdiv(TO_FIX_2_30(view->eye_distance), tx);
                /* You've got to be wondering 'What's up with this
                ** first_slice stuff. Well . . . when an object is not
                ** clipped to the sides of the view polygon, the texture
                ** column assigned to the first (leftmost) column of the
                ** object is column 0. However, if the object has been
                ** clipped to the left side of the screen, texture
                ** mapping needs to start someplace other than column 0.
                */
                        if (fb1 < 0)
                        {
                                first_slice = fixdiv(INT_TO_FIXED(-fb1),
                                        INT_TO_FIXED(fb2 - fb1));
                                fb1 = 0;
                        }

                        // Clip the right side of the object.
                        if (fb2 >= view_width)
                                fb2 = view_width - 1;
```

```
                              // Fill in the fields of the object start event.
                              start_obj->z = z;
                              start_obj->o = o;
                              start_obj->first_slice = first_slice;
                              start_obj->next = renderer->
                                             obj_start_lists[fb1].next;

                 // . . . and insert into the object start event list.
                              renderer->obj_start_lists[fb1].next = start_obj;

                              end_obj->o = o;
                              end_obj->next = renderer->obj_end_lists[fb2].next;
                              renderer->obj_end_lists[fb2].next = end_obj;
                     }
           }
     }
     }
```

Let's Create an Image—To the Screen We Go

All the wall and objects events have been created—here's where we actually start doing something with them. The function render_walls does not do any rendering itself, but it calls the functions which do. This is where everything starts to come together as an image on the screen.

```
static void render_walls(wtRenderer renderer, wtWorld world, wtView view)
{
        // Ugh . . . we really need to change the active list to be //  dynamic. It's
unlikely that there will ever be more than
        //   300 walls or 100 objects active at once (and there
        //   certainly won't be if there are less than these respective
        //   amounts of items in the world. Other places I'm pretty
        //   careful to make sure that the renderer won't break because
        //   of arbitrary limits, but I'd forgotten about this
        //   oversight.
        //
        static Active_wall active[300];
        static Active_object active_obj[100];
        int column;
        int active_count = 0, active_obj_count = 0;
        fixed Vx, Vy, dVy;


// Set up for fast calculation of view rays. The view rays are defined
//  by vectors in 2 space. The x component is always set to the
//   distance of the view line from the eye. The y component varies as
//   we render column by column. The view rays are used all over for
//   doing wall texture mapping, and it's more efficient to calculate
//   them once, incrementally, than it is to calculate them with
//   multplications whenever they're used.
        Vx = view->eye_distance;
        Vy = -view->view_plane_size;
```

```
        dVy = fixdiv(FIXED_DOUBLE(view->view_plane_size),
                INT_TO_FIXED(view_width));

// Render each column from left to right.
for (column = 0; column < view_width; column++)
{
        active_wall   *current, *last;
        Active_object *current_obj, *last_obj;
// Add walls and objects to the active list. Any walls or
//   objects for which there are start events are added to the
//   active lists.
        active_count = add_events(renderer, active, active_count,
                column);
        active_obj_count = add_obj_events(renderer,
        active_obj, active_obj_count, column);
// Call do_walls to render a column of the frame buffer. Only
//   walls and objects in the active lists are considered when
//   rendering the column.
        do_walls(active, active_count,
                active_obj, active_obj_count,
                column, view, Vx, Vy);

// Remove all objects from the active lists for which there are
//   end events at the current slot in the end events list.
        active_count   = remove_events(renderer, active,
                active_count, column);
        active_obj_count = remove_obj_events(renderer,
                active_obj, active_obj_count, column);
// Keep track of distances of walls in the active list. Notice
//   that we're not actually tracking the distances of walls,
//   but 1 / distance instead. That's because we can linearly
//   interpolate 1 / distance. Also, most calculations that
//   use distance are really using 1 / distance (i.e. distance
//   appears in the denominator.
        last = active + active_count;
        for (current = active; current < last; current++)
        {
                current->z += current->dz;

                // You know what z is; we will explain what
                //   pstart1, pend1, pstart2,
                //   and pend2 are in a bit.
                if (current->visible)
                {
                        current->pstart1 += current->dpstart1;
                        current->pend1 += current->dpend1;
                        current->pstart2 += current->dpstart2;
                        current->pend2 += current->dpend2;
                }
        }

        last_obj = active_obj + active_obj_count;
        for (current_obj = active_obj; current_obj < last_obj;
                        current_obj++)
                current_obj->x += current_obj->dx;
        Vy += dVy;
}
}
```

Add new walls to the active list. The active list is kept depth-sorted. We have
to be careful here. Correct depth ordering of the walls is vital for rendering. At
corners we have two or more walls at the same distance; however, there is still a
correct and incorrect ordering. If one wall is obscured by another, the visible wall
must be placed in front in the list.

```
static int add_events(wtRenderer renderer, Active_wall *active, int n_active, int
column)
{
        int j;
        Wall_start *1;


        // Add to the active list every wall in the start event list.
        FOREACH(1, &renderer->start_event_lists[column])
        {
                Wall_start *event = 1->next;
                wtWall wall = event->wall;
                fixed z = event->z;

                // Scan through the walls already in the active list and
                //  try to determine where to insert the new wall. THE
                //  WALLS MUST BE KEPT DEPTH ORDERED. The z comparisons
                //  might seem backwards, but
                //  remember: z is the *inverse* distance.
                for (j = 0; j < n_active; j++)
                {
                        wtWall wall2 = active[j].wall;
                        wtVertex common, v1, v2;

                        // Now the long awaited explanation of MAX_ERROR.
                        //  Because of accumulated error from repeatedly
                        //  incrementing z by dz, we can rely on z
                        //  values alone to provide depth ordering
                        //  information for us. Also, when walls join at
                        //  corners, their z values will be equal, yet we
                        //  still must determine which is in front of the
                        //  other. We can use z or an initial quick
                        //  check for depth ordering--if the z values that
                        //  we are comparing are farther apart than
                        //  MAX_ERROR (the maximum accumulated error) we
                        //  know right away which wall is behind the
                        //  other.
                        if (z < active[j].z - MAX_ERROR)
                                continue;
                        else if (z > active[j].z + MAX_ERROR)
                                break;

                        // See if the walls share a vertex. If they're
                        //  this close together they'd better.
                        if (wall->vertex1 == wall2->vertex1) {
                                common = wall->vertex1;
                                v1 = wall->vertex2;
                                v2 = wall2->vertex2;
                        } else if (wall->vertex1 == wall2->vertex2) {
                                common = wall->vertex1;
```

```
                                    v1 = wall->vertex2;
                                    v2 = wall2->vertex1;
                        } else if (wall->vertex2 == wall2->vertex1) {
                                    common = wall->vertex2;
                                    v1 = wall->vertex1;
                                    v2 = wall2->vertex2;
                        } else if (wall->vertex2 == wall2->vertex2) {
                                    common = wall->vertex2;
                                    v1 = wall->vertex1;
                                    v2 = wall2->vertex1;
                        } else {
                                    // We have two walls which are really close
            //   together, but share no vertices. Because
            //   of roundoff error, we don't know for certain
            //   which one is really in front. Ideally, this
            //   situation will be avoided by creating
                                    //   worldfiles which don't place non-adjoining
                                    //   walls extremely close together.
                                        if (z > active[j].z)
                                                break;
                                    else
                                                continue;
          }

                                    // we can't really demonstrate what's going on
                                    //   here very well without a diagram. See the
                                    //   function wall_obscured for our best attempt.
          if (!wall_obscured(common, v1, v2) &&
                                    wall_obscured(common, v2, v1))
                        break;
                        }

                        // Insert the wall into the active list.
                        memmove(active + j + 1,
                        active + j,
                        sizeof(Active_wall) * (n_active - j));

                        // Set the fields for the new active list entry. Most of
                        //   them are just copied from the even list entry.
                        active[j].wall = wall;
                        active[j].z = z;
                        active[j].dz = event->dz;
                        active[j].visible = FALSE;
                        active[j].is_back_view = event->is_back_view;
                        n_active++;
          }

          return n_active;
}
```

add_obj_events inserts objects from the object start event list into the depth-sorted active object list. This routine is straightforward and contains none of the complexities that plague the algorithm to determine which walls are in front of each other.

```
static int add_obj_events(wtRenderer renderer, Active_object *active, int n_active,
int column)
{
        int j;
        Object_start *l;


        FOREACH(l, &renderer->obj_start_lists[column])
        {
                Object_start *event = l->next;
                fixed z = event->z;
                wtObject o = event->o;

                // Scan through the current active list entries.
                for (j = 0; j < n_active && z < active[j].z; j++);

                // Insert the event into the active object list
                memmove(active + j + 1,
                active + j,
                sizeof(Active_object) * (n_active - j));

                // Set the fields of the active list entry
                active[j].z = z;
                active[j].o = o;

                // For walls, we call a function which intersects the
                //   view ray with the wall to determine which are of the
                //   texture to map onto the wall for a given screen
                //   column. Texture mapping is less complicated for
                //   objects since they are always parallel to the view
                //   plane. x is the current object texture column, and
                //   dx is the amount by which I increment it when we
                //   advance one screen column
                if (event->first_slice == FIXED_ZERO)
                        active[j].x = FIXED_ZERO;
                else
                        active[j].x = FIXED_SCALE(event->first_slice,
                                o->image->width);
                active[j].dx = fixdiv(INT_TO_FIXED(o->image->width * 2),
                fixmul(o->width, FIXED_SCALE(FROM_FIX_2_30(z),
                        view_width)));
                n_active++;
        }
        return n_active;
}


// Determine whether wall 1 is obscured by wall 2 from the view point.
//  This will be the case if a halfplane defined by wall 1 contains both the
//  view point and wall 2. Wall 1 is defined by the points common and v1;
//  wall2 is defined by command and v2. Note that this function uses the
//  transformed coordinates of the vertices, so the view point and view
//  direction need not be passed explicitly.
static BOOL wall_obscured(wtVertex common, wtVertex v1, wtVertex v2)
{
        fixed x1, y1, x2, y2;
        unsigned int sign1, sign2;


        x1 = common->tx - v1->tx;
```

```
y1 = common->ty - v1->ty;
x2 = common->tx - v2->tx;
y2 = common->ty - v2->ty;

// There's some tricky stuff done here to try to find the signs
//  of cross products without actually doing any
//  multiplication. I'm really not sure if avoiding a few
//  multiplies is worth the extra overhead of sign checking,
//  but the profiler shows this function as
//  taking a surprisingly small percentage of execution time.
//  we got this idea of computing the signs of products with
//  xor from something in Graphics Gems II.
if (FIXED_PRODUCT_SIGN(x1, y2) ^ FIXED_PRODUCT_SIGN(x2, y1))
        sign1 = FIXED_PRODUCT_SIGN(x1, y2);
else
        sign1 = FIXED_SIGN(fixmul(x1, y2) - fixmul(x2, y1));
if (FIXED_PRODUCT_SIGN(x1, common->ty) ^ FIXED_PRODUCT_SIGN(common->tx, y1))
        sign2 = FIXED_PRODUCT_SIGN(x1, common->ty);
else
        sign2 = FIXED_SIGN(fixmul(x1, common->ty) - fixmul(common->tx, y1));

if (sign1 ^ sign2)
        return FALSE;
else
        return TRUE;
}
```

remove_events and *remove_obj_events* are more event list management functions. We hope this event list stuff is starting to seem pretty routine. There's not much to either of these functions—they both operate in an incredibly straightforward (and none too efficient) manner.

```
// Remove walls from the active list. Return the number of walls
//  remaining in the active list.
static int remove_events(wtRenderer renderer,
Active_wall *active, int n_active, int column)
{
        int j;
        Wall_end *l;

        FOREACH(l, &renderer->end_event_lists[column])
        {
                Wall_end *event = l->next;
                Wall *wall = event->wall;

                for (j = 0; j < n_active && active[j].wall != wall; j++);
                n_active--;
                memmove(active + j, active + j + 1,
                        sizeof(Active_wall) * (n_active - j));
        }

        return n_active;
}
```

```
static int remove_obj_events(wtRenderer renderer,
Active_object *active, int n_active, int column)
{
        int j;
        Object_end *l;


        FOREACH(l, &renderer->obj_end_lists[column])
        {
                Object_end *event = l->next;
                Object *o = event->o;

                for (j = 0; j < n_active && active[j].o != o; j++);
                n_active--;
                memmove(active + j, active + j + 1,
                sizeof(Active_object) * (n_active - j));
        }

        return n_active;
}
```

This section contains the guts of the wall drawing functions. There are a number of static variables declared here which are used to pass information between these functions. They are not used anyplace else. If only C had a block structure like Pascal. . . .

```
static fixed pstart1, pend1, pstart2, pend2;
static fixed top, bottom;
static Region *front, *back;
```

Before you delve too far into this code, an explanation of the variables used here is in order. Depending on the regions on either side of a wall, the wall may have zero, one, or two visible segments. Refer to the description of the world structures of wt if you need to convince yourself of this again. pstart1 and pend1 are the bottom and top of the first wall segment, and pstart2 and pend2 are the bottom and top of the second segment. Top and bottom define the current clipping region. Front and back are the front (closest to the viewer) and back region of a wall.

```
// Walls can have up to two segments--one attached to the floor and one
//   attached to the ceiling. Draw wall segment calls draw_slice in
//   slice.c which is the function responsible for stuffing bits into
//   the framebuffer for walls drawing.
static void draw_wall_segment(fixed pstart, fixed pend, fixed start, fixed z, fixed
height, int fb_column, Pixel *tex_base, wtWall wall, fixed tex_dy)
{
        Pixel *fb_byte, *last_byte;
        int fb_start, fb_end;
```

```
fixed tex_y;

/*
** Here'a brief description of the parameters passed to
**  draw_wall_segment:
** pstart and pend are the top and bottom of the wall segment
** z is the inverse distance from the view line
** height
** tex_base is the address of the first pixel in the texture
**  column which we will map onto this wall column. Textures
**  are stored in memory rotated 90 degrees, so it is actually
**  a texture row that will map onto a wall column. This
**  weirdness was added to speed up the inner wall texture
**  mapping loop.
** fb_column is the column of the frame buffer which we are
**  currently rendering.
** wall is the wall that we are rendering.
** tex_dy is the amount by which to step through texture space
**  when we move a single pixel in screen space.
*/

// Clip the wall slice.
if (pstart < bottom)
{
        pstart = bottom;
        start = fixdiv(pstart, z) + height;
}
if (pend >= top)
        pend = top - 1;

// Determine the first and last row in the framebuffer for this
//  segment.
fb_start = (view_height >> 1) - 1 -
FIXED_TO_INT(FIXED_SCALE(pstart, view_height));
fb_end  = (view_height >> 1) - 1 -
FIXED_TO_INT(FIXED_SCALE(pend, view_height));

fb_column = view_width - fb_column - 1;
fb_byte  = fb + fb_column + view_constants.fb_rows[fb_start];
last_byte = fb + fb_column + view_constants.fb_rows[fb_end];
// If this is a sky wall, the texture mapping is independent of
//  the viewer's height.
if (wall->sky)
        tex_y = fixmul(view_constants.row_view[fb_start],
                wall->yfreq) + wall->yphase;
else
        tex_y = fixmul(start, wall->yfreq) + wall->yphase;

// Draw an opaque or transparent column of wall.
if (wall->opaque)
        draw_wall_slice(fb_byte, last_byte, tex_base, tex_y,
                tex_dy, view_width,
                wall->texture->log2height, fb_start - fb_end);
else
        draw_transparent_slice(fb_byte, last_byte, tex_base,
                tex_y, tex_dy,
                view_width, wall->texture->log2height,
        fb_start - fb_end);
}
```

Draw_wall() calls draw_wall_segment once, twice, or not at all depending
upon how many visible segments of the wall there are. It also determines which
column from a texture map to draw onto the current wall column.

```
static void draw_wall(wtWall wall, fixed z, fixed Vx, fixed Vy, wtView view, int
column)
{
        Pixel *tex_base;
        fixed tex_dy;
        int tex_column;
        BOOL do_floor, do_ceiling;
        wtTexture texture = wall->texture;
        fixed start1, start2;
        fixed t;


        start1 = front->floor;
        start2 = back->ceiling;

        if (pend1 > pend2)
                pend1 = pend2;
        if (pstart2 < pstart1)
                pstart2 = pstart1;

        texture = wall->texture;
        do_floor  = (pstart1 < top) && (pend1 > bottom) && (pend1 -
                pstart1 > FIXED_FUZZ);
        do_ceiling = (pstart2 < top) && (pend2 > bottom) && (pend2 -
                pstart2 > FIXED_FUZZ);

        // Don't do anything more with this wall if there's nothing to
        //  draw.
        if (!do_floor && !do_ceiling)
                return;

        // We compute the texture coordinates for sky walls and normal
        //  walls in fundamentally different ways.
        if (wall->sky)
        {
                fixed angle;

                // Compute the angle of this column. We will use the
                //  angle exclusively to determine which texture column
                //  to display for this slice of sky.
                angle = view->angle + fixdiv(FIXED_SCALE(view->arc,
                        column - (view_width >> 1)),
                INT_TO_FIXED(view_width));
                angle -= FIXED_SCALE(FIXED_2PI,
                FIXED_TO_INT(fixdiv(angle, FIXED_2PI)));
                angle = fixdiv(angle, FIXED_2PI);
                if (angle < FIXED_ZERO)
                angle = FIXED_ONE - angle;
                tex_column = FIXED_TO_INT(fixmul(angle, wall->xfreq))
                        &(texture->width - 1);
                tex_dy = fixdiv(wall->yfreq, INT_TO_FIXED(view_height));
        }
        else
```

```
{
        t = wall_ray_intersection(Vx, Vy, wall);
        // From t, calculate the integer coordinates in the
        //  texture bitmap. For efficiency, we assume that the
        //  width of the texture is a power of two.
        tex_column = FIXED_TO_INT(wall->xphase + fixmul(t,
                wall->xfreq)) &
                (texture->width - 1);
        // Test to avoid overflow here . . . if the wall is so
        //  far away that z (which is 1 / distance) is less than
        //  FIXED_FUZZ, then it will be so small when rendered
        //  that we can use a bogus value for tex_dy.
        if (z < FIXED_FUZZ)
                tex_dy = 0;
        else
                tex_dy = fixdiv(wall->yfreq, FIXED_SCALE(z,
                        view_height));
    }
    tex_base = texture->texels + (tex_column <<
            texture->log2height);
    if (do_floor)
            draw_wall_segment(pstart1, pend1, start1, z,
                    view->height, column,
                    tex_base, wall, tex_dy);

    if (do_ceiling)
            draw_wall_segment(pstart2, pend2, start2, z,
                    view->height,
                    column, tex_base, wall, tex_dy);
}
```

We have separated the object drawing and wall drawing functions. The texture mapping for objects is calculated somewhat differently than for walls. Also, with objects we don't need to worry about the possibility of having two separate segments to draw.

```
static void draw_object(wtObject o, fixed z, int tex_column,
            wtView view, int fb_column)
{
    fixed pstart, pend;
    fixed tex_y, tex_dy;
    int fb_start, fb_end;
    Pixel *fb_byte, *last_byte;
    Pixel *tex_base;


    // Project the bottom and top of the object onto the slice.
    pstart = fixmul(z, o->z - view->height);
    pend  = fixmul(z, o->height) + pstart;

    // See if the object is visible in this column.
    if (pstart > top || pend < bottom || pend - pstart < FIXED_FUZZ)
            return;
    tex_dy = fixdiv(INT_TO_FIXED(o->image->height),
    FIXED_SCALE(pend - pstart, view_height));
```

```
            // Clip the object slice.
            if (pstart < bottom)
            {
                    tex_y = fixmul(bottom - pstart, FIXED_SCALE(tex_dy,
                            view_height));
                    pstart = bottom;
            }
            else
                    tex_y = FIXED_ZERO;

            if (pend > top)
                    pend = top;

            fb_start = (view_height >> 1) - 1 -
                    FIXED_TO_INT(FIXED_SCALE(pstart, view_height));
            fb_end  = (view_height >> 1) - 1 -
                    FIXED_TO_INT(FIXED_SCALE(pend, view_height));
            fb_column = view_width - fb_column - 1;
            fb_byte  = fb + fb_column + view_constants.fb_rows[fb_start];
            last_byte = fb + fb_column + view_constants.fb_rows[fb_end];
            tex_base = o->image->texels + (tex_column <<
                    o->image->log2height);
            draw_transparent_slice(fb_byte, last_byte, tex_base, tex_y,
                    tex_dy, view_width,
                    o->image->log2height, fb_start - fb_end);
    }


typedef struct
{
        fixed top, bottom;
        Active_wall *active;
        Active_object *active_obj;
} Saved_wall;


#define MAX_TRANSPARENT_WALLS 100
static Saved_wall transparent_walls[MAX_TRANSPARENT_WALLS];


/* do_walls() draws all the walls for a screen column. */
static void do_walls(Active_wall *active, int n_active, Active_object *active_obj,
                int n_active_obj, int column, wtView view, fixed Vx, fixed Vy)
{
        fixed height = view->height;
        Saved_wall *last_saved = transparent_walls;


        // As we walk front to back through the active wall list, we
        //  track the top and bottom of the view port for this column.
        //  Because of the restrictions placed on world geometry, the
        //  view port will always be a single interval, making clipping
        //  extremely simple. When bottom is greater than top, the
        //  view port is closed--nothing behind the current wall will be
        //  visible.
        top  = FIXED_ONE_HALF;
        bottom = -FIXED_ONE_HALF;

        // This loop moves from front to back through the list of
        //  'active' walls. We stop when we reach the last wall in the
```

```
//  list, or when the walls we've already looked at completely
//  obscure anything behind them.
while (n_active-- > 0 && bottom < top)
{
        wtWall wall = active->wall;
        fixed z = active->z;
        fixed dz = active->dz;

        // See if there are any objects in front of this wall
        //  which need to be drawn. Since objects have
        //  transparent parts, drawing them must be deferred
        //  until after the opaque wall slices have
        //  been drawn. Transparent walls are handled in a
        //  similar manner later on in the loop.
        while (n_active_obj > 0 && active_obj->z >= z)
        {
                // Record the object in the save buffer.
                last_saved->top = top;
                last_saved->bottom = bottom;
                last_saved->active_obj = active_obj;
                last_saved->active = NULL;
                last_saved++;

                // Advance through the object list.
                n_active_obj--;
                active_obj++;
        }

        // Set up the front and back region pointers--if we're
        //  behind a wall, these need to be reversed.
        if (active->is_back_view)
        {
                front = wall->back;
                back = wall->front;
        }
        else
        {
                front = wall->front;
                back = wall->back;
        }

        // If this wall has not been visible before, set the
        //  visible flag
        //  and set up the projected coordinates and deltas.
        if (!active->visible)
        {
                active->pstart1 = fixmul2_30(TO_FIX_8_24(
                        front->floor - height), z);
                active->pend1  = fixmul2_30(TO_FIX_8_24(
                        back->floor - height), z);
                active->pstart2 = fixmul2_30(TO_FIX_8_24(
                        back->ceiling - height), z);
                active->pend2  = fixmul2_30(TO_FIX_8_24(
                        front->ceiling - height), z);
                active->dpstart1 = fixmul2_30(TO_FIX_8_24(
                        front->floor - height), dz);
                active->dpend1  = fixmul2_30(TO_FIX_8_24(
                        back->floor - height), dz);
                active->dpstart2 = fixmul2_30(TO_FIX_8_24(
                        back->ceiling - height), dz);
```

```
                    active->dpend2 = fixmul2_30(TO_FIX_8_24(
                            front->ceiling - height), dz);
                    active->visible = TRUE;
            }

            // If this wall is opaque, we draw it now and adjust
            //   bottom and top appropriately. Otherwise, we defer
            //   the drawing of the wall slice until later.
            if (active->wall->opaque)
            {
                    pstart1 = FROM_FIX_8_24(active->pstart1);
                    pend1 = FROM_FIX_8_24(active->pend1);
                    pstart2 = FROM_FIX_8_24(active->pstart2);
                    pend2 = FROM_FIX_8_24(active->pend2);

                    draw_wall(wall, FROM_FIX_2_30(z), Vx, Vy, view,
                            column);
                    if (bottom < pend1)
                            bottom = pend1;
                    if (bottom < pstart1)
                            bottom = pstart1;
                    if (top > pstart2)
                            top = pstart2;
                    if (top > pend2)
                            top = pend2;
            }
            else
            {
                    last_saved->top       = top;
                    last_saved->bottom    = bottom;
                    last_saved->active    = active;
                    last_saved->active_obj = NULL;
                    last_saved++;
            }
            active++;
    }

    // Now, handle the objects and transparent walls. last_saved
    //   points to an entry in the saved walls buffer. Each entry
    //   consists of the the active list entry plus the top and
    //   bottom clipping info.
    while (last_saved > transparent_walls)
    {
            Active_wall *active;
            Active_object *active_obj;

            last_saved--;
            top = last_saved->top;
            bottom = last_saved->bottom;
            active = last_saved->active;

            // If active is not NULL, this entry is a wall; if it is
            //   NULL,
            //   this entry is an object and active_obj is not null.
            if (active != NULL)
            {
                    pstart1 = FROM_FIX_8_24(active->pstart1);
                    pend1  = FROM_FIX_8_24(active->pend1);
                    pstart2 = FROM_FIX_8_24(active->pstart2);
                    pend2  = FROM_FIX_8_24(active->pend2);
```

```
                              draw_wall(active->wall, FROM_FIX_2_30(active->z),
                                      Vx, Vy, view, column);
                   }
                   else
                   {
                           active_obj = last_saved->active_obj;
                           draw_object(active_obj->o,
                                   FROM_FIX_2_30(active_obj->z),
                                   FIXED_TO_INT(active_obj->x), view, column);
                   }
          }
}


// Calculate the value of the parameter t at the intersection
//  of the view ray and the wall. t is 0 at the origin of
//  the wall, and 1 at the other endpoint.
static fixed wall_ray_intersection(fixed Vx, fixed Vy, wtWall wall)
{
          fixed denominator, Nx, Ny, Wx, Wy;
          Nx = -Vy;
          Ny = Vx;
          Wx = wall->vertex2->tx - wall->vertex1->tx;
          Wy = wall->vertex2->ty - wall->vertex1->ty;

          denominator = fixmul(Nx, Wx) + fixmul(Ny, Wy); /* N dot W */
          if (denominator < FIXED_FUZZ)
                  return FIXED_ONE - fixdiv(fixmul(Nx, wall->vertex1->tx) +
                          fixmul(Ny, wall->vertex1->ty), denominator);
          else
                  if (denominator > FIXED_FUZZ)
                          return fixdiv(fixmul(Nx, wall->vertex1->tx) +
                                  fixmul(Ny, wall->vertex1->ty),
                                  denominator);
                  else
                          return FIXED_ZERO;
}


static void init_buffers(wtRenderer renderer)
{
          int i;

          renderer->cur_start_event = renderer->start_events;
          renderer->cur_end_event = renderer->end_events;
          renderer->cur_start_obj = renderer->obj_start_events;
          renderer->cur_end_obj = renderer->obj_end_events;

          for (i = 0; i < renderer->width; i++)
          {
                  renderer->start_event_lists[i].next = NULL;
                  renderer->end_event_lists[i].next = NULL;
                  renderer->obj_start_lists[i].next = NULL;
                  renderer->obj_end_lists[i].next = NULL;
          }
}


static void clear_framebuffer(wtRenderer renderer)
```

```
{
         memset(renderer->framebuf, 0, renderer->height *
                renderer->width);
}


// Calculate values that are dependent only on the screen dimensions and
//   the view.
static void calc_view_constants(wtRenderer renderer, wtView view)
{
         int i;
         fixed x, y;


         fb = renderer->framebuf;
         view_width = renderer->width;
         view_height = renderer->height;
         view_constants.fb_rows = renderer->fb_rows;
         view_constants.row_view = renderer->row_view;
         view_constants.sin_tab = renderer->sin_tab;
         view_constants.cos_tab = renderer->cos_tab;

         view_constants.view_sin = FLOAT_TO_FIXED(sin(-
                FIXED_TO_FLOAT(view->angle)));
         view_constants.view_cos = FLOAT_TO_FIXED(cos(-
                FIXED_TO_FLOAT(view->angle)));
         view_constants.screen_dx = fixdiv(FIXED_DOUBLE(
                view->view_plane_size),
                INT_TO_FIXED(view_width));
         view_constants.screen_dy = fixdiv(FIXED_ONE,
                INT_TO_FIXED(view_height));
         view_constants.sin_dx = fixmul(view_constants.view_sin,
                view_constants.screen_dx);
         view_constants.cos_dx = fixmul(view_constants.view_cos,
         view_constants.screen_dx);
         y = FIXED_SCALE(view_constants.sin_dx, -(view_width >> 1));
         x = FIXED_SCALE(view_constants.cos_dx, -(view_width >> 1));

         for (i = 0; i < view_width; i++)
         {
                view_constants.sin_tab[i] = y;
                view_constants.cos_tab[i] = x;
                y += view_constants.sin_dx;
                x += view_constants.cos_dx;
         }


         y = FIXED_SCALE(view_constants.screen_dy, renderer->height >>
                1);

         for (i = 0; i < view_height; i++)
         {
                view_constants.row_view[i] = y;
                y -= view_constants.screen_dy;
         }
}
```

And by the way . . . wt stands for "what's this". . . .

PART IV

APPENDICES

PIVR WINDOWS

PIVR Windows Files

This appendix contains a list of all PIVR Windows files provided and their function.

Dir	File name	Description
	barproc.c	source code for slider bar control
	bitmap.c	source code for all bitmap-related functions
	dirproc.c	source code for compass control
	funcs.c	source code for miscellaneous functions
	includes.c	source code for pre-compiled header

	message.c	source code for Windows message processing functions
	spdproc.c	source code for speed control
	startup.c	source code for all one-time startup functions
	viewproc.c	source code for virtual view window functions
	vr.c	source code for Windows to VR engine interface functions
	winmain.c	source code for PIVR winmain function
	wndproc.c	source code for Windows message processing
	pivr.def	Microsoft-required .DEF file
	bitmap.h	function prototype definitions for functions in bitmap.c
	funcs.h	function prototype definitions for functions in funcs.c
	includes.h	application-wide definitions and precompiled headers
	message.h	function prototype definitions for functions in message.c
	resource.h	resource id definitions.
	startup.h	function prototype definitions for functions in startup.c
	vr.h	function prototype definitions for functions in vr.c
	pivr.hlp	Windows help file
	pivr.mak	Microsoft Visual Workbench make file
	pivr.rc	resource definitions file
res	autooff.bmp	autopilot bitmap (16 color)
res	autoon.bmp	autopilot bitmap (16 color)

res	bar.bmp	slider bar bitmap (16 color)
res	brp1x8.bmp	big red pushbutton, up bitmap (256 color)
res	brp1x8r.bmp	big red pushbutton, up bitmap (256 color, rainbow palette)
res	brp2x8.bmp	big red pushbutton, down bitmap (256 color)
res	brp2x8r.bmp	big red pushbutton, down bitmap (256 color, rainbow palette)
res	gauge.bmp	gauge outline bitmap (16 color)
res	lad.bmp	left arrow, down bitmap (16 color)
res	lau.bmp	left arrow, up bitmap (16 color)
res	pivrx24.bmp	pivr bitmap (true color)
res	pivrx8.bmp	pivr bitmap (256 color)
res	pivrx8r.bmp	pivr bitmap (256 color, rainbow palette)
res	rad.bmp	right arrow, down bitmap (16 color)
res	rau.bmp	right arrow, up bitmap (16 color)
res	slide.bmp	slider control bitmap (16 color)
res	icon1.ico	PIVR icon
hlp	help.doc	PIVR Windows help text (Microsoft Word 2.x format)
hlp	help.prj	help compiler project file

Don't Peek!

The line in question is in bold, a check for the current paint mode. Who cares what the paint mode is when we're trying to exit? Well, prior to adding that line, the app occasionally exhibited some very strange behavior. If it was closed (Alt+F4) during the opening monologue, whenever a **WaitFor()** function was executing, the message WM_CLOSE was processed as normal and the window was destroyed. That in turn caused a WM_DESTROY message to be generated which was also dutifully processed by **WndProc()**. However, since we were still in **WaitFor()**, gobbling up messages, the WM_QUIT message generated by **PostQuitMessage()** in the WM_DESTROY code *never made it to the message loop in WinMain()*. So the application literally missed its own exit line!

```
// ...WM_CLOSE...this message is received when Windows wants to close the
application.
// Use this time to decide whether or not the application can be closed or do any
// required cleanup. If OK to close the app, execute DestroyWindow() and return 0 or
// don't process it. Either way Windows will close the application. Return 0 without
// executing DestroyWindow() and nothing happens...

        case    WM_CLOSE:
        if (gnPaintMode != eNORMAL) return(0);
        DestroyWindow(hWnd);
        return(0);
```

The simplest solution, albeit not the best, is simply not to allow the application to exit when it's doing the startup monologue. Hence the mysterious line in bold.

It's only one line, but without a comment of some sort (and look how much it took to explain what was going on), you're begging for trouble.

APPENDIX B

RESOURCES

Network Resources

For those of you with net access. Information provided by Toni Emerson through her Web server (http://www.hitl.washington.edu) and the sci.virtual-worlds MetaFAQ and Bill Cockayne's VR Information Sites List (ftp://ftp.apple.com/pub/VR/vr_sites.*).

Web Sites

http://www.hitl.washington.edu
The HIT Lab at the University of Washington.

http://www.gatech.edu/gvu/multimedia/Multimedia.html
    Multimedia Computing Group at Georgia Tech.

http://www.gatech.edu/gvu/gvutop.html
    Graphics, Visualization and Usability Center at Georgia Tech.

http://isye.gatech.edu/CHMSR/
    Center for Human-Machine Systems Research at Georgia Tech.

http://www.gatech.edu/gvu/people/Masters/Rob.Kooper/Meta.VR.html
    VR Projects on the Net.

http://sunsite.unc.edu/
    University of North Carolina at Chapel Hill: SunSITE, UNC Chapel Hill,
    and more.

http://sunsite.unc.edu/exhibits/vmuseum/vmuseumhome.html
    UNC Virtual Museum.

FTP Sites

ftp://sunee.uwaterloo.ca/pub/vr   (129.97.50.50)
    Home of REND386 (freeware VR library/package), /pub (misc
    directories on pglove, raytracing, et al.)

ftp://ftp.u.washington.edu/public/virtual-worlds   (140.142.56.1)
    Home of sci.virtual-worlds, huge faq with a great deal of info, currently
    being updated.
    Current contents of /public/VirtualReality/:
        HITL/ Bibliographies, tech-reports, thesises, data files and more,
               from the HITLab.
        UNC/   Abstracts and tech-reports from the UNC-CH.
        misc/ Various papers and articles.

ftp://ftp.apple.com/pub/VR   (130.43.2.3)
    Sites list, Macintosh vr, CAD projects info, home of Gossamer and Dr.
    StrangeGlove

ftp://avalon.chinalake.navy.mil/pub   (129.131.31.11)
    Huge repository of 3-D objects in all types of formats

ftp://sunsite.unc.edu/pub/academic/computer-science/virtual-reality
    (152.2.22.81)
    Virtual reality demos, iris info, glasses, mirrors some of
    ftp.u.washington.edu, uforce info

ftp://src.doc.ic.ac.uk/usenet/comp.archives/auto/comp.sys.isis   (146.169.2.1)
    /usenet/comp.archives/auto/sci.virtual-worlds
    Great Usenet archives including stuff from sci.v-w; also has info on ISIS
    and a VR app for ISIS

ftp://wuarchive.wustl.edu   (128.252.135.4)
    Mirror of ftp.u.washington.edu VR archive, mirror of sugrfx.acs.syr.edu
    (which is now dead), docs for Sega glasses —> RS232 iface, Nintendo
    glove stuff. wuarchive is also a graphics archive with over 500 megs of
    graphics related info and source (/graphics)

ftp://cogsci.uwo.ca/pub/vr   (129.100.6.10)
    Mirrors some of sugrfx.syr.edu and karazm.math.uh.edu and has some
    local stuff

ftp://ftp.ipa.fhg.de/pub/VIRTUAL-REALITY   (129.233.17.68)
    Contains papers on work done at the IPA in Stuttgart

ftp://ftp.ncsa.uiuc.edu/VR   (141.142.20.50)
    Contains papers and systems built at NCSA

TELNET Sites

phantom.com   (38.145.218.228)
    Home of the MindVox system. telnet to and log in as guest. (You will be
    charged an access fee if you decide to become a user)

diaspar.com   (192.215.11.1)

Diaspar Virtual Reality Network supports Dmodem protocol, several VR discussion areas, fee for full access, demo account available, first month free. (also dial-up, see below)

Usenet Groups

sci.virtual-worlds	Virtual Reality technology and culture. (Mod)
sci.virtual-worlds.apps	Current and future uses of virtual-worlds tech. (Mod)
alt.3d	Discussions of three-dimensional imaging.
alt.cyberpunk	High-tech low-life.
alt.cyberpunk.chatsubo	Cyberpunk discussions.
alt.cyberpunk.tech	Cyberspace and Cyberpunk technology.
alt.cyberspace	Cyberspace and how it should work.
alt.education.distance	Learning over nets, etc.
alt.graphics.pixutils	Utilities for viewing computer graphic images.
alt.toys.high-tech	High-tech toys.
alt.uu.virtual-worlds.misc	Misc. virtual-worlds.
comp.ai	Artificial intelligence discussions.
comp.ai.fuzzy	Fuzzy set theory, aka fuzzy logic.
comp.arch	Computer architecture.
comp.cog-eng	Cognitive engineering.
comp.databases	Database and data management issues and theory.
comp.dsp	Digital signal processing.
comp.graphics	Computer graphics, art, animation, image processing.
comp.graphics.visualization	Computer graphics and scientific visualization.
comp.graphics.*	Many other graphics-related groups.

comp.human-factors	Issues related to human—computer interaction (HCI).
comp.infosystems.www	The World Wide Web information system.
comp.multimedia	Interactive multimedia technologies of all kinds.
comp.music	Applications of computers in music research.
comp.org.eff.news	News from the Electronic Frontiers Foundation. (Mod)
comp.os.research	Operating systems and related areas. (Mod)
comp.realtime	Issues related to real-time computing.
comp.research.japan	The nature of research in Japan. (Mod)
comp.risks	Risks to the public from computers & users. (Mod)
comp.robotics	All aspects of robots and their applications.
comp.simulation	Simulation methods, problems, uses. (Mod)
comp.society	The impact of technology on society. (Mod)
comp.speech	Research and applications in speech science and technology.
comp.sys.sgi.graphics	Graphics packages and issues on SGI machines.
comp.theory.dynamic-sys	Theory of dynamic systems.
rec.arts.cinema	Discussion of the art of cinema. (Mod)
rec.arts.int-fiction	Discussions about interactive fiction.
rec.arts.startrek.tech	Star Trek's depiction of future technologies.
rec.games.frp.cyber	Discussions of cyberpunk-related roleplaying games.
rec.games.mud.announce	Informational articles about multiuser dungeons. (Mod)
rec.games.mud.misc	Various aspects of multiuser computer games.
rec.games.netrek	Discussion of the X window system game Netrek.
rec.games.video.arcade	Discussions about coin-operated video games.

rec.games.video.misc	General discussion about home video games.
rec.games.video.sega	All Sega video game systems and software.
rec.parks.theme	Discussions of theme parks.
sci.cognitive	Perception, memory, judgment, and reasoning.
sci.electronics	Circuits, theory, electrons, and discussions.
sci.fractals	Objects of non-integral dimension and other chaos.
sci.med.telemedicine	Clinical consulting through computer networks.
sci.optics	Discussion relating to the science of optics.
sci.research	Research methods, funding, ethics, and whatever.

America Online

The VR discussion on AOL is sponsored by Virtus Corporation and can be found in their directory. To get to the discussion, use the keyword VIRTUS, and look in the "Let's Discuss" folder.

The Well

Telnet 192.132.30.2 or dial up and type "go vr".

BIX

The BIX conference is moderated by Dan Duncan and can be reached by typing "j virtual.world". There are a number of papers by such researchers as Bob Jacobson, Brenda Laurel, William Bricken, Brad Smith, Randy Walser, and others available on-line, as well as some lively discussion about the technical, philosophical, and political impact of VR. BIX can be called on your modem at 1-800-695-4882 for details and rates.

CompuServe

Once you are on CompuServe you can type "go graphdev" and look in the VR TECH areas for mail and libs. Or, you can type "go Cyberforum" or "go Cyber+".

Bulletin Boards

Diaspar Virtual Reality Network	
	(714) 376-1200 2400 bps
	(714) 376-1234 9600 bps
SENSE/NET	(801) 364-6227
Toronto Virtual Reality SIG	
	(416) 631-6625 16.8K baud
Virtual Space Driver [MD]	large DOS archives
	(301) 424-9133
Zarno [GA]	RIME carrier
	(706) 860-2927

Virtual References

Adam, John A. "Virtual Reality Is for Real." *IEEE Spectrum.* Oct. 1993: 22—29.

Airey, John M., John H. Rohlf, and Frederick P. Brooks, Jr. "Towards Image Realism with Interactive Update Rates in Complex Virtual Building Environments." Department of Computer Science, University of North Carolina, Chapel Hill, N.C.

Amato, Ivan. "In Search of the Human Touch." *Science* 258. 27 Nov. 1992: 1436—1437.

Antonoff, Michael. "Living in a Virtual World." *Popular Science.* July 1992: 83—86, 124—125.

Baecker, Ronald and Ian Small. "Animation at the Interface." *The Art of Human–Computer Interface Design*. Ed. Laurel, Brenda. Reading, Mass.: Addison-Wesley, 1990.

Benedikt, Michael. *Cyberspace: First Steps*. Cambridge, Mass.: MIT Press, 1993.

Brennan, Susan. "Conversation as Direct Manipulation: An Iconoclastic View." *The Art of Human–-Computer Interface Design*. Ed. Laurel, Brenda. Reading, Mass.: Addison-Wesley, 1990.

Brooks, Frederick P., Jr. "Grasping Reality through Illusions—Interactive Graphics Serving Science" TR88—007. *Proceedings of the Fifth Conference on Computers and Human Interaction*. 1–-11. Eds. E. Soloway, D. Frye, and S. Sheppard. Reading, Mass.: Addison-Wesley, 1988.

Brooks, Frederick P., Jr., *et al.* "Six Generations of Building Walkthroughs—Final Technical Report to the National Science Foundation." Department of Computer Science, University of North Carolina, Chapel Hill, N.C., June 1992.

Brooks, Frederick P., Jr., and William V. Wright. "Nineteenth Annual Progress Report Interactive Graphics for Molecular Studies." TR92-014. Department of Computer Science, University of North Carolina, Chapel Hill, N.C., April 1993.

Brooks, Frederick P., Jr., Ming Ouh-Young, James J. Batter, and P. Jerome Kilpatrick. "Project GROPE—Haptic Displays for Scientific Visualization." *ACM SIGGRAPH—Computer Graphics*. ACM-0-89791-344-2/90/8/177: 177–185. 1990.

Butterworth, Andrew Davidson, Stephen Hench, and T. Marc Olano. "3DM: A Three-Dimensional Modeler Using a Head-Mounted Display." *ACM SIGGRAPH—Computer Graphics*.ACM-0-89791-471-6/92/3/135: 135–-138, 226. 1992.

Campbell, Joseph. "Day of the Dead." 1988. As quoted in Rheingold, *Virtual Reality*.

Cheney, Margaret. *Tesla, Man out of Time*. New York: Dorset Press, 1989.

Cobb, Nathan. "Cyberpunk: Terminal Chic." *The Boston Globe,* 24 Nov. 1992. Living Arts: 29, 32. (As found on the Internet)

Cockayne, William. "On Law Enforcement Agencies in Cyberspace." billc@apple.com.

Cook, David A. *A History of Narrative Film.* New York: Summit Books, 1981. As quoted in Pimentel.

Coull, Tom, and Peter Rothman. "Virtual Reality for Decision Support Systems." *AI Expert.* Aug. 1993: 22—25.

Cramblitt, Bob. "World's Fastest Graphics Computer." *Computer Graphics World.* PennWell, 1993.

DeFanti, Thomas A., Daniel J. Sandin, and Carolina Cruz—Neira. "A 'room' with a 'view.'" *IEEE Spectrum.* Oct. 1993: 30—33.

Delaney, Ben. "Big Brother Is Watching." *AI Expert Virtual Reality Special Report.* July 1992: 35—38.

Department of Computer Science, University of North Carolina, Chapel Hill, N.C. "Head-Tracker Project Summary." Oct. 1993.

Department of Computer Science, University of North Carolina, Chapel Hill, N.C. "Pixel-Planes 5 Project Summary." Jul. 1993.

Dunn, Frank, ed. *VR Monitor* 2:1 Jan./Feb. 1993.

Edupage 8/10/93 quotes *New York Times.* 9 August 93, C2.

Eisenberg, Bart, Butler Hine, and Daryl Rasmussen. "Telerobotic Vehicle Control: NASA Preps for Mars." *AI Expert.* Aug. 1993: 19—21.

Fisher, Scott. "Virtual Interface Environments." *The Art of Human--Computer Interface Design.* Ed. Laurel, Brenda. Reading, Mass.: Addison-Wesley, 1990.

Fuchs, Henry, Gary Bishop, *et al.* "Research Directions in Virtual Environments."
    TR92—027. *ACM SIGGRAPH—Computer Graphics.* 26-3: 153—177. August
    1992.

Georgia Institute of Technology's Graphics, Visualization, and Usability Center
    Literature (GVU).

Gottschalk, Stefan, and John Hughes. "Autocalibration for Virtual Environments
    Tracking Hardware." *ACM SIGGRAPH—Computer Graphics.*
    ACM-0-89791-601-8/93/8/65: 65—72. 1993.

Graff, Gordon. "Virtual Acoustics Puts Sound in Its Place." Science 256. 1 May.
    1992: 616—617.

Hamilton, Joan, *et al.* "Virtual Reality: How a Computer-Generated World Could
    Change the Real World." *Business Week.* Oct. 5, 1992: 97—105.

Hancock, Dennis. "'Prototyping' the Hubble Fix." *IEEE Spectrum.* Oct. 1993:
    34—35.

Holloway, Richard, Henry Fuchs, and Warren Robinett. "Virtual—Worlds
    Research at the University of North Carolina at Chapel Hill as of
    February 1992." Department of Computer Science, University of North
    Carolina, Chapel Hill, N.C., Feb. 1992.

Human Interface Technology literature (see also Jones).

IVEX press releases and literature.

Jacobson, Linda. "The Business of Selling Virtual Reality." *AI Expert Virtual
    Reality Special Report.* July 1992: 39—41.

Jones, Alden, ed. *HIT Lab Review.* Number 3, Spring 1994.

Jones, Alden, ed. *HIT Lab Review.* Number 4, Autumn/Winter 1994.

Kay, Alan. "User Interface: A Personal View." *The Art of Human—Computer
    Interface Design.* Ed. Laurel, Brenda. Reading, Mass.: Addison-Wesley,
    1990.

Kerris, Richard. "Virtual Performers." *IRIS Universe* 20. Spring 1992: 12—13.

Krueger, Myron. "VIDEOPLACE and the Interface of the Future." *The Art of Human—Computer Interface Design.* Ed. Laurel, Brenda. Reading, Mass.: Addison-Wesley, 1990.

Lanier, Jaron. "A Brave New World: Virtual Reality Today." *AI Expert Virtual Reality Special Report.* July 1992: 11—17.

Latta, John. "The Business of Cyberspace." *AI Expert Virtual Reality Special Report.* July 1992: 27—33.

Laurel, Brenda, ed. *The Art of Human—Computer Interface Design.* Reading, Mass.: Addison-Wesley, 1990.

Laurel, Brenda. "Interface Agents: Metaphors with Character." *The Art of Human—Computer Interface Design.* Ed. Laurel, Brenda Reading, Mass.: Addison-Wesley, 1990.

Laurel, Brenda. "A New Opposable Thumb." *AI Expert Virtual Reality Special Report.* July 1992: 23—26.

Maddox, Tom. "After the Deluge: Cyberpunk in the '80s and '90s." Newsgroup alt.cyberpunk. tmaddox@netcom.com.

Molendi, Gloria, and Matteo Patriarca. "Virtual Reality: Medical Researches." Technical Report 1/92 *Universita' degli Studi di Milano Dipartimento di Scienze della Informazione.*

Naimark, Michael. "Realness and Interactivity." *The Art of Human—Computer Interface Design.* Ed. Laurel, Brenda. Reading, Mass.: Addison-Wesley, 1990.

Naj, A. K. *Wall Street Journal.* 3 March 93. B1, B8.

Negroponte, Nicholas. "Hospital Corners." *The Art of Human—Computer Interface Design.* Ed. Laurel, Brenda. Reading, Mass.: Addison-Wesley, 1990.

Negroponte, Nicholas. "The Noticeable Difference." *The Art of Human—Computer Interface Design.* Ed. Laurel, Brenda. Reading, Mass.: Addison-Wesley, 1990.

Newquist, Harvey P. III. "Reach Out and Touch Someone." *AI Expert.* Aug. 1993: 44–45.

Oren, Tim. "Designing a New Medium." *The Art of Human—Computer Interface Design.* Ed. Laurel, Brenda. Reading, Mass.: Addison-Wesley, 1990.

Park, Brian V. "The Cyberfactory: View of the Future." *AI Expert Virtual Reality Special Report.* July 1992: 59–64.

Parsons, Donald F. "History and Research on the Reliability of Telemedicine Diagnosis." Article 520 of newsgroups sci.med.telemedicine.

Peterson, Ivars. "Looking-Glass Worlds." *Science News* 141. Jan. 4, 1992: 8–10, 15.

Pfeiffer, John. *The Creative Explosions.* 1982. As quoted in Rheingold, *Virtual Reality.*

Pimentel, Ken, and Kevin Teixeira. *Virtual Reality: Through the New Looking Glass.* New York: Windcrest, 1993.

Reid, Elizabeth. "Electropolis: Communication and Community on Internet Relay Chat." Honours Thesis. University of Melbourne, 1991.

Rettig, Marc. "Virtual Reality and Artificial Life." *AI Expert.* Aug. 1993: 15–17.

Rheingold, Howard. "What's the Big Deal about Cyberspace?" *The Art of Human-Computer Interface Design.* Ed. Laurel, Brenda. Reading, Mass.: Addison-Wesley, 1990.

Rheingold, Howard. *Virtual Reality.* New York: Summit, 1991.

Rheingold, Howard. "A Slice of Life in My Virtual Community." hlr@well.sf.ca.us. June 1992.

Robinett, Warren, and Jannick Rolland. "A Computational Model for the Stereoscopic Optics of a Head-Mounted Display." *Presence*. 1:1 (Winter 1992): 45—62.

Robinett, Warren, and Richard Holloway. "Implementation of Flying, Scaling, and Grabbing in Virtual Worlds." *ACM SIGGRAPH—Computer Graphics*. ACM-0-89791-471-6/92/3/189: 189—192. 1992.

Robinett, Warren. "Electronic Expansion of Human Perception." *Whole Earth Review*. Fall 1991.

Rogoff, Leonard. "Virtual Reality." *The University Alumni Report*. University of North Carolina, Chapel Hill, N.C., Oct. 1991.

Sense 8 Corporation. *Universe*. 1:1 July 1992.

Simgraphics press releases.

Smith, Norris Parker. "Virtual Illusions." 9 July 1987. Daily news item from somewhere on the Internet.

Stix, Gary. "See-Through View." *Scientific American*. Sept. 1992: 166.

Sutherland, Ivan. "The Ultimate Display." *Proceedings of the IFIP Congress*. 1965: 506—508.

Swaine, Michael. "Psychedelic Technology." *Dr. Dobb's Journal*. April 1993: 99—102.

Taylor, Russell, Warren Robinett, *et al*. "The Nanomanipulator: A Virtual—Reality Interface for a Scanning Tunneling Microscope." *ACM SIGGRAPH—Computer Graphics*. ACM-0-89791-601-8/93/8/127: 127—134. 1993.

University of North Carolina's Department of Computer Science literature.

VPL Research, Inc. *Virtual World News*. 3:1 U.S. edition. Summer/Siggraph 1991.

Ward, Mark, Ronald Azuma, *et al.* "A Demonstrated Optical Tracker With Scalable Work Area for Head-Mounted Display Systems." Department of Computer Science, University of North Carolina, Chapel Hill, N.C.

Warner, Dave. "Medical Rehabilitation, Cyber-Style." *AI Expert Virtual Reality Special Report.* July 1992: 19—22.

Woolley, Benjamin. *Virtual Worlds: A Journey in Hype and Hyperreality.* Cambridge, Mass.: Blackwell, 1992.

Technical References

Arvo, James. *Graphics Gems II.* Cambridge, Mass.: AP Professional, 1991.

Foley, James., Andries van Dam, Steven Feiner, and John Hughes. *Computer Graphics Principles and Practice.* Reading, Mass.: Addison-Wesley, 2nd ed., 1990.

Gery, Ron. *The Palette Manager: How and Why.* Microsoft Developer Network Technology Group.

Glassner, Andrew S. *Graphics Gems.* Cambridge, Mass.: AP Professional, 1990.

Harrington, Stephen. *Computer Graphics, A Programming Approach.* New York: McGraw-Hill Book Company, 1987.

Heckbert, P. S. "Survey of Texture Mapping," *IEEE Computer Graphics and Applications,* 6 (11): 56—67. 1986.

Heckbert, P. S. *Graphics Gems IV.* Cambridge, Mass.: AP Professional, 1994.

Kirk, David. *Graphics Gems III.* Cambridge, Mass.: AP Professional, 1992.

Marsh, Kyle. *Classy Windows.* Microsoft Developer Network Technology Group.

Newman, W. M., and R. F. Sproull. *Principles of Interactive Computer Graphics.* New York: McGraw-Hill, 1981.

Petzold, Charles. *Programming Windows 3.1.* Microsoft Press, 1990.

Programmer's Reference, Volume 2: Functions. Microsoft Windows SDK.

Programmer's Reference, Volume 3: Messages, Structures and Macros. Microsoft Windows SDK.

Watkins, Christopher D., and Roger T. Stevens. *Advanced Graphics Programming in C and C++.* New York: Henry-Holt and M&T Publishing, Inc., 1991.

Watkins, Christopher D., and Roger T. Stevens. *Advanced Graphics Programming in Turbo Pascal.* New York: Henry-Holt and M&T Publishing, Inc., 1990.

Watkins, Christopher D., and Larry E. Sharp. *Programming in 3 Dimensions: 3-D Graphics, Ray Tracing and Animation.* New York: Henry-Holt and M&T Publishing, Inc., 1992.

Watkins, Christopher D., Stephen B. Coy, and Mark Finlay. *Photorealism and Ray Tracing in C.* New York: Henry-Holt and M&T Publishing, Inc., 1992.

Watkins, Christopher D., Alberto Sadun, and Stephen R. Marenka. *Modern Image Processing: Warping, Morphing and Classical Techniques.* Cambridge, Mass.: AP Professional, Inc., 1993.

Watkins, Christopher D., and Stephen R. Marenka. *Taking Flight: History, Fundamentals and Applications of Flight Simulation.* New York: Henry-Holt and M&T Publishing, Inc., 1994.

Watkins, Christopher D., and Stephen R. Marenka. *Virtual Reality ExCursions.* Cambridge, Mass.: AP Professional, Inc., 1994.

Watkins, Christopher D., Vincent Mallette, Stephen R. Marenka and Robert Johnson. *Exploring Photorealism and Ray Tracing.* New York: Henry-Holt and M&T Publishing, Inc., 1995.

Watt, Alan. *Fundamentals of Three-Dimensional Computer Graphics.* Reading, Mass.: Addison-Wesley, 1989.

References for Chapters 5-8

Endnotes for Chapter 5

[1] Fisher
[2] Fuchs

Endnotes for Chapter 6

[3] Tesla in Cheney p. 178
[4] Webster, p. 1026
[5] Sutherland, 1965
[6] Krueger p. 420
[7] Brand, the Media Lab, p. 139
[8] The Media Lab 5th Anniversary, 1990
[9] Negroponte, p. 352
[10] Sherry Posnick-Goodman, Peninsula
[11] Atlanta Journal and Constitution, Monday, Dec. 7, 1992, B1

Endnotes for Chapter 7

[12] UNC Literature
[13] HIT Lab info
[14] Lanier
[15] Lanier
[16] Hancock, pp. 34 - 39
[17] VPL & Lanier
[18] Sense 8, Hamilton, p. 99, and Coull, p. 23
[19] Adam, pp. 26-7 and Peterson, p. 10
[20] Hamilton, p. 100
[21] Eisenberg
[22] Eisenberg
[23] Brooks, 1990
[24] DeFanti, p. 30

[25] VRR June 1992
[26] SN: 6/22/91, p. 368 and Peterson, p. 9
[27] Dunn, p. 9
[28] Antonoff, p. 85
[29] Sense 8
[30] VRR, July/Aug. 92
[31] VPL
[32] Med & VR
[33] Molendi & VRR, May 1992
[34] Molendi
[35] Naj
[36] Brooks, 1990 and Holloway and Stix
[37] VRR June 1992
[38] Molendi, VRR July/Aug 92, Warner, p. 21
[39] Adam, p. 27 and Ga. Tech GVU
[40] Warner and Molendi
[41] Sinclair
[42] Molendi
[43] VRR, May 1992
[44] Molendi & Prothero

Endnotes for Chapter 8

[45] *Physics Today*, Dec. 1992, p. 25.
[46] Mishkin and Appenzeller, p. 83.
[47] *National Geographic*, Nov. 1992, p. 38.
[48] Ibid.
[49] *Scientific American*, May 1970, p. 124.
[50] Sedeen, p. 316.
[51] *Reader's Digest*, Mar. 1972, p. 94.
[52] Strother, p. 154.
[53] Patronis. Bracewell, pp. 86-95.
[54] Watkins and Marenka, p. 450.
[55] Sinclair.

APPENDIX C

ILLUSTRATIONS

Image Credits

All images associated with the Georgia Institute of Technology are copyright © 1993 by the individuals listed and the Georgia Institute of Technology, Atlanta, GA. Used by permission. All Georgia Institute of Technology images were generated using the GVU Center Virtual Environment Group's Simple Virtual Environment (SVE) Sofware, version 1.3, on Silicon Graphics Crimson Reality Engine and Reality Engine II/Onyx workstations, or tools developed in the Multimedia Technology Laboratory.

All images associated with IVEX Corporation are copyright © 1985—1993 by IVEX Corporation, Atlanta, GA. Used by permission.

Gray-Scale Inserts

Figure 5.1   HMD, DataGlove, and Elevator (worn by Thomas Meyer)
                   Photo Credits: Thomas Meyer/Rob Kooper
                   GVU Lab Project: ICV—Georgia Institute of Technology
                   (hmd.tif)

Figure 6.1   IVEX Corporation Flight Simulator
                   Image showing simulator cockpit and view
                   (ivex11.tif)

Figure 6.2   Stereo VR Glasses in the GVU Lab (worn by Rob Kooper)
                   Photo Credits: Thomas Meyer/Rob Kooper
                   GVU Lab Project: ICV—Georgia Institute of Technology
                   (glasses.tif)

Figure 6.3   Left: Virtual Research HMD (640 x 480 x 55° version) worn by
                   Tom Meyer
                   Right: Virtual Research HMD (320 x 240 x 80° version) worn
                   by E. J. Lee
                   Photo Credits: Thomas Meyer/Rob Kooper
                   GVU Lab Project: ICV—Georgia Institute of Technology
                   (hmd1.tif)

Figure 6.4   3-D Scanner
                   Photo Credit: Michael Sinclair
                   Multimedia Technology Lab Project—Georgia Institute of
                   Technology
                   (mattclr.tif)

Figure 6.5   View of Tech Campus and downtown Atlanta from the North
                   Photo Credits: Thomas Meyer/Larry Hodges
                   GVU Lab Project: DVE—Georgia Institute of Technology
                   (gatech1.tif)

Figure 6.6   Interaction with a 3-D widget using gesture recognition for
                    data visualization. A time step in molecular dynamics
                    simulation as seen in the virtual environment. Here a NaCl
                    cluster is smashing into a Ne surface with temperature
                    mapped onto atom color. In the foreground one can see how
                    color is attached, by direct manipulation, to the temperature
                    property of the glyph.
                    Data Credits: David Luedtke and Uzi Landman.
                    Photo Credits: Ron van Teylingen/Bill Ribarsky
                    GVU Lab Project: SV—Georgia Institute of Technology
                    (data2.tif)

Figure 7.1   VR Aerial View of GVU Center Lab
                    Photo Credits: Augusto Op den Bosch/Walter Patterson
                    GVU Lab Project: ICV—Georgia Institute of Technology
                    (lab1.tif)

Figure 7.2   Interaction with a three-dimensional visualization of
                    molecular data.
                    Glyph binder interface for mapping data variables onto
                    graphical elements in the virtual environment. The data is
                    classified by types, and here the user chooses the type
                    associated with a NaCl cluster.
                    Data Credits: David Luedtke and Uzi Landman.
                    Photo Credits: Ron van Teylingen/Bill Ribarsky
                    GVU Lab Project: SV—Georgia Institute of Technology
                    (data1.tif)

Figure 7.3   IVEX Corporation Flight Simulator
                    Image showing helicopter cockpit connected to simulator
                    system.
                    (ivex13.tif)

Figure 7.4   "A Virtual Party"
Left: Virtual Research HMD (320 x 240 x 80° version) and a
CyberGlove Data Glove worn by Tom Meyer
Middle: StereoGraphics StereoEyes Stereo Glasses
Right: Virtual Research HMD (640 x 480 x 55° version) worn
by E. J. Lee
Photo Credits: Thomas Meyer/Rob Kooper
GVU Lab Project: ICV—Georgia Institute of Technology
(hmd2.tif)

Figure 7.5   Ocular Surgery Simulator—Fusable Stereo Pair
In conjunction with the Medical College of Georgia
Photo Credit: Michael Sinclair
Multimedia Technology Lab Project—Georgia Institute of
Technology
(eyes4.tif)

Figure 7.6   View from a glass elevator over a lobby
Photo Credits: Rob Kooper/Thomas Meyer/Drew
Kessler/Larry Hodges
GVU Lab Project: Phobia—Georgia Institute of Technology
(elevator.tif)

Figure 8.1   The Human Eye

Figure 8.2   The Human Ear

Figure 8.3   Georgia Tech's 1996 Atlanta Torch Carrier used in City
Demonstration
3-D Model Credit: Kleizer-Walczak
Photo Credit: Michael Sinclair/Frank Witz
Multimedia Technology Lab Project—Georgia Institute of
Technology
(olytorch.tif)

APPENDIX D

INDEX

—X—

—Z—

Learning Windows™ Programming
with Virtual Reality

Christopher Watkins · Russell J. Berube Jr.

"About the Disk"

This disk contains all source code, executable files, and 3-D models to learn how to program Microsoft Windows™. These files may be used for personal use but are not to be included in "for sale" products. Licensing of 3-D graphics software may be arranged through Christopher Watkins, cwatkins@algorithm.com.

System Requirements:

Minimum 386 or compatible with or without coprocessor (preferably with) running Windows 3.1 and preferably Borland C/C++ compiler version 3.1. Can run with Microsoft C with minor adjustments.